D1230077

Selected Poems of Ai Qing

At home, Beijing, 1980
在北京家里（1980年）

SELECTED POEMS
OF
Ai Qing

艾 青 詩 選

Edited with
an Introduction and Notes by
Eugene Chen Eoyang

Translated by
Eugene Chen Eoyang, Peng Wenlan
and Marilyn Chin

PUBLISHED IN ASSOCIATION WITH THE
FOREIGN LANGUAGES PRESS, BEIJING

INDIANA UNIVERSITY PRESS • BLOOMINGTON

Manufactured in the United States of America
Library of Congress Cataloging in Publication Data
Ai, Ch'ng, 1910-
    Selected poems of Ai Qing.
    1. Ai, Ch'ng, 1910-   —Translations, English.
I. Chen, Eugene Eoyang. II. Title.
PL2833.I2A23   1981   895.1'15   82-47956
ISBN 0-253-34519-7   AACR2
ISBN 0-253-20302-3 (pbk.)
1 2 3 4 5 86 85 84 83 82

Contents

PHOTOGRAPHS FOLLOWING PAGE 218

Editor's Introduction

Ai Qing, A Poet of the People

The silence of a poet, particularly one whose work reflects the sufferings and yearnings of a people, is a terrible recrimination. One feels one owes such a poet not only the attention that is deserved, but the attention that was denied. We wonder about experiences he would have written about, now lost forever. We regret the neglect of feelings the poet would have explored in verse, that his poetry would have imprinted on our imaginations. We cannot help but wonder what the effect would have been, on the course of our lives, on the development of our sensibilities, had this lacuna of the imagination not occurred, when a poet, for whatever reason, falls silent.

The poet who calls himself Ai Qing has been writing poetry for half a century; but in that period of productivity, a break of some twenty years occurred. He first made his mark with a collection published in 1936, when he was 26 years old. He published poetry until the late fifties, 1957, when he was sent to a state farm in northwest China as part of the anti-Rightist campaign. Later, he was transferred to another state farm in Xinjiang. From this experience, he was to emerge, in 1975, blind in his right eye. During this interval of almost twenty years, he continued to write poetry, but all of the hundreds of poems he composed are lost. In order to estimate and to gauge the dimensions of this loss, one can only look at his early poetry. It is direct, without apparent artifice; it is personal, yet accessible, sincere but without idiosyncrasy; it is dramatic, populated with many characters, some described objectively, some more subjectively. He discovered that in speaking his own mind, in expressing his own feelings, in describing his own experiences, he was not so much reaching an audience as writing their poetry. His requirement of honesty to himself, therefore, took on an added responsibility, for in realizing that his voice happened to speak for the people, to be honest with himself, to himself, was in effect to keep faith with those he spoke for. He has never wavered from that self-dedication and that selflessness.

Chinese literary tradition has always taken seriously the genius of the people: its first classic, the *Shi Jing* ("The Book of Songs") was culled, in large measure, from the folk songs of the people; its lyric tradition was enriched by the lilting *zi-ye* songs of the countryside in the Six Dynasties Period; its *ci* poetry took its roots from the "entertainment quarters" and the singing girls who plied their trade; the legends of the people found their way into such "classic" works of fable and imagination as the *Feng-shen yanyi* ("The Investiture of the Spirits"), the *Xiyou ji* ("The Journey to the West"), and the *Liao-zhai zhi-yi* ("Strange Stories from a Studio"); the great collections of fiction in the late Ming — which made *xiao shuo* respectable as literature — derived much of their material from folk legends and anecdotes.

The poetry of Ai Qing takes its place comfortably in this tradition. He has many followers among the less educated but no less discerning segment of the population. The testimony of a coalminer from Kailuan Colliery is typical of this readership: the coalminer did not understand poetry, he confessed, but he could see his own life reflected in Ai Qing's poems. Ai Qing also has his adherents among the educated. The chairman of a Chinese department at a university in China, himself a specialist in pre-Tang Chinese literature, told me that when he was younger and could afford to buy but one book, that book was a volume of Ai

Qing's poems. To this day, he is still able to recite parts of Ai Qing's early works. It is clear that this reader, appreciating both the immediacy of the *Shi Jing* and its remoteness now, did not look for obscurity as the single hallmark of worthwhile literature. Sales figures of books published in China are not always easy to obtain, but we do know that over thirty thousand copies of the 1979 edition of Ai Qing's *Selected Poems* were sold; the 1957 edition went through six printings and sold over 50,000 copies. These figures indicate that Ai Qing is not a "coterie" poet. Even allowing for the factors of a greater population and a lower list price for books, these figures would still compare favorably with the sales of a successful volume of poetry in America, where 3,000 copies is considered impressive.

The poetry of Ai Qing is about time-honored themes: a beggar woman by the side of the road; the selfless love and devotion of a hired wet-nurse; the sense of desolation that accompanies a heavy snowfall — particularly with the associations of death in the color white for the Chinese. The people in Ai Qing's poetry are authentic; they seem familiar and inevitable. He is unremitting in his dedication to a full expression of true feeling. Readers embarrassed by intense feelings, who regard any hint of emotion as sentimentality, will find Ai Qing's poetry not to their taste. There are few "new" insights here; rare are the phrases that mark the conceit and the contrivance of a "dandy" poet. He takes what might be called "clichés" and sees them through. He would probably agree with the critic who observed that "a cliché is merely a truth rubbed so smooth that it deflects thought". Earlier in his career, Ai Qing was told that he had the ability to write poetry both for the sake of art and for the sake of the people. However forced and false the dichotomy might be, his answer was, nevertheless, unequivocal: given the choice, he would write the poetry of the people. It is true that one hears in Ai Qing's poetry, not

one voice, but many. One sees not the face of one poet, but
the many faces of the people. One lives the life not of one
man, but of humanity.

Yet for all this ingenuousness, here is a true poet, a
voice of passion, one whose eloquence derives from the
mainsprings of experience, not rhetoric. His early poetry
showed a tendency toward metrical and metaphorical ex-
periment: "Paris", for example, written when he had just
returned from Europe in the early thirties, bears the vestiges
of Rimbaud's "sonnet, *Voyelles*". His first great success
was an autobiographical poem about the woman, a wet-nurse,
who raised him. It is written with a ruminative intensity,
the rhythms evocative, insistent, the language repetitive — as
if recollection were the evidence of feeling, and memory the
warrant of emotion. "Dayanhe — My Wet-nurse" both
explains and reflects some of Ai Qing's lifelong attitudes: his
ambivalent feelings toward tradition, devotion and compas-
sion toward its quiet heroism, distrust and indignation at its
backwardness; his outrage at the indignities of the present,
and his inextinguishable hope for the future; his abiding faith
in the individual. Other poems, like "The Bugler" and "He
Dies a Second Time", are evocations of a dramatic scene,
which brilliantly combine description with characterization
and an uncanny sense of narrative. These poems are more
than "set-pieces", for Ai Qing is able to find the meaningful
in the commonplace — as in his characterization of the young
bugler whose habit it is to stir before sunrise, yet gets up
before he needs to. What rouses the young bugler, Ai Qing
observes, is "his passionate impatience for the dawn". The
phrase reverberates with wide impact. In China today, not
only the buglers are passionately impatient for the dawn. In
a country of early risers, more dependent on daylight than
some more "advanced", energy-profligate countries, the dawn
of a new day holds special-promise. More recent poems, such
as "Hush, a Voice Is Speaking. . . ." and "On the Crest of

a Wave", try to capture the tumultuous events in China of
the past decade, and to celebrate that watershed in history,
the Tiananmen Incident, which occurred on April 5, 1976.
These poems speak for the sacrifice of the young, their dis-
illusionment and their courage, in the face of unspeakable
deceits. Ai Qing continues to write, and — happily — to
publish. He can still command a substantial audience. When
he spoke on poetry at the Beijing Library on March 14, 1981,
thousands turned out to hear him, and to listen to the recita-
tion, by three radio announcers, of "Snow Falls on China's
Land", "The Announcement of the Dawn", and "The Cockpit
of Ancient Rome" (all translated and included in this
volume).

Ai Qing has acknowledged a number of influences: Ver-
haeren, the Belgian poet, Rimbaud, Yessenin, Whitman,
Mayakovsky. Of these, perhaps Whitman is the most ap-
posite: his sympathies and his sensibilities are Whitmanesque,
but there is one important difference — Ai Qing lacks Whit-
man's all-encompassing ego. Where Whitman spoke as the
embodiment of the people, the poet *as* the people, Ai Qing
has assumed a more modest stance: he has been content to
be, from time to time, a poet *of* the people. But he derives
his inspiration from the same source. He has been impelled
to write when the pressure of circumstances, the sufferings
of the populace, and the agonies of his countrymen were so
unbearable that they moved him to poetry. He has said that
he wrote most of his poems during times of war, but for all
that, he is not a war poet, no more than Du Fu is a war poet.
Both Du Fu and Ai Qing found many readers during the
fighting that has ravaged China, off and on, for the last half-
century — the Sino-Japanese War, a struggle for national
survival; the War of Liberation, a struggle to found a new
nation; to say nothing of the internal turmoil known as
the "cultural revolution". The contrasts of style, of
language, of form, of diction, could not, of course, be more

striking in the two poets, yet they do not seem as important as their similarities. For both are moral poets, both have large sympathies, both are enormously touched by the lives of other human beings. The Chinese have a special place for poets who speak their suffering, who capture and exalt into art the mundane, mind-numbing grind of daily life, the tragedy and senselessness of war, the simple joys of family life and of that feeling between people which goes by the facile name of "love" in English, but which is not as readily expressed in Chinese. In times of national crisis, it appears that Du Fu among traditional poets and Ai Qing among modern poets have sustained the most readers.

The derivation of the pen-name "Ai Qing", makes an interesting anecdote in itself. According to the poet, when he was in France from 1929 to 1932, he was once mistaken by a hotel manager for Chiang Kai-shek, because the French transliteration of their two names at the time were similar ("Tchiang Kai-tchek" and "Tchiang Hai-tcheng"). Later, when he returned to China and was put in prison by the Kuomintang, he chose a pen-name by crossing out the phonetic in his family name: this left a cross under a grass radical, which in Chinese forms the "word for "*ai*" 艾 . The second word in the pen-name was chosen because it was homophonic in his native Zhejiang dialect with "*cheng*" 澄, the second word in his given name.

Whatever the derivation of the pen-name, readers may retain their own associations. The word "*ai*" can suggest something, or someone, fine, beautiful, or good, as in the expression "*shao ai*" 少艾 for "a young beauty". The word "*qing*" 青 suggests youth and freshness as in the expression "*qing-nian*" 青年 for "young people". "Ai Qing",[1]

---

[1] The pronunciation of Ai Qing ("*eye-ching*") may resemble popular mispronunciations of the *I Ching* as "*eye-ching*" (instead of "*ee-jing*"). The Chinese for the poet's pen-name is, of course, in no way similar to the Chinese for the ancient treatise on geomancy.

therefore, has a certain buoyant sound. It will not surprise us if a poet who has chosen this pen-name is unabashedly romantic. For all that he deplores, for all that he finds cruel and unjust, Ai Qing loves life. He has looked into the depths of misery and pain, and — far from recoiling in disillusionment — he reaffirms a belief in the ultimate goodness of life and of people. This optimism may be ill-founded in the minds of some, but there are innumerable readers who share with Ai Qing his affirmations of life. It is this buoyant resiliency, this dauntlessness in the face of difficulty and disappointment, that gives Ai Qing's poetry its special appeal. It is the same buoyant resiliency that has enabled individual Chinese, to say nothing of China as a nation, to survive. It is the same buoyancy that China will need if she is to achieve her great objectives by the dawn of the twenty-first century.

A Word on Translation

The translation of literature, under the best of circumstances, is a hazardous enterprise; the translation of poetry (in light of Frost's famous dictum that "Poetry is what gets lost in translation") even more so. Still, whatever the impossibilities of translation and the inadequacies of translators, the task of transmitting worthwhile literature to readers in other languages is an honorable and laudable enterprise. The preparation of this volume has involved both collaboration and cooperation, and some explanation of this process may be of interest, partly because it provides some background on current activities in translation and partly because that background may herald future developments in translations involving Chinese and English.

The majority of the translations of over fifty poems in this collection were prepared by Eugene Chen Eoyang, who also assumed overall editorial responsibilities for the English text. New translations by Peng Wenlan and Marilyn Chin have been included, as well as a handful of translations previously published in *Chinese Literature*. In a project of this complexity, involving transoceanic exchanges, the encouragement as well as the advice, to say nothing of the helpful corrections, of colleagues in China and the United States has been essential, and is hereby gratefully acknowledged. As this volume is one of the earliest to be co-published by the Foreign Languages Press in Beijing and the Indiana University Press in Bloomington, it is fitting that consultants at both institutions were actively involved in reviewing the manuscript for the press. At Indiana University, Leo Lee and Irving Lo read early versions of the typescript. Leo Lee, in particular, went over each translation and clarified many points not immediately clear to at least one translator. In Beijing, Sun Zhilong did a lot of work in editing the Chinese text, and Shen Zhen, Bonnie McDougall and Huang Jingying offered their criticisms and suggestions for improvement. Most of the translations are by a single hand, but in those cases where more than one translator made substantial contributions, joint attribution is given. The selection of the poems to be translated was a joint effort, and reflected the consultants of both Presses, the translators, and of Ai Qing and his wife, Gao Ying. Despite this widespread consultation, errors of interpretation and of translation may have occurred. One can rely on reviewers to point them out. For these errors, the translator bears the sole responsibility (except in joint efforts, where it will be duly shared).

The task of publishing modern Chinese written in *baihua* poses certain special problems for the translator. One of these might be characterized as "the unending modifier". In German, long clauses modifying a noun may precede that noun, sometimes deferring it until it is almost forgotten. (The reader of German, it is said, needs a long memory.) This feature is found in much modern *baihua* poetry in

Chinese, but there are two important differences. First, the lines are rarely if ever as long as equivalent phrases would be in German: long modifiers in a *mono*syllabic language will never seem as long as long modifiers in a *multi*syllabic language. Second, the modifiers in Chinese will not be marked with the grammatical declensions found in German, with the result that there is, in Chinese, perhaps less clarity as to what is done to what (or whom) when. In actual practice, however, this does not pose a very serious problem, since context makes the meaning clear in all but a few instances.

The translator, faced with presenting these "unending modifiers" in fluent English, cannot merely adopt the solution of citing the genitives one after another: A of B of C of D, or, in Chinese, D 的 C 的 B 的 A. The solution may be a discreet use of the subordinate clause, the apposite phrase, the parenthetical epithet. Two examples, from Ai Qing's "A Lament for Paris", might serve as illustrations. In a version preserving the original word order, the translation would read: "Is her (*de*) brave (*de*) people's (*de*) blood written with (*de*)." The first and third "*de*" function as possessives; the second and fourth as genitives. In fluent English, this emerges as: "Has been written with the blood of its brave people." Another, more convoluted example would be, from the same poem: "It (the time) will give love-freedom, love-democracy (*de*)/France's people be victorious." In a fluent version, this may be rendered: "The time that will deliver victory/To those who love freedom and democracy, the people of France." In this last example, the emphasis on "victorious" in the Chinese at the end of the line (which is also the end of the section), is sacrificed in English. But the alternative, ending the lines with an invocation to "the people of France" perhaps achieves a commensurate effect.

Still, a gain in fluency may suffer two kinds of loss: first, it sometimes loses the almost repetitive force of the structure in Chinese; second, it sometimes elongates the line

unduly with the addition of conjunctions and relative pro-
nouns, to say nothing of repeated subjects. Ai Qing writes
free verse that is often impressionistic, generally unpunctuat-
ed, so a certain syntactical freedom may be exercised on occa-
sion; however, while the translations may reverse the order
of the modifier and the word modified, this reversal extends
beyond one line only when more than one line forms a single
syntactical unit. The objective is to preserve the fluency
in the original, and yet retain the powerful effect of modifiers
piled one on top of another until final release is achieved in
the last nominal substantive. How well each translation man-
ages this, the reader must judge. (For the reference of
specialists, the Chinese text of the poems is appended at the
back.)

Special problems relating to individual poems are also
glossed at the back in order not to mar the presentation of
the translations as poems, not texts. Footnotes are added
only when an allusion is considered unfamiliar enough to
warrant explanation. The poet's footnotes are printed without
markings; the editor's footnotes will be indicated.

The *pinyin* system of transliteration has been used except
when time-honored custom sanctions another spelling. But,
for the most part, transliterations are avoided in favor of
translations, except when the word or phrase is so familiar
as to be unrecognizable in any other form (there is no point,
for example, rendering "Shanghai" as "On the Sea").

Eugene Chen Eoyang

Beijing
May 1, 1981*

* I wish to express my gratitude to the Lilly Endowment for an
award of a Lilly Faculty Open Fellowship, which enabled me to travel
to Beijing to confer with colleagues at the Foreign Languages Press. And
to those colleagues at the Foreign Languages Press, whose courtesies to
me during my stay extended beyond the professional, I owe many happy
and instructive hours. Their solicitude has made me a translator, if no
less errant, then not so hapless, nor so helpless.

Author's Preface

I

"We've been searching for you for twenty years.
We've been waiting for you for twenty years. . . ."

"During the upheaval of the 'Gang of Four' days, none of us knew what had happened to you. I thought you were probably dead. . . ."

The above extracts come from letters received from readers, almost all of which convey similar sentiments. These letters have been coming in since the end of April this year (1977), after the publication of my first poem in quite some time, and they show the concern that readers have had for me.

"A writer who doesn't write, or who does not have any works published, might just as well not exist."

And not to exist is the same as being dead, and I'm far from being dead.

For many years Lin Biao and the Gang of Four wanted to ban all forms of poetry. Works produced by writers who did not belong to their own clique were blacklisted and shelved.

But, as long as poetry belongs to the people, it will be safeguarded by the people.

"I went all over the place to buy your poems, but I still couldn't get them anywhere. . . ."

"We looked high and low for your poems. Whenever we came

1

across one, we would copy it down and hide it. . . ."

"In order to keep my copy of your poems safe, I wrapped it up in a plastic bag and hid it in the rice jar. . . ."

"After the Tangshan earthquake, I found an edition of your poems under a cupboard. . . ."

A friend of mine recently showed me a copy of *Dayanhe*, published forty-two years ago, and asked me for my autograph. I wrote the following poem on the title page:

Like an orphan
Lost on the earth,
Who has so often seen the flames of war
And smelled the smoke of gunpowder,
Who has suffered so much torment and misery,
I have been separated from you for forty years or more,
And now at last we meet again —
You, covered with bruises and scars
But your face preserved intact —
How remarkable!

A coalminer from the Kailuan Colliery wrote to me:

"I cannot understand poetry. I was born in the countryside and whenever I read your poems, they bring back memories of the place where I spent my childhood and they make me think of my sorry little village. . . . How is it that the magic of poetry can be so powerful? . . . I only know that I, a common laborer, often think of you and am concerned about you. . . . As long as you get this letter and see for yourself the feelings of one who has often thought of you for the last twenty years or more, my mind will be at rest. . . ."

Practically all my readers who have sent me letters have expressed delight at the fact that I have begun writing poems again: "Everything's fine now," "At last you've come out," "You're still alive and in good health. You ought to start writing again!"

I am sixty-eight this year. As regards age, this is not considered old, but many of my young friends are already dead, while I, like a walnut lost in some small corner, have managed to survive.

II

I was born in 1910 on the seventeenth day of the second month, according to the lunar calendar. I'm from Jinhua in Zhejiang Province and my native home is in the mountains. They say that my mother labored mightily when she gave birth to me. A fortune-teller said that I would be too much for my parents, and so, I became an object of aversion to the extent that I was not even allowed to call my parents "father" and "mother" but had to address them as "uncle" and "aunt". It was as if I had no parents. This made me detest fortune-telling and superstitions in general, and confirmed me an atheist as well.

In my early youth, I sought consolation in painting.

I was already nine years old at the outbreak of the May 4th Movement. Our primary school textbook contained some enlightening views demanding democracy and science.

Women students were becoming liberated, "unbinding their feet."[1]

The first time my middle school teacher set us an essay topic, about our ideas on private study, I wrote a composition entitled, "Each Age Has Its Own Literature", in which I spoke against the reading of classical Chinese works. My teacher wrote: "Your knowledge on this subject is insufficient. You must not think the words of Hu Shi and Lu Xun[2]

[1] In feudal China girls had their feet bound at the age of six or seven. — *Ed.*

[2] Hu Shi (1891-1962) was an important figure in the Literary Reform Movement, beginning in 1917. Lu Xun (1881-1936), a short story writer, poet, essayist, and critic, was one of the prime advocates of the May Fourth Movement that began in 1919. — *Ed.*

infallible." There was nothing wrong with what my teacher had written, but still I drew a big × across his comments.

"The rising wind forebodes an impending storm." Students frequently held demonstrations in the streets, waving flags and shouting slogans, overturned shops that sold Japanese goods, and broke into "Opium Control Centers".[1] The storm of revolution shook this ancient city in the south. A mimeographed copy of *An Elementary Introduction to Historical Materialism* (where I got it, I don't know) made me grasp for the first time the concept of Marxist class struggle, a concept which finally became bound up with my destiny and which determined the course of my life.

During my summer vacation in 1928, after graduating from junior middle school, I passed the entrance examination for the Painting Department of the West Lake National School of Fine Arts (now known as the Hangzhou Academy of Fine Arts). Before the end of the first term, the Director of the School sought me out. He told me, "You won't learn anything here. You'd better go abroad."

And so, in the spring of the following year I left for France, my head filled with Romanticism.

I was a penniless student in Paris. My parents were not willing to give me any financial help so I found a job in a small arts and crafts factory, and in my spare time I studied a little bit on my own, going to a "free art studio" in Montparnasse to learn figure painting and sketching. I also read a few books on philosophy and literature translated into Chinese; Russian novels of critical realism; and novels and poems on the Soviet October Revolution. Sometimes I went to Lenin Hall in the workers' district and saw films that had been banned. I also read a few modern French poems. My

---

[1] These "Control Centers" actually sold opium surreptitiously. — *Ed.*

favorites were those of the great Belgian poet Verhaeren. His poems left a deep impression on me. They sharply expose the unrestricted expansion of cities in the capitalist world and the consequent destruction of the countryside. In short, in my three years in Paris, I was a free spirit, even if I was indigent.

III

The September 18th Incident of 1931[1] intensified the national crisis for the people of China.

Four months later, on the very day that the January 28th Incident[2] broke out, I set out from Marseilles to return to China. But when the steamer reached Hong Kong around the first ten days of April, it stopped for four days. The Kuomintang was busy negotiating the Shanghai Ceasefire Agreement with the Japanese imperialists.

When I arrived in Shanghai, the war had already ended. But once again, China whimpered in humiliation. . . . Totally confused, I went back home to Jinhua, only to leave less than a month later.

I arrived in Shanghai in May and joined the League of Left-wing Artists, and, together with some other members, organized the Spring Soil Art Society.

When I was in Paris, I had tried my hand at poetry. I would jot down in my sketchbook a few lines when they suddenly flashed through my mind.

On the journey back from Paris, now, I wrote a few short poems. But I had never thought of actually becoming a poet by profession.

[1] The Shenyang Incident ("The Mukden Incident") marked the Japanese invasion of Northeast China, which some consider the event that "sounded the bell" for the Second World War. — *Ed.*

[2] When Japanese forces opened up a second front, this time against Shanghai, to divert attention from Manchuria. — *Ed.*

Then, one day, my roommate, himself a poet, saw a poem of mine on the table called "Gathering", which records the scene of the meeting held in Paris by the Eastern Branch of the Great Anti-Imperialist League. He took it in his head to write a note: "Dear Editor: I am sending you a poem. If you cannot use it, please return it", and sent the note along with the poem to a left-wing periodical of the time, "The Dipper". I didn't imagine it would actually be printed. It was after this small incident that I began to shift from painting to literature and finally decided to devote myself entirely to literature.

In June, the Spring Soil Art Society held an exhibition in Shanghai on the second floor of the Y. M. C. A. building. Lu Xun gave us his support and even loaned us his precious collection of prints by the German artist Käthe Kollwitz to add to our exhibition. Lu Xun came in person to look at the exhibition and left his tiny signature in the visitors' book. He also contributed five *yuan* (for we had to pay for the rental of the hall), and when I handed the receipt to him, he silently crumpled it up and threw it away.

This was the only time I ever met Lu Xun.

On the night of July 12th, the Spring Soil Art Society was just holding an Esperanto class when we were suddenly raided by secret agents from the police station in the French concession. After being searched for half an hour, I was arrested along with twelve other young artists.

The Kuomintang charged our group of defenseless young people with "subverting the government", taking advantage of their notorious "Emergency Decree to Deal with Actions Endangering the Republic".

We were kept under surveillance for a protracted period. I wrote a considerable number of poems. Some were smuggled out by our lawyer and close friends during their visits; they were subsequently published.

In order to avoid arousing the suspicion of the prison

authorities, I began to use the penname Ai Qing from 1933, when I wrote *Dayanhe — My Wet-nurse.* I have been using this penname now for a good forty-five years.

I was released in October 1935. The following year I published my first collection of poems under the title *Dayanhe.*

IV

On the 7th of July, 1937, the War of Resistance Against Japan broke out. The day before, I had a premonition and wrote a poem entitled *Our Land Reborn*:

For our land that had once been dead
Has, under the brilliant sky,
Been reborn!
— Miseries are no more than memories.
In the warm bosom of the earth
Will flow once more
The surging blood of our warriors.

The people of China, the great people of China, with our own living blood, have washed away the humiliation that has enslaved us for the last hundred years.

I left Shanghai for Wuhan, and from there I went on to Linfen in Shanxi Province. Next I went to Xi'an and then returned to Wuhan. Finally, I ended up in Guilin, where I was editor of *The South*, a supplement of the *Guangxi Daily*. I published my collection of poems, *The North*.

During the latter half of 1939, after having taught for a month at Xinning in Hunan, I went to Chongqing.

In the spring of 1940, I took my long poem *Torch* with me to Chongqing, then the cultural center of the "Great Interior".

Soon after, I was granted an interview with Comrade Zhou Enlai. Our meeting took place in Beipei on the outskirts of Chongqing. At the appointed time, he strode down from the high, thickly shaded stone steps, wearing a light gray cadre suit, looking very smart and trim.

In a talk he gave at the Yucai School, he made a point of saying that he hoped I would go to Yan'an, where I would be able "to devote myself to writing". At that time, everyone addressed him familiarly as "Vice-Chairman Zhou" (i.e., Vice-Chairman of the Military Commission).

The Southern Anhui Incident[1] occurred at the beginning of 1941, shaking the country and the whole world. The Kuomintang launched the third "Anti-Communist Onslaught". Progressive writers in Chongqing were intimidated, or were kept under close surveillance. Luckily, Comrade Zhou Enlai helped me out. Along with four other writers, I shook off the Kuomintang secret agents, but we were stopped and searched forty-seven times before we finally arrived safe and sound in Yan'an.

One early summer evening, after we were notified, we went to a cave dwelling in the Yangjia Mountains, and there, for the first time, we met the most impressive person I've ever encountered in my life — the great leader of the Chinese people, Mao Zedong. His stalwart figure and his affable smile left an indelible impression on me.

In November, I was elected a delegate to the Assembly of Representatives of the Shaanxi-Gansu-Ningxia border region where I wrote my first eulogy to Mao Zedong.

During the spring of 1942, Chairman Mao received me on several occasions. The first time, I was told that he had something to discuss with me. I went to see him.

---

[1] The Southern Anhui Incident occurred in January 1941 when the Communist New Fourth Army and the Kuomintang Army agreed to join forces to repel the Japanese invaders. On the way north, at southern Anhui, the 9,000 troops of the New Fourth Army were surrounded by 80,000 Kuomintang troops and — but for a thousand or more who managed to break through — were wiped out.

He told me about "some articles on which everybody had their opinion. What do you think we should do?" To be frank, I didn't think there was anything to worry about at the time. I said, in all innocence, "Call a meeting. You can explain things then." He said, "Will anyone listen to what I have to say?" I answered, "At least I will be there."

Afterwards, he wrote me a letter, saying, "With regard to the principles of literature and art that we discussed yesterday, I'd like you to go around collecting opposing points of view." The words "opposing points of view" were circled.

I did not collect any opposing views, but merely wrote out my own personal opinions.

After reading them he wrote to me again, and said, "Eager to have a talk with you." During our conversation, he raised many questions, which included questions of literature, art and politics, and of the functions of censure and praise. I made alterations to what I had written, according to his suggestions, and had it published under the title, "My Views on What Should Be Done About Literature and Art Today".

Later, in May, the Yan'an Forum on Literature and Art was held in Chairman Mao's name. It lasted several days and the discussions were lively.

During the forum, I remember Commander-in-chief Zhu De making a penetrating interpretation of two lines from Li Bai[1] that I had quoted in my article. They were:

In this life, rather a friend of Han Jingzhou
Than a marquis with ten thousand households.

Zhu De said, "Our Han Jingzhou is the worker, the peasant, and the soldier." Actually, he was pointing out the direction that artists and writers should follow.

At dusk on the day the talks came to an end, Chairman Mao issued his famous "Talks at the Yan'an Forum on

[1] Tang poet (701-762) — *Ed.*

Literature and Art", which has since become a classic, in which he developed the Marxist theory on literature and art, clearly and correctly reaffirming Lenin's principles on art and literature for the Party.

After the forum, I wrote to Chairman Mao stating my wish to go to the front. In his reply he wrote, "We approve of your going to northwest Shanxi, but you are advised not to wander too far, as the Datong-Puzhou railway line is difficult to cross. For the present we hope you will stay in Yan'an and study a little Marxism-Leninism, especially historical materialism. Then you can go to the front, where you can observe closely the class-relations in the countryside. Otherwise you will never understand China's war situation. . . ."

Telling me to study Marxism-Leninism, and especially historical materialism, was in fact telling me to throw myself into the "rectification movement" that was soon to follow. We were to be armed with Marxism-Leninism and, with this, overthrow abstract idealism in all realms of life.

V

In August 1945, Japan capitulated.

In October, I followed the Literature and Art Troupe of North China to Zhangjiakou. The troupe was merged into the United University of North China, where it became its School of Literature and Art. Soon after, it withdrew from Zhangjiakou and moved to the area covering central and southern Hebei. During the War of Liberation, I stayed with the School of Literature and Art carrying out administrative work. I also participated in land reform in several areas. My series of poems, *The Cuckoo*, was written then.

In early 1949, Beijing was liberated. My first job on entering the city was to take charge of the "Central Academy of Fine Arts" in the capacity of "Occupation Staff". I also took part in organizing the China Federation of Literary and Art Circles and the Chinese Writers' Association, attended the first session of the Chinese People's Political Consultative Conference and finally became the deputy chief editor of *Renmin Wenxue* (People's Literature).

In 1950, I visited the Soviet Union with a delegation from the Central Committee of the Chinese Communist Party, and all the poems that I had written so far appeared in *A Red Star of Ruby*.

In 1953, I went home and collected historical materials on eastern Zhejiang during the Anti-Japanese War period, but my epic poem, *The Tale of the Hidden Guns,* written in the style of a folk song, was a failure.

In July 1954, when I received an invitation from the Chilean Chamber of Deputies to visit their country, I wrote a series of poems entitled *South American Travels* and, after this series, a long sequel, *The Atlantic.*

In 1956, the People's Literature Press published my second collection of poems, *Spring.* In the postscript, I wrote:

> My works cannot possibly do justice to this great era. It can
> be reflected only by a multitude of choruses and orchestras. I
> am but one flautist from amid countless orchestras, and it is
> only because I am roused by this great era that I wish to cele-
> brate the bright prospects ahead.

In 1957, I had originally planned to write *The Hungarian Incident.* I had already finished the first two parts — *Flora* and *Lake Balaton,* but put them aside for lack of material. Then I left for Shanghai and collected historical materials concerning the imperialist invasion of China's economy. I wrote the section *The Bund,* but once again, in the press of business, I put it aside.

In April 1958, with the help of a general and the consent of Premier Zhou Enlai, I went to a state farm in the northeast to "observe and learn from real life". I was deputy head of a tree farm and spent a year and a half there living together with lumberjacks. During my stay I wrote two long poems, *Trampling Across the Wasteland Through a Thousand Miles of Snow* and *Rose-colored Dawn over the River Hamatong.* Unfortunately, both works were lost.

In the winter of 1959, I went to Xinjiang where I spent sixteen years in a reclamation area with a production and construction corps.

I made many friends there. I am determined to sing the praises of these warriors, these transformers of nature, and I have already gathered copious material in preparation for poems on this mechanized reclamation area.

In 1972, a doctor examined me and found out that my right eye had been losing its vision for the past four or five years because of a cataract.

In the spring of 1975, my superior approved my going to Beijing so I could receive treatment for my eye.

Then came 1976 — what an unforgettable year that was! The Chinese people lost three leaders in a row; the whole country was plunged into imminent danger — the pernicious Gang of Four extended their sinister, greedy reach in all directions. . . . Thanks to the Party Central Committee crushing the Gang of Four, our great motherland turned from disaster to stability. I, too, was liberated for the second time.

VI

The poet must speak the truth.

You hear people say, "So-and-so's poems are popular because they express what is in the hearts of the people." I don't think that explains it all. I would say, "So-and-so's poems are popular because he speaks the truth — straight from his heart."

Everybody loves to hear the truth and a poet can only touch the hearts of the people with words that are sincere. He must also stand with the people, sharing their loves and hates, their joys and sorrows. Only when the poet's wisdom and courage come from the people will he win the people's trust.

The people do not like falsehoods. No matter how well you camouflage it, no matter how high-sounding it appears, it will not stir the people's hearts. In his own heart, everyone has a scale on which he weighs your words.

There are people who brag about their "political savvy". They always praise those who are in power and attack those who have fallen.

Such people write "poetry" with one eye on changes in the weather.

But we live in such a rapidly changing world that such "poets" have to run their legs off, hopping from one extreme to another, like a speculator at the stock market. Though they have the slipperiness of a philistine, they just can't help sometimes betting on the wrong horse.

"Political savvy" is, of course, necessary — the sharper the better — but it must be in accord with the will of the people. If one is motivated by selfish, egoistic considerations, one won't be able to smell out the real thing.

This means that the poet's sensitivity must be at one with the sensitivity of the people and he must also have the political resilience of the people.

A "Bounce-back Greybeard"[1] is only a toy, never an example for human behavior.

---

[1] A stuffed doll in the shape of an old man, so weighted as to always right itself when knocked down — like the "Schmoo"-dolls of Al Capp — *Ed.*

Nobody can be excited by everything. Even a cicada knows when to get excited.

There are people who think you don't need "inspiration" to write poetry. They are probably people who advocate artificial insemination, but they are unlikely to be poets.

People who think that anything they don't understand or can't explain does not exist or is unscientific can only live out their lives in a small shell like a snail.

The objective world is constantly changing. It sometimes rains, sometimes the wind blows. People too are moved, now by joy, now by sorrow.

"Inspiration," if we must call it that, is nothing more than a poet responding to something in a new way: it is a sudden passion, a flash or spark lighting up the heart if only for an instant. "Inspiration," so-called, is the happiest possible encounter of the poet's subjective world with objective reality. It should be the poet's best friend. Why exile inspiration to the deserts of subjectivism?

There can be no contradiction without difference.

To be excited about everything is to be excited about nothing.

A poet must be true to his feelings. Feelings are his reaction to the objective world.

Not every poem is about the poet himself, but every poem is written by him, and that means it comes from his heart.

To affect excitement when there is none means you must learn to lie. If one is not stirred by anything to write about, one cannot stir the feelings of others.

Of course, telling the truth may cause trouble, or even represent a risk, but if you want to write poetry, you shouldn't do it at the expense of your own conscience by telling lies.

VII

One doesn't write poetry for the sake of playing around with verbal skills; on the other hand, one must have these skills in order to write poetry. Even when we talk, there is such a thing as talking to the point or not talking to the point.

The activity of the human mind, which produces the imagination and the ability to associate ideas, is nothing but a synthesis of life's experiences. In the course of synthesizing these experiences, metaphors occur. The object of metaphor is for one experience to corroborate another experience.

> The sense of touch and the sense of sight are mutually complementary, so that, after a while, we can speak of the outer form of something as something susceptible to touch.

What a clever notion, that of something being "mutually complementary." Engels' use of this phrase, "mutually complementary," although it relates to the senses, also applies to the relationships between things and to the relationships between thoughts. It grasps the interrelatedness and the connections between everything in creation.

The activity of the imagination consists of crystallizing all sorts of things that are difficult to grasp, all sorts of things that are vague and elusive, and presenting them clearly before the reader, as clearly as the print on a page.

The activity of the imagination consists of converting something abstract to concrete terms — something that will touch the emotions.

The activity of the imagination causes something heavy and leaden to sprout wings; or, the reverse, to freeze and fix something flowing and in flux.

In the realm of the imagination, one can grasp hands across ten thousand miles; or, one could cause hands that hold each other to wave goodbye.

The way of the imagination is the way that draws "mutual complementarities" from the abstract and the concrete.

The way of the imagination is poetry, and it is the basic tool in the creation of poetry as well as other literature.

Even in theoretical work (including works based on "logical thinking"), one sees the workings of the imagination. For example, "The Communist Manifesto":

> The aristocracy, in order to rally the people to them, waved the proletarian alms-bag in front for a banner. But the people, as often as it joined them, saw on their hindquarters the old feudal coat of arms, and deserted them with loud and irreverent laughter.

Take the case of Shakespeare, a writer who simply was unable to write except imaginatively. In his works, there is not one instance when the light of the imagination did not flash.

For example, "gold" is but a concept, but in his *Timon of Athens*, "gold" is transformed into a "person" with concrete attributes:

> O thou sweet king-killer, and dear divorce
> 'Twist natural son and sire, thou bright defiler
> Of Hymen's purest bed, thou valiant Mars,
> Thou ever young, fresh, loved, and delicate wooer,
> Whose blush doth thaw the consecrated snow
> That lies on Dian's lap. Thou visible god,
> That solder'st close impossibilities
> And mak'st them kiss. . . .

> *Timon of Athens*, IV, iii, 386-393

This is a metaphor that runs through the thoughts like a thread, which presents the deepest and sharpest indictment of the world controlled by capitalism.

Only when poetry can achieve this kind of penetrating imagination can it produce a perdurable appeal.

Those who write poetry will often develop an image to explore a concept. For example, my "Pearl":

In the sea of azure-blue
Which takes in the energy of the sun
You are the embodiment of the rainbow
Iridescent like the rosy glimmer of dawn

The image of flowered dew, of frozen thought
The essence of beloved white crystal
A concept nurtured in the heart
That forms beads of genuine pearl

"Concept" is abstract, but to form "beads of genuine pearl" is to create something with its own radiance, something that can be grasped.

"Resistance" is an abstraction that belongs to the category of words of the spirit. "Wherever there is oppression, there you will find resistance." Resistance arises naturally in people who are oppressed.

Aren't there still people who oppress other people who should be resisted?

Those countries and those people who seek their own right to life, when they suffer unremitting oppression, what should they do?

One wave after another
Makes its relentless assault.
Each wave falls at its feet,
Dashed to bring foam, and dispersed. . . .

The face and body of the reef,
As if slashed by a knife;
But it stands there still
With a faint smile, gazing out at the sea. . . .

This point of view is only seen from the angle of the "reef", against which the waves "Makes its relentless assault" — what other choice does it have?

There are those who say that a reef is "hostile to all

ships, big or small", that "it is too arrogant" — it should yield. This completely overlooks the fact that a reef is immobile, and that "ships, big and small" should not go bumping into the obstinate, intractable reef. This is an example of how two different conclusions might be drawn from two different perspectives.

The metaphors that emerge out a lively imagination are not themselves primary things, which is why Lenin said: "All metaphors are cripples." Because of this, metaphors are most easily distorted and can be used for the vilest slander: — history knows many cases of "imputed literary wrong doings"[1] that have been constructed as a result of metaphor.

VIII

The era in which I now live has been a turbulent, vital, brilliant, colorful time. Like those of my age, I have survived various kinds of war and I have encountered diverse sorts of enemy as well. The times have really been unpredictable!

In the winter of 1941, I wrote a long poem titled "Era"; in it, the most important words seem to apply to what has happened in the last few years:

> Even if I knew that it would bring me
> Neither the merriment of a festival day
> Nor the gay laughter from a playground
> But a sight more bloody than a thousand slaughterhouses,
> I should still have rushed into its arms,
> With all the fervor that life can possess.
> . . . .
> In order to rise from the abyss of time,
> I would welcome greater praise or slander more vile,
> Undying enmity and a threatening attack . . .

[1] This refers to the practice — particularly characteristic of suspicious emperors — of looking for arcane treasons in the writings of suspected officials and scholars — *Ed.*

. . . .
I am faithful and devoted to the era; but I keep silence,
Unwilling, like a captured prisoner
Who is silent before he is escorted to the execution grounds,
I keep silence, because I do not have words brilliant enough
To express my emotions, my passionate entreaties,
Like thunder rolling in an overcast sky in early summer.
I offer to that which has so gratified and so pleased me,
My love for it surpasses my love for anything else.
I would willingly give my life for its advent —
To it I offer both my body and my soul.
Before it I will so humble myself
As to lie supine on the ground,
And let it, like a horse's hooves, trample on my chest.

This is the kind of poem that clearly celebrates the era, an era for which we fought and gave our lives: "Before it I will so humble myself/As to lie supine on the ground/And let it, like a horse's hooves, trample on my chest."

Such a poem, however, was willfully distorted by that literary mountebank, Yao Wenyuan, who vilified it as "the cry of an individualist braggart!" and had the unmitigated gall to say that it was a poem attacking Yan'an!

It was this very literary mountebank who said that I never praised the proletariat! But, in four of my poems, I mentioned the first proletarian political group, the Paris Commune:

In *Paris* (1932), I spoke about "the birth of the Commune"; in *Mourning Paris* (1940), I wrote: "there will be the birth of a Second Commune"; in *Commemorating Romain Rolland* (1945), I said: "selling out the sons of the Commune that they became themselves captives"; and in *The Resistance of Toulon* (1942), I wrote: "The heirs of the Commune will be liberated again!"

This phony "Marxist theorist" exposed himself as an anti-Marxist long ago, as early as twenty years before.

After his article was published, I received a letter from a general who wrote these words of encouragement: "You have praised the Commune's children, you should continue to write poetry."

What a striking contrast between these two responses!

I do not know how many times I have mentioned the leaders and the soldiers of the proletariat. . . . How could it be said that I have never praised the proletariat? Is one counted among the proletariat only when one adopts a label that reads: "Proletariat"?

The literary mountebank also distorted the following lines from "The Song of the Sun" from my long poem *Facing the Sun*:

> The sun
> Makes me think . . .
>
> . . . .
>
> Of the *Marseillaise*, the *Internationale*,
> Of Washington, Lenin, Sun Yat-sen
>   And all the names of those figures
>   Who delivered mankind from misery.

The literary mountebank said, "But the *Internationale* and Lenin have been placed side by side with the *Marseillaise*, Washington, and Sun Yat-sen; they are not singled out at all." Thus he passed the following political "judgement" on me: "He is merely obsessed with bourgeois freedom and democracy." That's some word, "merely"!

I wrote the long poem *Facing the Sun* in April 1938 in Wuchang, then under Kuomintang control. That was the period when the Kuomintang showed passive resistance against Japan, but active opposition to the Chinese Communist Party. Was I wrong, then, at that time, to talk about freedom and democracy?

A full twenty years later, in 1958, in Shanghai, Yao was living in the "writer's studio", run by his turncoat father, Yao Pengzi. Sitting casually on the sofa, he laughed scornfully at the poems I had written during the White Terror period. He was apparently quite pleased with himself. He even said that I had added "Lenin" and the *Internationale* just for show!

And all this because he enjoyed the freedom to beat people up as he liked and to libel them at his whim.

Today, we have the chance to review the way this literary mountebank rose to power and rank, and to see even more clearly the fascist despotism of the Gang of Four in the cultural sphere, for which they had a dry run some twenty years ago.

Such a gangster, who charged about like one about to enter Limbo, became a "Colossus" through fraud, seizing complete control in the fields of art and literature over a period of twenty years. Is this not something to make us wonder?

But, happily, all this is finally behind us.

Now, the mighty current of the times has swept me away to a new harbor about to brim with sunshine and, in the prolonged sound of horns in the fog, my life begins a new voyage.

Middle of December, 1978

(Translated by Peng Wenlan
and Eugene Chen Eoyang)

Transparent Night

Transparent night.

. . . A burst of hearty laughter in the fields . . .
A band of winebibbers, gazing
At the deep slumbering village,
Noisily wind their way . . .
To the village
Where the bark of a dog sets a-quiver
The scattered stars filling the sky.

To the village
Through the slumbering street
Through the slumbering square, they rush
Into a bustling tavern.

Wine, lamplight, drunken faces,
Dissipated laughter fused together. . . .

"Let's go to the slaughter house,
Let's drink beef broth. . . ."

2

The winebibbers make their way to the edge of the village
And enter the door gaping with lamplight,

The smell of blood, piles of meat, and the hot stench
Of cowhide. . . .
People shouting, people shouting.
Like a prairie fire, the oil lamp casts its light
Upon dozens of mud-colored faces
Among the grassland dwellers.

Here's our recreation center,
Such familiar faces,
We take up
Steaming hot joints of beef,
Mouths open wide, and chew and chew. . . .

"Wine! Wine!
Give us wine!"
Like a prairie fire, the oil lamp casts its light
Upon cow's blood, the butcher's bloodstained arms,
And the butcher's
        Blood-besplattered brow.

Like a prairie fire, the oil lamp casts its light
Upon our burning muscles, and
— inside —
The strength of pain, wrath, and hate.

Like a prairie fire, the oil lamp casts its light
Upon night prowlers
Drunkards
Loafers
Highway robbers
Cattle thieves
Coming out from every which corner. . . .

"Wine! Wine!
Give us wine!"

3

. . . .
"By the light of the stars, shivering
    We go. . . ."
A burst of laughter in the fields . . .
A band of winebibbers leaving
The slumbering village, making for
The slumbering grassland
Noisily they wind their way. . . .

Night! Transparent
Night!

September 10, 1932

(Translated by Peng Wenlan)

Dayanhe — My Wet-Nurse

Dayanhe, my wet-nurse:
Her name was the name of the village which gave her birth;
She was a child-bride:
My wet-nurse, Dayanhe.

I am the son of a landlord,
But I have been brought up on Dayanhe's milk:
The son of Dayanhe.
Raising me Dayanhe raised her own family;
I am one who was raised on your milk,
Oh Dayanhe, my wet-nurse.

Dayanhe, today, looking at the snow falling makes me think
   of you:
Your grass-covered, snow-laden grave,
The withered weeds on the tiled eaves of your shut-up house,
Your garden-plot, ten-foot square, and mortgaged,
Your stone seat just outside the gate, overgrown with moss,
Dayanhe, today, looking at the snow falling makes me think
   of you.

With your great big hands, you cradled me to your breast,
   soothing me;
After you had stoked the fire in the oven,
After you had brushed off the coal-ashes from your apron,
After you had tasted for yourself whether the rice was cooked,
After you had set the bowls of black soybeans on the black
   table,

After you had mended your sons' clothes, torn by thorns on
    the mountain ridge,

After you had bandaged the hand of your little son, nicked
    with a cleaver,

After you had squeezed to death, one by one, the lice on
    your children's shirts,

After you had collected the first egg of the day,

With your great big hands, you cradled me to your breast,
    soothing me.

I am the son of a landlord,

After I had taken all the milk you had to offer,

I was taken back to my home by the parents who gave me
    birth.

Ah, Dayanhe, why are you crying?

I was a newcomer to the parents who gave me birth!

I touched the red-lacquered, floral-carved furniture,

I touched the ornate brocade on my parents' bed,

I looked dumbly at the "Bless This House" sign above the
    door — which I couldn't read,

I touched the buttons of my new clothes, made of silk and
    mother-of-pearl,

I saw in my mother's arms a sister whom I scarcely knew,

I sat on a lacquered stool with a small brazier set underneath,

I ate white rice which had been milled three times.

Still, I was bashful and shy! Because I,

I was a newcomer to the parents who gave me birth.

Dayanhe, in order to survive,

After her milk had run dry,

She began to put those arms, arms that had cradled me, to
    work,

Smiling, she washed our clothes,

Smiling, she carried the vegetables, and rinsed them in the
    icy pond by the village,

Smiling, she sliced the turnips frozen through and through,
Smiling, she stirred the swill in the pigs' trough,
Smiling, she fanned the flames under the stove with the
     broiling meat,
Smiling, she carried the baling baskets of beans and grain to
     the open square where they baked in the sun,
Dayanhe, in order to survive,
After the milk in her had run dry,
She put those arms, arms that had cradled me, to work.

Dayanhe was so devoted to her foster-child, whom she
     suckled;
At New Year's, she'd busy herself cutting winter-rice candy
     for him,
For him, who would steal off to her house by the village,
For him, who would walk up to her and call her "Mama",
Dayanhe, she would stick his drawing of Guan Yu, the war
     god, bright green and bright red, on the wall by the
     stove,
Dayanhe, how she would boast and brag to her neighbors
     about her foster-child.
Dayanhe, once she dreamt a dream she could tell no one,
In her dream, she was drinking a wedding toast to her foster-
     child,
Sitting in a resplendent hall bedecked with silk,
And the beautiful young bride called her affectionately,
     "Mother."
. . . .
Dayanhe, she was so devoted to her foster-child!

Dayanhe, in a dream from which she has not awakened, has
     died.
When she died, her foster-child was not at her side,
When she died, the husband who often beat her shed tears
     for her.

Her five sons each cried bitter tears,
When she died, feebly, she called out the name of her foster-
    child,
Dayanhe is dead:
When she died, her foster-child was not at her side.

Dayanhe, she went with tears in her eyes!
Along with forty-nine years, a lifetime of humiliation at the
    hands of the world,
Along with the innumerable sufferings of a slave,
Along with a two-bit casket and some bundles of rice-straw,
Along with a plot of ground to bury a casket in a few square
    feet,
Along with a handful of ashes, from paper money burned,
Dayanhe, she went with tears in her eyes.

But these are the things that Dayanhe did not know:
That her drunkard husband is dead,
That her eldest son became a bandit,
That her second died in the smoke of war,
That her third, her fourth, her fifth,
Live on, vilified by their teachers and their landlords,
And I — I write condemnations of this unjust world.
When I, after drifting about for a long time, went home
On the mountain ridge, in the wilds,
When I saw my brothers, we were closer than we were 6 or
    7 years ago,
This, this is what you, Dayanhe, calmly sleeping in repose,
This is what you do not know!

Dayanhe, today, your foster-child is in jail,
Writing a poem of praise, dedicated to you,
Dedicated to your spirit, purple shade under the brown soil,
Dedicated to your outstretched arms that embraced me,
Dedicated to your lips that kissed me,

Dedicated to your face, warm and soft, the color of earth,
Dedicated to your breasts that suckled me,
Dedicated to your sons, my brothers,
Dedicated to all of them on earth,
The wet-nurses like my Dayanhe, and all their sons,
Dedicated to Dayanhe, who loved me as she loved her own
    sons.

Dayanhe,
I am one who grew up suckling at your breasts,
Your son.
I pay tribute to you,
With all my love.

On a snowy morning,
January 14, 1933

(Translated by Eugene Chen Eoyang)

Paris

Paris
Facing you
At dawn, in the twilight
At noon, in the deep of night
— I have seen
You in your own moods:
Anger, joy
Agony, happiness and high spirits!
All day long
You would, without pause
Beat with your fists at your own breast
Blow after blow!
Or crane your neck, looking straight up towards the skies
Shouting out!
Or droop your head mournfully, eyes shut tight
Absorbed in deep, dark meditation,
Or loosen your long, golden tresses
And sing out,
Or else,
Undo your crimson dress
Laying bare a piece of luscious flesh
Lascivious wanton that you are!
To me only
And to sojourners by the hundreds of thousands
You have sent out
Your irresistible and seductive call. . . .
Paris,
You beautiful, hysterical whore

. . . .
Look at the trolleys one after the other
Going towards the end of the long boulevard
And disappearing. . . .
Then, once again, one after another, coming back!
Listen, the trolley
Ding ding ding ding ding fly past. . . .
The surging crowds of people
Rush in from the big streets
And into the small alleys,
Then, from each alley, they double back
To form a floodtide
Amassing
On the boulevards
On the open squares
Not stopping for one minute
Swirling about!
Swirling about!
Shouting all at once
Shifting back and forth and around
Buildings in every direction
Piled up one on top of another
Or the memorial obelisk
Or around the bronze statues
Or in front of the large emporia,
Stores side by side
In the light of the sun
In the light of the lamps
Shining on and on forever
Trippingly
Festively
Lighting up like Severini's brilliant, glowing canvas
"The Shimmering Dance". . . .
From the *Radio*
And the music from Les Marchés Aux Puces,

Together with the violent
Vociferous
Clamor
Of men at work —
Magnificent hymn,
Glory's high-blown sentences,
Iron-sinewed verse —
And from chapter after chapter
Buses, trolleys, *le Métro,* fully stocked,
A scintillating alphabet,
Asphalt streets, trolley tracks, byways are the animating
    sentences,
Wheel + wheel + wheel are punctuations of action,
Whistle + whistle + whistle are exclamation points! —
All these now mix together in an everlastingly beautiful
    prose —
Flourishing, from the different tongues of different in-
    dividuals
From different elements,
Into one entirely fantastic "creation"
An entirely fresh and resonant chorus!
You are —
What makes an "individual"
With a subtle and particular "character";
That has seeped into
The masses, like endless drops of water,
Converted and manifest in
Tens of thousands —
The most magnificent
The most demented
The most bizarre "character".
You are preposterous, Paris!
How many centuries
In exchanges between generations and peoples
Have they put their own favorite coloring

And dabbed it on your face.
Every life, every movement
Every massacre, every battle clambering on your streets —
Even the smallest wedding party —
Are all of a piece with
Louis the Sixteenth mounting the guillotine
Revolution
Riot
The birth of the Commune
The Assault on the Bastille:
All are part of a meaning that is indelible
That we dutifully record here:
Your growth
Your age
Your nature and your disposition
Your joys as well as your grief.
Paris,
You are now strong!
Your heaven-soaring flames are now a magnet
Attracting people from every nation, every race,
From all over the world,
Who have, with a venturesome spirit
Rushed to you
Embraced you with love
Or detested you to the very marrow of their being!
— You do not know
From what kind of far-off clump of grass I
Jumped out of,
Reaching out to you
With trembling arms
And goading myself
To greater and greater hardships!
Paris
You rare and precious creation
You want to live life with courage

Like reckless men rushing to their deaths!
You use
Aphrodisiacs, bronzes of Napoleon, alcohol, the Arc de
    Triomphe
The Eiffel Tower, women
The Louvre, l'Opéra
La Bourse, the banks
To beckon:
All the world's —
Idiots, gamblers, pimps
Drunks, pot-bellied merchants
Adventurers, boxers
Dreamers, speculators. . . .
Ah, Paris!
For your captivating smile
How many people
Have abandoned
Their deep-rooted, loving family ties,
And thrown them away for your dubious attractions
How many hundreds of thousands
Have all expended their energies,
Poured out the sweat of their labor
To entreat you
To give them some of your sympathy
And some of your love!
But
You —
Huge metropolis,
Are nothing but this
Iron-hearted, stone-faced being!
We are, finally,
Discouraged by suffering and by defeat
And yet the stronger for it.
You have shot off dazzling sparks
With your haughtiness! And you

Yet casting them off in their misery,
Like so much trash,
Have absolutely no pity!
Paris,
I hate you and I love you with all my strength.
Don't mock me when my arms fall limp
Walking my despondent way home,
I am still young!
And
On the field of life, of those who have been routed
I am by no means the only one!
— Indeed, compared to those you dote on,
There are incomparably more of us!
We all have to
Distance ourselves from you
— Gain a little experience
Temper our sinews
Until the day arrives
When an army of troops congregates
And rises up against you!
Then,
We will be in the vanguard of the attack
And when we conquer you
We will
Take you out on the town
Embrace you
We would have you on our arms
Singing wildly amusing songs!
Paris, you — you
Profligate
So profligate
And bewitching a woman!

(Translated by Eugene Chen Eoyang)

The Sun

From the graves of the ancient past,
From the ages of darkness,
From this death stream of humanity,
Awakening mountains from their slumber,
Like a wheel of fire over the sand dunes
The sun rolls on towards me. . . .

With invincible rays
It gives breath to life,
Making the branches of trees dance towards it,
Making the rivers rush forward with song.

When it comes I can hear
The sleeping insects turning underground,
The people talking loudly in the squares,
The cities beckoning it from the distance
With electricity and steel.
Then my breast
Is torn open by the hands of fire,
My rotten soul
Gets discarded by the river,
And I gain faith once more
In the resurgence of humanity.

Spring, 1937

(From *Chinese Literature*)

Coal's Reply

Where do you live?

I live in ten thousand years of steep mountain
I live in ten thousand years of crag-rock

And your age?

My age is greater than the mountain's
Greater than the crag-rock's

How long have you been silenced?
Since the dinosaurs governed the earth
Since the earth felt its first tremor

Have you perished in this deep rancor and bitterness?

Death?   No, no, I'm still alive
Please, give me a light, give me a light

Spring 1937

(Translated by Marilyn Chin)

A Smile

I don't trust archaeologists —

After several thousand years have passed,
By the shores bare of human footprints,
In the ruins that once bustled with activity,
Someone will pick up a fragment of dry bone
— A dry bone from my body.
How will he know that this fragment of dry bone
Was singed and charred back in the twentieth century?

And who can, in the earth's strata,
Find
The teardrops of the victims
Who suffered the ultimate torments?
Those teardrops
Were locked behind a thousand iron bars,
With only one key
That could unlock that kind of prison gate.
But the countless brave men who tried to get that key
Have all been killed, fallen
Under the guns and the swords of the defenders.

If I could pick one of those teardrops
To keep by my pillow,
More than the pearl recovered from a thousand fathoms deep,
It would shine on and on,
Radiating through all time and space!
Haven't all of us,

Each in our own time,
Been nailed on a cross?
And this crucifixion
Is surely no less excruciating than
Being crucified by the people of Nazareth.

By the hands of our enemy,
A crown of thorns has been placed on our head,
From our brow, deathly pale and lacerated,
Drip drops of blood, crimson,
But even this cannot signify
The bitter anguish in our heart!
It is true
That we should not harbor any hopes in vain,
But we would wish some day,
When people think of us,
As one thinks of things long ago,
Of ancestors who wrestled with primeval monsters,
A smile will flit across their faces,
A smile both serene and generous —
Perhaps even a little indulgent —
Oh, how willing I would be,
To lay down my life for such a smile!

May 8, 1937

(Translated by Eugene Chen Eoyang)

The Land Reborn

The putrid days
Have long since sunk down to the riverbed.
May the currents wash them clean,
So that soon no trace of them will be left.

On the river bank,
Where spring has passed through, stepping lightly,
Everywhere flowers flourish and grass is lush;
And from over there, from that grove,
Emanates
The loud chirpings of a hundred birds
Celebrating the season.

Oh, sowers of the seed,
It is time to sow your seed:
Let us toil with might and main, so that
The earth might bring forth
Golden kernels of grain.

Now is also the time
For you — oh poet of sorrow and suffering,
To cast off the dolors of days long past,
Let hope revive,
In your long, long suffering hearts.

For our land that had once been dead,
Has, under the brilliant sky,
Been reborn!

— Miseries are no more than memories.
In the warm bosom of the earth
Will flow once more
The surging blood of our warriors.

On the Shanghai-Hangzhou Railroad
July 6, 1937

(Translated by Eugene Chen Eoyang)

He Has Risen

He has risen —
From dozens of years of humiliation,
By the deep pit dug for him by the enemy.

His brow dripping with blood,
His chest also running with blood,
But he is laughing —
He has never laughed like this before.

He is laughing,
His eyes looking forward, gleaming,
As if searching
For the enemy that felled him to the ground.

He has risen.
When he stands,
He will be fiercer than all beasts,
And wiser than all men.

He must be like this,
For he must snatch back his own life
From the death of the enemy.

October 12, 1937, Hangzhou

(From *Chinese Literature*)

43

Snow Falls on China's Land

Snow falls on China's land;
Cold blockades China....

Wind,
Like a grief-stricken old woman
Closely following behind,
Stretching out her icy claws,
Tugs at the travellers' clothes.
With words as old as the land,
Her nagging never ends...
Coming from the forests
In horse-drawn carts,
You, there, farmers of China,
Wearing fur hats,
Braving the blizzard —
Where are you going?

I tell you,
I too am a descendant of farmers.
From your wrinkled faces etched with pain,
I understand deeply
The years and years of toil
Of the men who make their lives on the prairie.

Yet I
Am no happier than you
— Lying in the river of time.
Turbulent waves of hardship
Have so often swallowed me up,
Only to spew me forth.

I have lost the most precious days
Of my youth
In roaming and in prisons.
My life
Like yours
Is haggard.

Snow falls on China's land;
Cold blockades China. . . .

On the river of this snowy night,
One small oil lamp drifts slowly
In a rickety boat with a black canopy.
Who sits in there
In the lamplight, head bowed?

— Ah, it's you,
Tousle-haired and grubby-faced young woman.
Wasn't it
Your home
— That warm and happy nest —
Was burnt to the ground
By the brutal enemy?
Wasn't it
A night like this
Bereft of the protection of a man
That, in the terror of death,
You were teased and poked by enemy bayonets?

On such cold nights as tonight,
Our countless
Aged mothers
Huddle together in homes not theirs —
Like strangers
Not knowing
Where tomorrow's wheel

Will take them.
And China's roads
Are so rugged
And so muddy.

Snow falls on China's land;
Cold blockades China. . . .

Passing over the prairies in this snowy night,
Over regions chewed raw by the beacons of war,
Countless, the tillers of the virgin soil
Lost, the animals they nurtured;
Lost, their fertile fields.
They crowd together
In life's hopeless squalor:
On famine's earth,
Gazing at the dark sky,
They reach out, trembling,
And beg for succor.

Oh, the pain and misery of China,
As long and vast as this snowy night!
Snow falls on China's land;
Snow blockades China. . . .

China,
The feeble poem I write
On this lampless night,
Can it bring you a little warmth?

In the night
December 28, 1937

(Translated by Marilyn Chin)

Wheelbarrow

In the territory where the Yellow River once flowed,
In the numberless dried-up riverbeds,
The wheelbarrow,
With its single wheel,
Lets out a squeal that shakes the lugubrious sky,
Piercing the wintry chill, the desolate stillness.
From the foot of this mountain
To the foot of that mountain,
The sound cuts right through
The sorrow of the northern people.

On frost-bitten, snow-chilled days,
In and around destitute little villages,
The wheelbarrow,
With its solitary wheel,
Carves out its deep ruts in the pale-yellow layers of earth,
Cutting through the vastness and the desolation,
From this road
To that road,
It knits together
The sorrow of the northern people.

Early 1938

(Translated by Eugene Chen Eoyang)

The North

One day a poet from the grasslands of Keerqin
said to me, "The north is wretched."

Yes,
The north is wretched,
From beyond the frontier blows
The wind from the desert,
Scraping off the fertile greensward in the north,
And with it, the glory of the seasons
— Now a stretch of pallid ashen yellow,
Covered with a layer, an impenetrable miasma of sand,
That howling gale that hurries over here from the horizon
And brings with it a terror,
Maniacally
Sweeping over the land;
Vast and desolate hinterlands,
Frozen in the cold winds of December,
Villages, yes, mountainsides, yes, riverbanks too,
Crumbling walls and unkempt graves, as well,
All covered with a dusty mantle of misery....
A solitary traveller,
His body leaning forward,
His hand shielding his face,
In the wind-swept sand,
Gasps hard for breath,
One step after another,
Still manages to move on ...
A number of donkeys

48

— Those beasts with their mournful eyes
  And drooping ears,
Bear the heavy weight
Of the suffering in the land;
Their weary tread
Steps laboriously
Over the north
And its interminable, desolate roads. . . .

Those streams have long since dried up,
And the riverbeds are lined with wheel tracks.
The people and the land of the north,
Are thirsty,
Oh, so thirsty for the fresh, life-giving spring.
The withered forests,
And low-lying houses,
Are sparse, forlorn,
Scattered under the dark-gray backdrop of the sky.
In the sky,
The sun can't be seen,
Just a flock of wild geese in formation,
Agitated, these wild geese,
Beat their black wings,
Cry out their uncertainty and distress,
And from this cold wasteland, flee,
Flee to
The south where green foliage blots out the sky. . . .

The north is wretched.
The Yellow River, thousands of miles long,
Its waves, turbulent and muddy,
Has given this vast area in the north
Torrents of calamity and misfortune;
Oh, how the winds and frosts down through the years
Have etched

The vast northern landscape
Of squalor and starvation.

And I
— I, this sojourner from the south,
Oh, how I love this wretched land in the north.
Its windy sands that pelt the face,
And its cold air that seeps into the bones,
Will not cause me to curse it,
I love this wretched land,
An endless stretch of desolate hinterland;
Yet, it brings out my devotion.
— I see them,
Our forebears,
Leading their flocks of sheep,
Blowing on the reed-pipes,
Overwhelmed in this great desert dusk;
We have trod
This age-old, loamy brown layer of earth,
Where the skeletons of our forebears are buried,
— This earth that they first broke open with the plow,
Thousands of years ago
They were already here
Battling the Nature that made them fight for survival.
When they defended their territory,
They never once disgraced themselves.
They are dead now,
Leaving the legacy of the land to us —
I love this wretched country,
Her vast, barren soil,
Which gave us a language pure and simple,
And a capacious spirit as well.
I believe this language and this spirit,
Strong and sturdy, will survive on the land,
Never to be extinguished.

I love this wretched country,
    This age-old country,
This country
That has nourished what I have loved:
The world's most long-suffering
And most venerable people.

Tongguan
February 4, 1938

(Translated by Eugene Chen Eoyang)

The Woman Mending Clothes

The woman mending clothes sits by the roadside.
When people pass by
Dust rises up,
Dust coats her kerchief,
Dust grays her clothes.

Her baby begins crying,
The child's tears are dried by the sun;
She does not notice it.
Silently she thinks of her home,
Its shelter destroyed by gunfire.
Silently she mends clothes for people,
And lets her child's eyes,
Those poor reddened eyes,
Stare at the empty basket.

The woman mending clothes sits by the roadside.
The road stretches away endlessly.
She mends socks for some passer-by,
And the passer-by goes on.

At a station on the Beiping-Hankou Railway
February 1938

(From *Chinese Literature*)

Facing the Sun

From the graves of the ancient past,
From the ages of darkness,
From this death stream of humanity,
Awakening mountains from their slumber,
Like a wheel of fire over the sand dunes
The sun rolls on towards me. . . .

From an earlier poem, "The Sun"

1. I Get Up

I get up —
Like a drowsy beast
An injured beast
From the forest of dry scattered leaves
From an ice-cold rock
Struggling for some time
I manage to prop my body up
And open my eyes
To seek out the horizon. . . .

I —
Am a traveller,
Come from far-off mountain regions
From mountain regions yet uncultivated
To this city of millions
Who labor with their hands
Who yell with the mouths
Who tramp over the streets of the city

53

And my body
My aching body
Is left with a persistent fatigue
From running a long distance
In the wind and rain last night

Still
I get up at last

I open the window
And with the eyes of a prisoner who sees light for the first
  time
I see the dawn
— Ah, the dawn as it really is
(From afar
There seems to come the sound of people singing)
Then — I decide to go into the street

2. On the Street

Good morning,
Policeman who stands at the intersection
Waving your white-sleeved arm
As the traffic goes by;
Good morning,
Grocer from the outskirts
Toting baskets brimming with vegetables;
Good morning,
Red-skirted street-cleaner
Sweeping up the thoroughfares;
Good morning,
Brown-skinned, young housewife
Bringing your basket, the first to arrive at the market.
I don't believe

Any of you could have spent the night
As I did
Pursued by ceaseless wind and rain,
Entangled in an endless nightmare:
You all slept better than I!

3.   Yesterday

Yesterday
Upon this earth
With my pathetic hopes
I nurse out my days
Just like those widows
Wearing mourning clothes
Who take their pathetic memories
And nurse out their days

Yesterday
I thought of my own country
     As a "sick bay"
— I had contracted an incurable disease
There has not been a day
That I have not looked
With dazed eyes at
     The interminable life of suffering on this land. . . .
There has not been a day
That I have not listened
With stupefied ears to
     The unremitting groans of agony on this land

Yesterday
I locked myself
In the prison of my mind —
All around me high gray walls

Not a sound
I followed the high wall
And walked, and walked,
My soul —
Whether night or day —
Intoning over and over
A sad song about the destiny of mankind

Yesterday
I ran wildly
Through the sunless fields
Under a dark, overcast sky
To the mountaintop
Fell down on the purple rock
And shedding hot tears
I wept for this, our century

But now all is well
Everything is past and gone

4.   Sunrise

The sun has risen. . . .
When it appears. . . .
"The cities beckon to it from the distance
With electricity and steel."

Quote from earlier poem "The Sun"

The sun rises
From behind the tall buildings in the distance
— Those mountains built of cement and steel
With their smokestacks by the hundreds
Their utility poles by the thousands
Their rooftops by the ten thousands
Forming in its network

A dense overgrown forest

On the Pacific
On the Indian Ocean
On the Red Sea
On the Mediterranean
In my first fervent hopes for the world
And in my youth when I sailed upon a boundless blue sea
I have seen beautiful sunrises
But at this moment
In the city that I breathe in
A city that spews out the smell of paraffin
The smell of tar
A city full of miscellaneous smells
A city which exposes a metal body
A mineral body
An electric body
A city which receives with open arms
Dawn's tender care
I see a sunrise
More beautiful than any other

5. The Song of the Sun

Yes
The sun is altogether more beautiful
More than fair virgins
More than flower-petals drinking in the dew
More than white snow
More than blue seas
The sun is a golden red orb
A brilliant orb
An expanding orb

Whitman
Was inspired by the sun
With a breadth of mind as vast as the sea
He wrote poems as vast as the sea

Van Gogh
Was inspired by the sun
With a burning brush
He dipped into burning colors
And painted farmers tilling the land
He painted sunflowers

Duncan
Was inspired by the sun
With her lofty bearing
She conveyed to us the rhythm of the universe

The sun
It rises higher
It grows brighter
It reddens like blood

The sun
Makes me think of the French and American Revolutions
Of "Liberté, Egalité et Fraternité"
Of democracy
Of the *Marseillaise,* the *Internationale,*
Of Washington, Lenin, Sun Yat-sen
        And all the names of those figures
        Who delivered mankind from misery.

Yes
The sun is beautiful
And, moreover, immortal

6. The Sun Shines Upon . . .

The rising sun
Shines upon our heads
Shines upon our heads — bowed for so long
    Never looking up
The sun shines upon our cities and villages
Shines upon our cities and villages —
    So long inhabited and yet so long under usurped power
The sun shines upon our fields, rivers, and mountains
Shines upon our fields, rivers, and mountains
    Where tortured souls have writhed in pain for so long

Today
The sun's dazzling rays
Rouses us from the sleep of despair
From the miasma shrouding our ceaseless suffering
It rouses our cities and villages
From the mist veiling our endless melancholy
It rouses our fields, rivers and mountains
We have lifted our heavy heads
From the sodden ground
And together
We shout to the lofty sky
"Look at us!
We are
Laughing like the sun!"

7. Beneath the Sun

    "Look at us!
    We are
    Laughing like the sun!"

Over there
A wounded soldier

Propped up on wooden crutches
Goes along the length of the wall
Advances with large strides
The sun shines upon his face
Shines upon his honest, simple, smiling face
He moves forward step by step
Unaware that I am watching him from a distance
As his tall figure draped in a gray uniform bearing a Red
      Cross
Approaches me
This true and noble figure under the sun
I feel
Is more magnificent than Napoleon's bronze image

The sun shines
In the sky above the city

The people in the street
So many, so many
It's not that they greet me
But as I walk towards them
I watch each one passing me by
I no longer feel
They are strangers

The sun shines upon their faces
Shines on their
      Bright youthful faces
      Wrinkled old faces
      Flushed girlish faces
      Kind grandmotherly faces
And all those
      Faces, gloomy yesterday but smiling today,
Pass quickly by
Limbs in motion

In the radiance of the sun
Coming and going, they walk
— As though prompted by a common desire —
Their smiling faces
Seem to say in unison
    "We love this day
    Not because we
      Do not see our own suffering
    Not because we
      Do not know hunger and death
    We love this day
    Because this day has brought us
    The most reliable news
    Of a glorious tomorrow

The sunlight
Glistens upon the ancient stone bridge. . . .
A few young women —
    Ah, those symbols of felicity!
Almsbags on their backs
Upon the stone bridge
Beneath the sun
Are singing fresh songs
    "We are angels
    Wholesome and pure
    Our loved ones are
    Young and brave
    Some ride war-horses
    Galloping across the wilderness
    Some fly airplanes
    Winging across the sky. . . ."
(Their song breaks off as they beg for alms)
Now
They sing again
    "On the battlefield

Bravely they cut the enemy down
While we at the rear
Provide comfort and cheer
One day we will triumph
And happily gather together ..."
Their songs
How melodious
The sun shines upon their breast
Thrust out with pride
Their bare arms
Their noble fronts, radiant in honor,
Their song
Floats to the other side of the bridge. . . .

The sunlight
Floods the street

On the other side of the street
Bathed in the sunlight
A group of workers dressed in clothes dirty with soot
Are carrying a machine
— White light glinting off its hard-edged metal
The sun shines
Upon their sweaty faces
As they move forward with each step
They utter a slow, heavy cry
"Heave-ho!
Heave-ho!
We are workers
Workers most pitiful
Born in squalor
Brought up in hard work
Busy through the year
For the sake of food and clothing
Not enough food to fill the belly

Nor enough clothing for warmth
Heave-ho!
Heave-ho!
Since August 13th
The enemy has been attacking
The factory has been bombed
Everything is stolen
Millions of fellow workers
Are starving and cast adrift
We in the rear
Must speed up our labors
Produce for the country
Sweat for the resistance
One day we will triumph
And then we'll have food and clothing
Heave-ho!
Heave-ho! . . ."
Uttering their ceaseless "Heave-ho!"
They turn the corner. . . .

Sunlight
Floods the large drill-yard

In the drill-yard
Thousands of soldiers wearing straw-colored uniforms
    Are practicing drills
Helmets on their heads
    And bayonets on their rifles
Flash in the sun
In solemn silence
They await
Orders to come through
Now
They start marching
And as they march in step

I hear
     "One! Two! Three! Four!
     One! Two! Three! Four!
     We come from the fields
     We come from mountain villages
     We live in thatched huts
     We breathe in the pig-sty
     We till the fields
     The fields are our life
     But today
     The enemy has arrived in our villages
     Our thatched huts are burned down
     Our animals devoured
     Our parents slaughtered
     Our women raped
     We no longer have sickles and hoes
     Only bullets and guns to carry
     We must use our gleaming bayonets
     To seize back our fields
     Return to our villages
     And destroy our enemy
     Wherever the enemy plants his feet
     There his blood will flow
     . . . .
     One! Two! Three! Four!
     One! Two! Three! Four!
     . . . ."

Ah, what an encounter that would be! . . .

8.   Today

Today
Rushing along the sunlit road

I no longer hang my head
  Hands in my pockets
Nor whistle that lonesome tune
I do not look at the clouds drifting on the horizon
Nor pace to and fro aimlessly on the pavement

Today
In the midst of crowds in the sun
I will no longer search for
Those with faces as downtrodden as mine

Today
The sun caresses my cheek on which tears flowed last night
Caresses my eyes weary of gazing at the world's shame
Caresses my lips whose voice is hoarse from crying for justice
Caresses my still young but already aging
Ah! almost bowed arthritic back

Today
I hear
The sun saying to me
  "Come to me
  From now on
  You should be a little happier. . . ."

And thus
Bewitched by this newborn day
I relish the distant bugle call from beyond the city in the
  early morning
I relish the push and shove of the busy crowd
I relish the sound of gongs and drums that pass along the
  street
I relish the spectacle of the circus troupe
  And when I see those primeval, crude, but wholesome
   turns

I begin to relish them deeply
— Just as deeply as I relish the sun

Today
I thank the sun
For the sun has summoned me back my childhood

9. I Go to the Sun

I rush forth
On the wheels of old passion as before
The sun above me
Shines with a radiance more powerful than any other
Scorches the flesh on my body
With its fervent inspiration
In a voice that's hoarse
I sing:
    "And so, my breast
    Is ripped open at the hands of fire
    My putrid soul
    Is cast off by the river. . . ."
At this moment
Towards what I see what I hear
I feel a generosity and a passion I've never felt before
I would even die in this glorious moment. . . .

Wuchang
April 1938

(Translated by Peng Wenlan
and Eugene Chen Eoyang)

I Love This Land

If I were a bird,
I would sing with my hoarse voice
Of this land buffeted by storms,
Of this river turbulent with our grief,
Of these angry winds ceaselessly blowing,
And of the dawn, infinitely gentle over the woods. . . .
— Then I would die
And even my feathers would rot in the soil.

Why are my eyes always brimming with tears?
Because I love this land so deeply. . . .

November 17, 1938

(From *Chinese Literature*)

Beggar

In the north,
Beggars pace to and fro on both banks of the Yellow River,
Pace to and fro on both sides of the railroad tracks.

In the north,
Beggars with the most excruciating voices
Cry out their suffering,
And say they have come from a devastated area,
Or from the battlefield.

Hunger and starvation are frightful things:
They make the old forget their kindness,
And teach the young how to hate.

In the north
Beggars use dull, fixed stares
To freeze you with their eyes,
To see whatever you are eating,
Or the way you pick your teeth with your fingernails.

In the north
Beggars extend their always outstretched hands,
Their hands black as soot,
Asking for a copper or two,

From anyone,
Even the soldiers without a copper to their name.

Longhai Railway
Spring 1939

(Translated by Eugene Chen Eoyang)

Street

I once lived on this street —
Those who lived there have been driven off by the alarms of
    war:
Child-bearing women, sick men, asthmatic old men,
Old ladies raising little babies. . . .

Every day was spent in bedlam,
Numberless the people who were shipped in trucks to this
    small town;
The street teemed with refugees, wounded soldiers, youths
    dropped out of school,
The ears buzzed with a variety of different dialects.

The street changed, the war made it flourish:
On both sides, vending booths of all types cropped up,
Beancurd shops turned into restaurants, groceries into hotels,
The house opposite my home became a temporary hospital.

One day, the skies above this little town were blotted out
    with black wings,
One bombing run sent cataclysms through this little town;
The enemy rained down deadly fire and destruction on the
    street —
Half of the town was left in ruins.

Look: the roof of that house has been ripped off,
Walls don't come together any more,
The wells are choked with debris,

The rafters have been fired into charcoal.

People have all fled in this disaster
(Who's interested in where they all went?)
But there was still one I had met before,
A girl who lived in the same compound as I —

She walked over from another street,
And greeted me with a carefree air . . .
— Her hair cut short, legs in puttees,
She was already wearing military green!

Guilin
Spring 1939

(Translated by Eugene Chen Eoyang)

The Bugler

It seems that I once heard someone say that the destiny of a bugler is doomed, that when he presses his lips against the brass metal to produce the sounds, he blows out as well imperceptible traces of his own blood. . . .

Buglers' faces are often sallow. . . .

I

Among the tired troops curled up on the bed of rice-straw,
Among the filthy troops wearing their ash-gray uniforms,
He is the first to wake up —
He wakes up, starts up all of a sudden,
It's as if he were — every day — startled awake.
Yes, he is startled awake:
What startles him
Are the wheels of the chariots that bring the dawn
Rolling down along the edge of heaven.

He opens his eyes wide,
In the dim lamplight that burned through the night.
He sees the bugle hanging by him,
Looks at it in a daze,
As someone just roused from sleep
Would look at his beloved upon first opening his eyes,
And with the same affection —
In all the days given to live out this life,
He can do nothing but love his bugle.

The bugle is beautiful —
Throughout its length,
Glints a vibrant brilliance;
On its throat
A scarlet tassel is tied.

The bugler has risen from his bed of rice-straw on the ground,
Harboring no grudge that he had to sleep on this damp mud
    floor.
He quickly ties on his leggings,
With ice-cold water he washes his face.
He looks over at his weary comrades snoring,
Then extends his arm to take up his bugle.

Outside, it is still gloomy and dark;
Day has not yet broken,
What startled him awake —
Was his own passionate impatience
For the dawn.

He walks up the slope of the mountain,
And stands there for some time,
Until, finally, he sees this mundane marvel unfold before
    him:
Dark night drawing back her mysterious veil
The stars wane, and one by one, disperse and disappear . . .
Dawn — ah, the bride of the day,
Riding a chariot with golden wheels
Approaches from the far side of the sky;
Our world, in welcoming her,
Has already hung down in the east a million-mile curtain of
    light . . .
Look,
Between heaven and earth, a sacred and stately ceremony
    takes place. . . .

2

Now, he begins,
Standing underneath the blue and lucent dome of heaven,
He begins, and, with the fresh fragrant air of the open
     country,
Blows his breath through the bugle,
— And, along with it, perhaps a trace of blood?
From the bugle, out of deep feeling,
A fresh, full sound is given back to the countryside,
— With devotion to the beautiful dawn,
He blows the sounds of reveille:
How that sound resounds for miles and miles! . . .

Everything on earth,
Brimming over with joy,
Responds to the call of the bugle.

The forests are awake,
And broadcast, wave upon wave, the clamorings of birds;
The rivers are awake,
And summon herds of horses to lap up their waters;
The farmlands are awake,
And the peasant women scurry down the diked furrows;
The assembly ground is awake,
And the soldiers in their ash-gray uniforms,
Burst out of their broken-down barracks bathed in the
     morning light,
And scramble into position for the roll call. . . .

Then, he gets down from the mountain slope,
And loses himself
In the numberless gray-uniformed throng standing at atten-
     tion.
After he has finished sounding the call to breakfast,

He blows the call for assembly;
Later, in the glorious radiance that rains down from the sun,
Dazzling every reach of the overarching sky,
With fervor and urgency,
He sounds the call to arms.

3

That road
Stretches out to the edge of a heaven with no stopping point;
That road
Has been laid out by the trampings of ten thousand feet,
The mud tracks of a thousand trucks;
That road
Joins one village to yet another village;
That road
Having crossed over one hill climbs yet another hill.
And now
The sun gilds that road with a layer of gold,
And our bugler,
At the head of long columns of sun-drenched troops,
Sounds the call to advance
And gives to the troops on the move
A stirring beat to march to.

4

The gray figures,
Spread out in the open country —
But, the countryside today,
This boundless expanse of green grass, this darkling plain,
Will become for us a solemn and sacred altar;
Listen, an ear-splitting blast

Explodes over the horizon;
We breathe in the fragrance of grass mixed with mud,
And we also breathe in the exhalations of far-off explosions.
We crouch in our battle trenches,
Wordlessly, solemnly, awaiting our orders,
Like expectant mothers
Waiting in pain for the birth of their offspring;
In our hearts,
We have never felt, as we feel today, this overwhelming
    sense of love,
Ordained by the times in which we live
— A lot each of us has chosen for himself,
This last day of our lives.
There is not one among us unmoved by a pure and sacred
    ambition:
We are prepared to win in battle the glory of our sacrifice!

5

Now, the vicious onslaught begins —
Countless numbers of combatants
Bolt out of their trenches, startled by the flashes of light,
All across the front, charging furiously ahead,
Menacing the enemy by their advance . . .
In the death-dealing, earth-shattering noise,
In the forward surge of soldiers who cannot afford to look
    back,
In the mad dash, the rushing waves of humanity,
In the continuous, high density bomb bursts,
Our bugler,
With the excitement that fate has instilled in him,
Rushes forth at the same time as he blows that
Staccato, urgent, stirring

Call to charge, a call that nothing short of death will inter-
   rupt.

That sound soared high above us,
And was more beautiful than anything else.
Just then, when, as if making an irrefutable declaration,
He let forth a strain to celebrate the victory,
He was felled by a bullet drilled into his heart.
He collapsed, forlorn;
No one had seen him fall,
But in the very last moment of his fall,
   On the earth that he had loved so much,
At that moment, his hand
Still clutched the bugle tight in his grip.

On that smooth, polished brass,
Was reflected the blood of the dead,
And his pale, sallow face;
It reflected the never-ending movement
   of soldiers with guns firing, rushing forward,
   of horses whinnying,
   of trucks clanking . . .
But the sun, the sun
Made that bugle glint and flash in its light. . . .

Listen:
That bugle seems to be sounding still. . . .

End of March, 1939

(Translated by Eugene Chen Eoyang)

He Dies a Second Time

1. Stretcher

When he wakes up
He is already lying on the stretcher
He knows that he is still alive
Two of his comrades carry him
They do not say a word

The air is thick with the cold of the winter wind
The clouds hang low and are on the move
And silently the wind shakes the treetops
They hurry along
Carrying the stretcher
Through the woods of winter

Having undergone searing, excruciating pain
His heart is now at peace
Just as the battleground which has recently seen horrendous
    atrocities
Is now also at peace, and in the same way

Just now his blood
Seeping through the gauze bandages on his arms
Still, drop by drop,
Drips down on the wintry roads of the motherland

But on that very evening
Going the direction opposite to the stretcher

A mighty deployment, ten times larger than the one before,
With the steps of ten thousand
Will stamp out the mottled traces of the scarlet blood drops
    he's left behind.

2.   Hospital

Where are our rifles gone to?
And our dusty, bloodstained clothes?
Our helmets are being worn by other comrades
We wear cotton clothes with the Red Cross stitched on
We are stretched out, stretched out
Seeing countless human bodies gnawed away
By corrosive acids and poison gases
Each one of us with dark apprehension in our eyes
And unending moans on our lips
Days come and go without number
Like the coming and going of a procession of black coffins
Where we are
No one's pain
Will be less than anyone else's
Everyone has, with nothing less than their lives,
Resisted the onslaught of the enemy
Absorbed the murderous fire —
We have all shed our own blood
On to the land that we have defended. . . .
But today, we are stretched out, stretched out
We are told that this is our glory
But it is not the kind of glory we seek
We are stretched out, the battleground is in our hearts
Even more than the villages where we were raised
We would still like to
Charge ahead amidst the flames of war
But we are now, today,

Like a bunch of trussed-up animals
Moaning on iron beds
— We are hurt, and we are expectant
For how long?

3.   Hands

Every day at a set time comes
A nurse in white uniform and white cap
Who walks in and walks out without a word
Unwinding the gauze bandages on the wounds of the
    wounded
Gently pulling out wads of cotton soaked in iodine
She cleans off the festering pus and blood
Her slender graceful hands are deft and soothing
We would not find a wife like this
Our sisters would also not be like this
Cleaning off the pus and blood and wrapping up the wound
Deft and soothing, using every one of her ten fingers
Using all those slender, spotless fingers
On one of the ten fingers there is a golden radiance
That shines on our wounds
And shines into a particular place in our hearts. . . .
She walks away without so much as a word
But after she walks away, I look at my own hand
A hand that once held a hoe, that once raised a rifle
A hand that has been made clumsy and coarse with hard
    work
Now it lies limp, useless, on my chest
A hand that grew from the arm that sustained the wound
Looking at my own hand, then looking at her hand
Thinking and wondering
Wondering and thinking
Oh, what, in the end, was the portion of fate

That two such different hands should come together?

4.   Healing

Time passes in a void
He left the hospital
Like a felon leaving prison
His body free from cumbersome cotton clothes
He wears a light gray-colored uniform
On the lapel is still stitched a Red Cross
Freedom, sunshine, the world has already turned into spring
Numberless the people on the street
Make him feel estranged and yet at home
The sun beats down on the street
And from a long deep sleep suddenly startled awake
Life quickens in the radiance
People pass by at a frenetic pace
He alone is still tired like this
No one has even noticed him —
A wounded soldier, today his wound
Is healed, and he is happy
But he is sobered by the realization
Of the deeper meaning in his recovery
Which he senses only just at this moment
He is a soldier
A soldier must suffer injury on the battlefield
When he has healed he must return to the fight
He thinks as he walks
But there is something wrong in every step
His pallid face looks terrible
People walk by, with not a one
Who sees on his face the visage of pain
Only the sun, at noon
Sends down its flashing fingers

And soothes his sorry-looking, jaundiced face
That face with a wan smile through the pain. . . .

5.   Bearing

He puts a gray uniform with a Red Cross stitched on it
His jacket wrapped over his shoulder, its sleeves hanging limp
He walks on the broad street of a city at night
He walks on the broad city street which makes him heady
From all sides, the hum of activity, the sound of crowds,
The sound of cars, the sound of horns and police whistles
There he is crushed, shoved, and poked
There on the smooth pavement
There under the dazzling lights
There on the slippery tar roads
There alongside processions of late model automobiles
There in front of women who wear beautiful clothes
Oh, how conspicuous he is in his shabbiness
Yet nevertheless he seems to lengthen his stride
(Because he is wearing his proudest outfit)
He feels that it's only right
To walk with this bearing when out in the world
And only those who are just like him can
Walk out in the world in this way

Then, just when he thinks to walk about in this way
— Chin up, in his gray uniform, taking large strides
He thinks all eyes are on him as he walks
His face, bathed in the electric light,
Begins to flush with embarrassment
For fear that all those people
Have already guessed the secret in his heart —
Actually, no one even notices him at all

6. Farmlands

This is a bright, beautiful day
He makes for the farmlands
As if something were calling to him

Today, as his feet walk on
The soft, loamy earth of the furrows
He senses an unnameable joy
He sheds his shoes
And dips his feet into a shallow ditch
Splashing the flowing water with his hands
For some time now — he has lived through
Days controlled by Red Cross signs
And the days that are left to him
Will also be controlled by Red Cross signs
But today, he must return to these farmlands
As if it might be for the last time
Looking for something that seems to be beckoning him
That something which he does not know himself
He sees the paddy-fields
He sees a farmer
He sees an ox pulling the plow
Oh, it's all the same
It's all the same everywhere
— People say that this is China
The trees are green, the grounds covered with grass
Those mud walls, places further away
Those tiled homesteads, people walking
— He thinks of people saying this is China
He walks and he walks
What a day this is!
He is now happy, foolishly happy
Even Spring Festival Days do not bring happiness such as
     this

Everything glistens in the radiance of the day
Every place glistens in the radiance of the day
He smiles to the farmer busy at his work
He doesn't even know himself why he smiles
Nor does the farmer notice that he is smiling

7.   A Glimpse

Along the route stretching out to the outskirts
On a road lined by trees, he walks in the deep blue shadows
Shielding himself from the piercing sunlight, in the shade
He sees: some horse-drawn carts, nimbly
Rolling on, and sitting inside
Some very neatly dressed boys and girls
From their mouths stream forth gales of laughter
And clear-voiced chatter that he finds unsettling
He walks on, like a broken-down old man
Slowly, he approaches a park
Towards the entrance to the park
And at the base of an arched marble gateway
He sees: a crippled soldier
His heart is suddenly startled by a certain sense
Whereupon he thinks: maybe this crippled comrade
Was braver than anyone else, maybe
He had hoped that he would be buried on the battlefield
But now, he is stretched out and moaning
Moaning and stretched out
To spend the remaining years of his life
Ah, who has the heart to look at something like this?
Whoever sees this must sense a seething fury in his heart
Let us go and fight again
Let us go and die happily in the midst of battle
Don't let us come back with only one leg left
Crying and weeping in front of everybody

Stretching out a filthy hand, and starving
Begging for pity and charity!

8.   An Exchange

He took off the gray uniform with the Red Cross insignia
    stitched on
And put on once again the grass-green army clothes of
    several months ago
Where are the bloodstains on the army clothes?
And the place where the bullet made a hole is all patched up
When he wears it, he feels a thrill in his heart
A thrill greater than he felt when he first enlisted
He sensed somehow that these army clothes and that Red
    Cross uniform
Seemed to be associated for all time
He would forever be wearing them, exchanging one for the
    other
That's right, exchanging one for the other, this is the way
    it should be
For a soldier, for himself
Before the end of the War of Liberation for his country
These two kinds of uniform were the flags in his life
These flags should fly
Fluttering over the trampled motherland. . . .

9.   Send-off

Led on by the unremitting sound of firecrackers
Led on by the sound of the bugle which rouses everyone on
    the street
Led on by the roar of people crowded on both sides of the
    avenue

Let us go on the road that is paved with the hopes of the
    people
Let us go on the road that leads from today's world to
    tomorrow's world
Let us go on the road that those who come after will
    remember and be moved by
Our chests are puffed up
Our pace is measured
We have crossed over among the small walls built by the
    populace
We have crossed over in between self-confidence and pride
We think of nothing in our hearts except glory
We think of nothing except the pursuit of glory
We think of nothing except a welcome death in pursuit of
    glory. . . .

10.   Reflections

Did you not know
What death is like?
— To live on, to die off
Insects and flora
Evolve even as they shed their skins and their husks in
    life. . . .
In all this, what can you imagine
All this is about?
To be a soldier, quite right,
Is to give one's life to the battle
To die on the banks of a river!
To die in the wilds!
Our torsos frozen stiff by the cold dew
Our corpses rotting in the clumps of wild grass
For how many generations now

Man has used his own life
To fertilize the soil
And used the soil to nourish
His own life
Who can escape this law of nature?
— Well, then, for us to die for this
What's wrong with that?
Shouldering our rifles
We sway back and forth, marching down rank and file
Haven't your hearts often been
Afflicted by something stronger than love?
On the day you set out, to march into battle
Don't you often
Feel that you have lived your life
But that now you should die
— This death would be
For those beyond counting who come after
So that their life might be happier than yours?
All the glory
All the hymns of praise
What use are they
If we do not think of
Our dying for our own sacred mission?
— And this, in the end, isn't this also part of
The great and incontrovertible will of the people?

11.   Charge Ahead

Charge ahead, be brave
Fix bayonets, comrades-in-arms
Forge thousands of dedicated souls
Into one common purpose:
To struggle for liberation of the motherland!
What is there for us to fear —

When we have realized the glory of death in battle?
Charge ahead, be brave
Towards the spot where the shelling is the most intense
Towards the trenches spitting out bullets
Look, how the lily-livered enemy
Trembles before the sounds of our onrushing advance!
Charge ahead, be brave
Shame and humiliation
Must come to an end —
We must wrest back from the hands of the enemy
The destiny of the motherland
Only this sacred struggle
Will deliver us our freedom and our happiness. . . .
Charge ahead, be brave
This glorious day
Is ours to seize!
Our lives
Must engage.in unflagging, hard-fought struggle
To make valiant and strong!
Comrades-in-arms, fix bayonets,
Be brave, charge ahead!

12.   He Is Felled

It was so very quick
Not allowing a moment's thought
A moment as sudden as a bolt of lightning
An exploding bullet
For the second — and the last — time
Pierced through his body
His life
Had already passed on from the life of the world
In the end, like a tree,
He was felled, cut down by an enormous axe

Through the windows from which he saw the world
Before those eyes, just now filled with tears of joy
Are closed forever
He can think of nothing at all
— His mother is dead
And he had no wife to love
It was all very simple

A soldier
Does not know about a lot of things
He only knows
That he should die for this war of liberation
When he falls
All he knows is
That he is laid out in the soil of his motherland
— Because people
Those people who understand more than he did
Have already told him about this

After a while, his comrades-in-arms
Will go out looking for him again
— This will be the last visit they pay to him
But this time
What they bring is not a stretcher
But a stub-handled shovel

And picking no place in particular
In a spot he once defended with his life
Not far from the banks of a river
They dig out a shallow grave. . . .

After the mud that mixes with the spring grass
Covered over his corpse
He leaves behind to the world
One of those poor, innumerable earthmounds

Scattered like stars over the wasteland
On these earthmounds
People have never marked the names of the dead
— Even if they were to mark them
What would be the point?

End of spring, 1939

(Translated by Eugene Chen Eoyang)

The Desolate Wilds

Oh, how the thin mists veil the desolate wilds . . .

One cannot see far into the distance —
One cannot see what once stood under a translucent sky,
The pine trees at the horizon,
Or, behind the pine trees,
The chalk cliffs that glimmered in greeting the sun;
In front, faintly visible,
The gradually diminishing outlines
Of a dusky, tortuous road,
And on both sides of the road,
Fields that are dim and parched.

The fields already lie in waste —
Strewn with overturned clods of earth,
And withered wild grasses,
And rotting stalks of grain,
Mixed in with the wild grasses;
In the vast, ash-white expanse emerges
Here and there a meld of colors:
A swatch of earth brown, dark ochre, and burnt tea-
leaves. . . .
Only a few patches of turnips and vegetables —
White frost covering them,
Leaving spots of green —
Adorn
This drab, monotonous, crude
And lowly countryside.

In all those ponds, one after another,
Because of a long drought,
The accumulated water is about to dry up;
In the impenetrable white glaze
Wriggles several lines of pale brown
Wayward dikes;
Once a luxuriant green,
These water weeds, these lotus leaves,
Have long since mired in the riverbeds;
What is left:
Gnarled and crooked stems
Standing stubbornly
In the vapors that rise slowly from the ponds. . . .

A mountain slope stretches across in front,
A road winds its way up the slope,
And follows its rise and fall,
Disappears down into the sparse woods. . . .
On the slope,
On both sides of the ash-brown road,
Reflecting the pervasive gloom and desolation,
There are only scattered grave mounds
And dark stone tablets
About to be buried in oblivion.

Everything is like this:
Still, cold, and palpably forlorn. . . .

Oh, ash-brown, twisting road!
People walk and walk
In every which direction,
Yet, as if forever following the same shadow,
Ending up with the same fate;
In the endless, arduous, and woebegone way ahead,
What lie in wait are calamity, sickness, and death —

Those who have been wandering in these desolate wilds,
Who among them has ever enjoyed his life?

Still,
The desolate wilds of winter;
Are what I feel closest to —
In the bone-chilling frost,
I have walked over the uneven embankments,
Along the desolate edge of the ponds,
And the dark-drab, brown mountain slopes,
Each step heavy-laden, until I feel distressed
— Like an old buffalo finished with plowing the fields,
Bringing back his burden of weariness. . . .

And oh! the mist —
Gray-white and turbid,
Vast and unfathomable
Before me,
One power line, one utility pole after another
Diminishes in the distance
The mist unfolds before me
A limitless vastness and profundity. . . .

You, melancholy, open-hearted,
Oh so hard-working and impoverished wilds. . . .

There is not a sound:
Everything seems as if muffled by mist;
Only by that
Clump of bushes one can scarcely make out,
Comes a stream of twitterings
From sparrows, wings shivering,
And fearful of the bitter cold.

Within those surrounding hedges of thorn and bramble

Several little huts are huddled together —
They are all alike,
With firewood strewn helter-skelter by the wall,
And tattered clothes hanging from a bamboo pole,
Lamenting
Their futile, never-ending toil;
Rising from the frosted tree-bark covering the hovels,
The kitchen smoke wafts up lazily in the fog;
Painting a picture
Of inescapable squalor. . . .

People in those hovels,
What brutally dismal days do they lead!
They are enshrouded in the gloom of life. . . .
Where, it seems, the light of day never dawns.
They and their livestock breathe the same air,
— Their beds are like animal pens
And their ragged coverlets,
Are as dingy and as hard
As hardened clay. . . .

And so, cold and hunger,
Ignorance and superstition,
Wrap their iron grip
On these hovels. . . .

A farmer, toting a bamboo basket,
Walks out of the mist,
With nothing but scallions and garlic in his basket;
His felt cap is torn beyond repair,
His face as filthy as his clothes,
His hands, chapped by the frost,
Slipped under his waistband,
His bare feet
Treading the frost-crusted road:

Quietly,
He carries his softly creaking shoulder-pole
And slowly
He disappears into the mist before him. . . .

Oh, desolate wilds —
Will you forever grieve and suffer
Injustice and yet keep silent?

Oh, how the thin mists veil the desolate wilds!

Early morning
January 3, 1940

(Translated by Eugene Chen Eoyang)

Winter Pond

Winter pond,
Lonely, like an old man's heart —
A heart that has known too much the bitterness in the world.
Winter pond,
Dried up, like an old man's eyes —
Eyes with their luster rubbed dim by toil.
Winter pond,
Wasted, like an old man's hair —
Hair of ashen color, as sparse as winter grass.
Winter pond,
Somber, like a grieved old man —
An old man bent over beneath the gloom of the sky.

January 11, 1940

(Translated by Peng Wenlan)

Trees

One tree, another tree,
Each standing alone and erect
The wind and air
Tell their distance apart

But beneath the cover of earth
Their roots reach out
And at depths that cannot be seen
The roots of the trees intertwine

Spring 1940

(Translated by Peng Wenlan)

Carrying Them In

Please make way
Please walk on the sidewalk
Let us carry them in
Please don't shove
Please stand to one side of the street
Let us carry them in
Please don't shout
Please pay your respects with your silence
Let us carry them in

This is a woman
Whose skull is burst open with shrapnel
Let her close her eyes and sleep soundly
That she might wake up gradually after a while
Let us carry her home
Let her family, in tears and bitterness, take care of matters.

This is one of the service personnel
On his gray uniform, he still wears an armband
Do you know who he is? — his face all covered with dust
A merciless fragment of shrapnel broke his hard-working arm
Please make way, please show him some consideration
He has suffered his wounds to limit your losses.

Please don't shove, there are still more to come
Wounded soldiers who stayed at the hospital for the
    wounded;
Wounded at the front, they were lying in their hospital beds

Waiting for their wounds to heal so they could return to the
    battlefield
Now the ruthless enemy has bombed even the hospitals
And the wounds of the wounded are compounded.

Please make way
Let us carry them in
Please, everyone stand aside
Let us come in with the stretchers
Please, keep in mind
These are all debts bought with blood. . . .

Chongqing
June 11, 1940

(Translated by Eugene Chen Eoyang)

Lament for Paris

Berlin, at 6 p.m., on the 14th of June, a bulletin from the Transoceanic News Agency: "According to official dispatches, the German Army has, this morning, entered Paris."

The tricolor of red, white, and blue
Drops down:
In its place, and flapping
On the banks of the Seine,
Over the *Place de la Concorde*,
Is a flag with a black swastika against the color of blood.

Now, in the waters of the Seine,
With sad murmurs, day and night,
Slowly flow
The tears of a city that has fallen. . . .

The imposing buildings have now fallen,
Fallen as well
Are "Liberté, Egalité, Fraternité"
Inscribed on their great big doors. . . .

In front of the *Panthéon*
And *Les Invalides*
Marches a triumphal procession
More pretentious than at the time of the First Consul
And in that long and solemn parade
Strides a man

More reckless than Napoleon;

The bronze statues of Rousseau, Voltaire, and Danton,
Are knocked down by the pitiless sledgehammer;
And in their places
Stand
Hitler, Goebbels, Goering
In poses with both arms akimbo

The history of humanity
Has added a page —
An utterly comic and ridiculous chapter —
And on the other side of that page
Flow, in secret,
Grave and innocent tears

France —
You have been praised by the poet[1] who praised democracy
As "the most beautiful name in the world."
Today, the hands of the Germans
Are to efface your name
And replace you with the harsh guttural
"Deutsch!"
On the boulevards where I used to stroll
There are no more Americans looking for a good time,
No refined ladies used to coquetry and kisses —
They have taken the silk masks they wore at costume balls,
As well as their black lace gloves,
And have left for the banks of the Congo in North Africa.

Broad and spacious
Champs Elysées
Where Marguerite's carriage

___
[1] Walt Whitman (1819-1892) — *Ed.*

Went for a ride,
Now, tanks bearing
The swastika insignia rush over you,
Along with mounted troops, shouting "Heil Hitler!"

Here come the stalwarts of National Socialism!
Their high, sharp-spurred boots
Resound on the streets with an ear-piercing sound
They force their way into a cafe closed now for a week
Bullying a trembling old woman
Into serving them enough liquor to get drunk on.

Oh, city of culture and art,
Today, crack German troops
Have come to knock down the doors of your museums.
They use their bayonets to poke into
The canvasses of Delacroix and David;
And Ingres' "The Turkish Bath"
Has been commandeered by General Headquarters;
And in all the libraries and fine arts institutes
Copies of *Mein Kampf* are distributed,
And "The Portrait of the March Into Paris" hung.

Paris, your spineless governors
Have abandoned you —
Daladier and Reynaud have said:
"If we are shoved out of Europe
Then we will move to North Africa,
So that one day, if it is necessary,
We can migrate to our colonies in America."
— They are still
Drunk in their paltry delusions of power;

And now, it is you —
Splendid, upright

People of France —
Who are, in the end, exiled
"Refugees propping up their aged, dragging their young
. . . Like an enormous long snake,
Slithering along without end . . ."
And it is for you, people of France,
That I grieve. . . .

No!
The people of France are brave.
This is not the first time
That Prussian soldiers have entered Paris;
Each time those who threw back the invaders
Were the people of France themselves.
France's glorious history
Has been written with the blood of its brave people.

We will still keep faith with the time —
The time that will deliver victory
To those who love freedom and democracy, the people of
    France.

Just at this moment,
When I am absorbed in my memories of Paris,
In my ears
Still ring
"The *Marseillaise*" and "The *Internationale*";
Before my eyes
I can still see workers coming out
Of Lenin Hall in stalwart rank and file . . .
I have faith: when Daladier and Reynaud
Haul away the wealth of France along with their girls and
    perfumes
From Bordeaux to North Africa or South America,
The people of France will rise up even mightier,

Once again they will man
The barricades in the streets
To struggle against their own enemies
And then a Second Commune will be born!

Chongqing
June 15, 1940

(Translated by Eugene Chen Eoyang)

Highway

Just like Americans
Moving down a California road
I move down the high plateau of Western China
On a newly opened highway

I come from a valley nestled in a mountain range
A very humble little village
I come from a small, dismal, soot-covered, tile-roofed house
With a farmer's forthrightness and the passion borne of suf-
     fering
I rush up the mountain —
And let the air and the sunshine
And the open country spread out before me on the mountain.
     like an ocean
Brushing away my daily irritations
As well as life's troubles,
And I let the vast expanse of a limitlessly bright sky
And its infinitely unobstructed perspective
Ease my oh so long suffocating heart. . . .

The long ribbon of road
Follows the contours of the mountain
Meandering snugly up the side, going up
People are climbing slowly up the mountain
Gradually distancing themselves from the world below.
Walking through the upper reaches of the atmosphere
Is like floating in mid-air

We are tired
At the base of an old tree, we could
Sit down and rest
And listen to the mountain stream come crashing down
From craggy cliffs
And watch the eagles and the hawks
Screech and soar
Near where we are standing. . . .

A line of mules carrying sacks of coal on their backs,
Led on by mule-drivers in tattered clothes,
With lackadaisical "giddyaps" and lifeless cracks of the whip,
Passes raggedly by this way
And then turns into a forsaken mountain gorge.
We could follow their steps
And imagine in this gorge, next to a crumbling old temple,
A row of houses where simple, rustic articles are crafted.

Those trucks, so loaded down,
Roll through with a cheerful rumble
With the cargo in them jostling about
Those young men
Seeing me, a traveller on foot,
Hail me and wave their arms
On this kind of day
Even though their impulses
And my impulses do not originate from the same source
My heart is also full of irrepressible buoyancy.

And then there are the fleet automobiles
Glinting with flashes of light off the chrome,
Sending out wings of white light,
Exhilarated by the speed,
On the crest of the mountain
They fly past fearlessly,

Enticing me, my feelings and my thoughts,
To soar with them into the sky.

And so
My soul sensed at once a liberation
My lungs breathed in new air
My eyes opened wide to the ultimate horizons
My feet, limp from joy, walked over the face of the earth.

With strong arms and heavy steel hammers to cleave asunder,
With powerful dynamite to blast open the rocky cliffs,
On the side of summits thousands of feet high,
With rock and mud and cement,
The sweat of workers by the thousands and ten thousands
Coagulates into a road thousands of miles long.
Above, the vault of heaven
— A stretch of mind-boggling blue;
Below, the great river,
The river torrents flowing on without end,
Numberless dark riverboats and their ragged sails
Float — almost motionless — on the surface of the water.
From this point
They appear as insignificant gray dots.
When one walks up to the mountain heights
One leaves far behind the trouble and distress of home.
Oh, the piteous heart, the ingenuous heart:
At last, from innocence and openness
It is once more revived into
A life of dignity and pride —
Even if I were an ant
Or a grasshopper with rigid wings
To crawl up or to fly down this kind of road
Would be the utmost joy. . . .

Today, I wear straw sandals,

A cool, rattan-weave sun-hat on my head
Walking on this newly opened highway
My heart following its bent
And sensing a limitless joy:
The road stretched out before me
Is so broad, so smooth,
So independent and without obstruction,
Leading off into the distance —
We can see it clearly
Wriggling its way to the edge of heaven
Heroically battening down the landscape.
From my spot, I gaze off in all directions and see
Rivers, hillocks, roads, houses,
And here and there a beautiful cluster of trees,
All blending and melding in, incomparably, with the atmos-
    phere:
In the end, I have this manifest feeling,
That I am standing on the summit of the world.

Autumn 1940

(Translated by Eugene Chen Eoyang)

Boy Reaping

The evening sun burns the entire plain scarlet.
The boy reaper reaps the grass in silence.
Head bent, body curled, hands quick with work;
From one side he slowly moves on to the other.

Grass buries his tiny body —
We see only, in the dense clumps of grass,
One bamboo basket, a few mounds of grass,
And in the evening sun, gold flashes off the sickle.

1940

(Translated by Marilyn Chin)

Old Man

By a long, long row of gourd-trellises
Stretches a long, long mud furrow
A hunchbacked old man turns the soil
Thinking to sow some new seeds.

And thus he works wearily away
His hunchback raised higher than his head
He turns the soil over, then clears the ground,
Flinging weeds and stones to either side

His clothes are dark like black mud
His skin dull ochre like dun earth
From high above, the sun shines on his face
Creased with wrinkles like the bark of a tree

Hoe in hand, he works away with all his might
Sweat streaming from his brow to his jaw
A slight breeze blows and he coughs softly a few times
While the bright sunshine lights up his somber face

August 17, 1940

(Translated by Peng Wenlan)

My Father

These days I often see my father in my dreams —
His face shows a "kindliness" it never had before,
Betraying toward me a touch of "forgiveness";
His tone of voice is also very warm,
As if all the pains he took, and all his plans,
Were for the purpose of protecting me, his son.

Last year, around spring, he wrote me several times,
With heartfelt feeling he hoped I would return home,
There were important things he wanted to tell me,
Some matters concerning landholdings and property;
But, with some irritation, I disregarded his wish,
And didn't make a move to go back to my village,
I was afraid the family would thrust such duties on me,
As to thwart my youthful destiny.

One day, when pomegranate trees had blossomed in May,
He left this world, with disappointment in his heart.

2

I am his eldest son,
He was twenty-one when I was born,
Studying in a secondary school;
In the last year of Manchu rule.

111

He showed a warm and upright character,
Wearing a long robe, a queue on his head,
He was portly, with a dark complexion,
His big round eyes bulged out,
His ears seem appended, just behind his cheeks,
People remarked that he had a "happy face",
So that he would be one "content within himself".

Satisfied with the lot assigned to him,
He spent mundane and mediocre days,
Puffing on his hookah, sipping rice wine,
Stretched out on a bamboo cot reading "Strange Tales from a
      Studio",
With its stories of female spirits and fox fairies.

When he was sixteen, my grandfather died;
My grandmother had been a child bride,
And often took abuse from my grandfather's concubine;
My uncle was an opium addict,
Who held gambling parties, and sought out women;
But he, my father,
Was bent on "self-cultivation" and "investigation of things"
      to learn about life —
A good son to his mother
And a good husband to his wife.

Influenced by the ideas of Liang Qichao,[1]
He knew that "Progress has no limits".
He became a supporter of the Reform Group,
And in that poor, backward little town,
He was the first to cut off his jet-black queue.
A reader of the magazine "Eastern Miscellany,"[2]

[1] Liang Qichao (1873-1929), one of the reformist leaders who launched the Reform Movement of 1898 towards the end of China's last feudal dynasty, the Qing (1644-1911) — Ed.

[2] A monthly journal published in Shanghai in the thirties — Ed.

A subscriber to the newspaper "Shenbao",[1]
A member of the International Savings Association,
He had a chiming clock in his hall,
And a "Shell" gas lamp in his bedroom.

In the town we had a store handed down by my great-grand-
 father —
Products from Peking, and from overseas, foodstuffs, wine,
 "anything you want,"
It provided our whole family with its clothing,
Daily provisions and snacks for tea,
With a chit, we could take whatever we wanted;
Thirty-nine employees worked busily for 365 days.
At the end of the year, the proprietor rakes in the pro-
 ceeds.

He had a few hundred plots of land in the village
And several score tenant farmers hovering around him
At home, every year, we had four farmhands,
A bondmaid, an old servant-woman,
And with these, we lived a life of leisure.

No passion! He tried nothing risky!
With his own interests and predilections,
He wanted to build a "new family",
His daughter he sent to a missionary school,
His sons he pressed to learn English.

With a slap and a whip he disciplined his children,
He became a tyrant in the house.
Frugality was what he taught us,
Obedience was what he swore us to.
In addition, he wanted us to study hard,

[1] An influential Shanghai newspaper in the forties — *Ed.*

To pay close attention to our grades,
He knew that knowledge was a useful thing —
First, it was something one could show off,
Second, it was a way of protecting property.
These were his most honored guests:
A retired army general,
A teacher of Chinese from the high school in the provincial
    capital,
Economics and law students from the university,
The chief of police in town,
And the magistrate in the prefecture.

He often scanned an atlas of the world,
Read up on meteorology, probed the stars.
From *The Theory of Evolution,* he knew that monkeys were
    man's ancestors;
But when he offered ritual sacrifices,
He feigned the ardor of faith as before.
On this, he was very clear in his mind:
For those who owed him rent or taxes,
Graven images of Yama, King of Hell,
Were far more effective than Darwin's theory.

Listlessly he waited around for "progress",
Nonchalantly, he welcomed "revolution",
He knew this was "the tide of the times",
And avoided being caught up in the rush,
He merely watched at a discreet distance....

In 1926
The Nationalist Revolutionary Army set out from the south
And passed through my village,
At the time, I was thinking of applying to the Whampoa
    Military Academy,

But my father remained impassive,
His eyes were glazed, and he did not respond.

The revolution was like a sudden storm: it came and then it
    went.

Countless numbers of brave young men,
They all became sacrificial victims of the times,
When I saw my fill of terror and sorrow,
My heart was like a boat that's lost its sails
Drifting about in a restless, boundless sea. . . .

Landlords all hope their sons will make money, take office,
They want them to study economics and law
But with the colors I dipped my brush in,
I dabbed off a little landscape
And the figure of a toiling farmer.

The passions and ambitions of youth,
Often moved me to get away from home:
In order to go to a faraway capital,
I used many practical arguments,
To wheedle his consent out of my father.

One night, from under the floorboards,
He took out a thousand Mexican silver dollars,
His hands trembling, his face dark,
He counted the money as he admonished me:
"You come back after a few years,
Don't let fun make you forget to come back home!"

Then, when it was time for me to go,
He saw me off at the edge of the village,
I didn't have the nerve to consider

How heavy the hopes were he had placed on me,
My heart could only urge:
"Get out of here fast —
This wretched farmland,
This poor little town,
Wander about by yourself,
Roam around in freedom!"

3

Years afterwards, a dejected figure
Returned to that run-down village,
Nothing in his hands, not a thing —
Save for a bunch of books on rebellion,
Some passionate paintings,
And a deep sense of shame and resentment
For people who have been "colonized".

In July, I was locked up in jail,
In August, sentence was passed;
From the dashed hopes he had for his son,
My father cried all night right up to the dawn.

In those dark, depressing months and years,
He sent a stream of temperate letters,
Telling me to be "a model" to my brothers and sisters,
To follow the "wishes of the family";
He also used old-fashioned expressions and tender feelings,
And a prearranged scheme for happiness
To win me over to his side.
When I was set free once again,
He watched eagerly for my return,

He sent to me
Just enough money to come home.

He repeated to me what others had said
(Heaven knows where he heard them from!)
He said that China had no capitalist class,
No American-type large corporations,
No coldblooded exploitation and profit-mongering.
He said: "Never have I,
Oppressed my workers,
But if they really want revolution,
Then what's to become of me?"
Whereupon he opened up his account book,
And opened up a thick ledger on grain deals.
Then, with a sympathetic glance, he looked at me
And on his mustachioed mouth there was a smile,
Fingering the abacus with one hand,
And speaking in a low voice,
He urged me to look after the future of my brothers and
    sisters.

But, in the end, he flew into a rage —
He frowned, he bit hard into his lower lip,
He seemed upset,
Knocking on the table with extended fingers.
He was furious at the *insouciant* attitude of his son,
— That he would take his own home
As nothing but a waystation for tourists,
And see as nothing but filth
The legacy his ancestors had left him.

In order to save myself from the ruins,
In order to seek out an ideal of ultimate good,
Once again, I left my home town,

And even if my heels should have bled from walking,
I would still have gone on ahead ...

Now my father is dead,
He contracted tympanites and died,
He can never again reproach me,
So what more is there to say?

He was a very ordinary man;
Timid by nature, he accepted his lot,
In the most violent of times,
He led a most peaceable life,
Like all the landlords of China:
The Golden Mean, conservative, stingy, smug,
Making of those depressed little villages
A fiefdom that would never change;
And the legacy inherited from his ancestors,
He was to leave to his descendants,
Neither less than nor greater than it was!
That's the way it was —
And that's where I feel pity for him.

Now my father
Rests in peace in the earth.
At his funeral,
I did not post the flag of mourning for him
Nor did I wear the customary coarse hemp clothes;
For just at that time, I was yelling myself hoarse,
Rushing into the fires of the War of Liberation. . . .

My mother wrote asking me to go home,
She wanted me to look after the family,
But I didn't want to bury myself alive,
So heartlessly, I thwarted her wishes,
Thrilled by the excitement that war provided,

I turned my back on my home town —
Because I, I knew for myself
That there were higher ideals in this world,
What I wanted to devote myself to was not my own family,
But something that would belong to millions —
A transcendent faith.

August 1941

(Translated by Eugene Chen Eoyang)

A Poem Dedicated to a Village

My poem is dedicated to a very small village in China —
Tucked away in the hollow of one arm of a mountain ridge.
On the ridge stand: old pine trees that creak in the wind,
Maples with red leaves splayed like duck's feet;
Tall beeches bearing fruit, hooded by a cap,
And an old locust tree, its trunk split asunder by lightning.
These old trees are bunched together in a grove on the ridge,
Giving shade to an ancient village and its denizens.

I think of a clear lake by the village —
Surrounded by a thick row of lush-green willows,
On its surface floats leaves of water-chestnut, water hyacinth,
    and the white flowers of the water-lily.
The faithful companion of the sky, the lake reflects its laughter
    and its tears;
It is a vanity for the clouds, a mirror for sunlight, moonlight,
    and birds in flight;
A spa for the stars, a swimming pond for water fowl;
Enormous and diligent water buffalo poke their heads out
    of the water,
And watch the village women squatting on rocky ledges
    washing clothes and vegetables.

I think of the quiet, shaded orchards in the village —
The orchards full of peach, apricot, plum, pomegranate, and
    crabapple,
Marked off from the outside with a retaining wall or a bam-
    boo fence

On the wall and on the fence, ivy and creeper climb:
That's where magpies nest, where sparrows play,
A honey-factory for bees, a warehouse for ants;
A practice room for crickets, a studio for weaving maidens;
And where the heartless spider slyly weaves a net to snare
    butterflies.

I think of the wells by the roads in the village —
These six-sided wells of dark stone are the reservoirs for
    the village;
Drawing water over the years, the ropes have left ruts on
    their rim,
Dark and dank, green moss also lines the perimeter inside,
I think of the paths across the fields in the village —
These winding, narrow paths of cobblestone and stepping-
    stone,
They lead up to the rivulets, the ridges, and the groves,
As well as to another village behind the great forest over the
    ridge.

I think of the small brook near the village —
Day and night bringing in running water from afar,
Pouring onto the fields, the orchards, and into the wells,
Providing the people of the village with all they need to
    drink.
I think of the wooden bridge over the brook nearby the
    village —
A mere husk of a structure after repeated use,
Year after year, its skinny struts barely visible in the water,
So that the people of the village can cross over its hump-
    backed spine.

I think of the open area in the middle of the town —
A playground for the children, a place to wrestle and tumble,

Where grownups thresh wheat, shell peas, husk grain, and
   sift rice . . .
And on long bamboo poles, clothes flutter in the wind, not
   quite dry;
Where, on large mats, barley, soybeans, and buckwheat are
   set out in the sun;
On summer evenings, people would gather there, to chat,
   catch the breeze, even argue amongst themselves,
On winter mornings, they loosen their clothes, pick off lice,
   take in some sun;
And if a cow should fall down a cliff, this field would become
   a slaughterhouse.

I think of the simple dwellings in that village —
They were huddled together, like people shivering from the
   cold,
They have been blackened by the soot of charred wood, and
   coated with dust;
Inside, the sound of women scolding and of children bawling;
From the rafters hang sunflower and turnip seeds,
Or wrinkled red peppers on a string, and yellowing dried
   vegetables;
Tiny little windows gaze out upon the road leading out of
   the village,
Looking beyond to the mountain ranges, and to the settle-
   ments at their base.

I think of the oldest man in the village —
His hair and beard ash-white, teeth gone, ears deaf;
His hands like wisteria gnarled around his walking stick;
And those just back from market shout when they tell him
   the current prices;
I think of the oldest woman in the village —
Once married into this village, she has never left,
She has never seen a sailboat, let alone a train or a steamship,

Her children and grandchildren have all died off, but she
    carries on undaunted.

I think of the much oppressed farmers of the village —
Their faces as sullen as pine forests, their skins as wrinkled
    as pine bark,
Their eyes rubbed dim by disillusionment and despair;
I think of the faithful wives of these farmers —
Their anemic faces looking as drab-brown as the soil,
All day long, they're busy husking grain, pounding rice,
    cooking meals, tending pigs;
Mending shoes at the same time they stuff their nipples into
    the mouths of their suckling babes.

I think of the young cowherds in the village —
Of the child-brides who rub their eyes with filthy hands,
Of tenant farmers with no land and no oxen,
Of farmhands with nothing of their own except their bodies
    and the clothes on them,
Of the carpenters, the stonemasons, the plasterers who built
    the houses.
Of the butchers, the blacksmiths, the tailors,
Of all the people who have been worn down by poverty —
Who have worked for years, but have not yet received their
    reward.

My poem is dedicated to the luckless people of the village —
No matter where I go, I will keep their memory alive,
The memory of people who are cut off from the world by a
    mountain barrier,
Who are, like wild boars, both taciturn and fierce,
They have been — for so long — hoodwinked, cheated, and
    ridiculed;
Every face masks a seething resentment that has yet to ex-
    plode.

In their clothing, they hide long, sharp, pointed blades,
Kept for now in their sheaths, but they will, one day, show
    their edge in vengeance.

I dedicate my poem to the little village where I was born and
    raised —
A lowly, hardly remarkable tiny little village,
There must be a million such villages in China.
It lives in my heart, as a mother lives in the heart of a son.
Though brilliant landscapes and wretched lives form sharp
    contrasts,
Still, the benevolence of Nature does not make up for the
    misfortunes of the people.
This is unjust: the village should be in consonance with
    Nature;
To repel deceit and oppression, this village will wake, one day,
    from its slumber.

September 7, 1942

(Translated by Eugene Chen Eoyang)

Mao Zedong

Wherever Mao Zedong appears
Thunderous applause fills the air —

"The people's leader" — not a hollow term of praise;
He wins the people's trust by giving them his love.

He takes root in this vast and ancient land of China,
Bearing history's chronicles upon his own back.

Worry often spreads across his face,
His eyes reflect the people's misery.

Statesman, poet, military commander,
Revolutionary — applying thought to action;

Always pondering, always summarizing,
One hand casting aside the enemy, the other receiving more
    friends;

"Concentration" is his ingenious strategy —
Focussing the greatest force on the biggest enemy,

A new slogan determines a new direction:
"Give your all for the death of Fascism!"

During the Assembly of Representatives of the Shaanxi-
Gansu-Ningxia Border Region
November 6, 1941

(Translated by Peng Wenlan)

Words from the Sun

Open up your windows
Open up your plank doors
Let me enter, let me enter
Enter your tiny home

I bring you golden-yellow flowers
I bring you the fragrance of a forest
I bring you brilliance and warmth
I bring you dew for your whole body

Hurry, wake up, wake up
Lift your head from your pillow
Open wide your eyes covered by thick lashes
Let your eyes witness my arrival

Open your hearts, like tiny wooden chambers
Open their windows which have been closed for so long
Let me fill the space in your hearts
With flowers, fragrance, light, warmth, dew

January 14, 1942

(Translated by Marilyn Chin)

Wild Fire

Set these black nights ablaze
On these lofty mountaintops
Extend your arms of flame
Embrace night's broad bosom
Embrace her dark-blue, ice-cold bosom
From the tips of your high-leaping flames
Let your sparks fly out
Let them descend, like a host of sprites
Down the unfathomable, dark-cold abyss
Let them flash on the souls fast asleep there
Let them, even if only in dazed dreaming
Dance, for once, the dance of joy

Set these black nights ablaze
Let the flames climb higher and higher!
Let your joyous configurations
Rise from the ground to the heavens
Inspire this wearisome world of ours
With the dance of your spirited fire
Rise up and soar!
Let the thousand eyes of this dark night
Look to you
Let the hearts on this dark night
All heed your earth-shaking summons
Oh, your joyous flames
Oh, your trembling flames

Listen! From what profound corner
Comes this song that hymns your praise like a waterfall. . . .

Northern Shaanxi
1942

(Translated by Eugene Chen Eoyang)

The Announcement of the Dawn

This is my plea
Ah, poet, please rise

And tell the others
What they've been waiting for is coming

Say that I've trampled dew to get here
I've followed the glimmer of the last star

I have come from the east
From the sea of turbulent billows

I shall bring light for the world
I shall bring warmth for mankind

With your honest words
Bring forth my news

Announce to mankind whose eyes are burnt by longing
And the distant towns and villages filled with despair

Ask them to come welcome me --
The messenger of light, the herald of day

Open all windows to welcome me
Open all doors to welcome me

Welcome me, please, with steam whistles

Welcome me, please, with bugles blowing

Ask street cleaners to sweep the streets clean
Ask garbage trucks to move the garbage

Let workers walk the streets with long strides
Let vehicles in gleaming ranks glide through the broad square

Tell the villages to awaken from the damp fog
Tell them to open their fence gates in welcome

Ask village women to open up their chicken coops
Ask farmers to lead their oxen out from the barns

Announce to them in your passionate words
That I have come from the mountains, from the forests

Tell them to sweep their drying-yards clean
And their eternally filthy courtyards

Open your windows, decorated with paper flowers
Open your doors, adorned with the new year's mottoes

Please wake up the courteous women
And the snoring young men

Wake up the young lovers
And the girls, so fond of sleeping

Please wake up exhausted mothers
And the babies by their side

Please wake up everyone
Even the sick and mothers lying-in

Even the old and feeble
Even those groaning in bed

Even those who are wounded, who fought for our righteous
      cause
And those wandering refugees whose homes were destroyed

Please wake up all the unfortunate ones
I could comfort them as well

Please wake those who love life
Workers, engineers, and painters

Singers, please come welcome me with songs
In the sound of dew that seep into the grass

Dancers, please come welcome me with dancing
In their morning robes of white mist

Please wake up the healthy and beautiful
I am coming at once to knock on their windows

You, poet loyal to time, please
Bring to mankind your message of comfort

Tell them to get ready to welcome me
I shall arrive in the rooster's last cry

Tell them to gaze at the horizon with their faithful eyes
For I will shine on those who expect me, the most benign
      light

Hurry, before the night is over, tell all
That what they've been waiting for is coming

                              (Translated by Marilyn Chin)

Reef

One wave after another
Makes its relentless assault.
Each wave falls at its feet,
Dashed to briny foam, and dispersed.

The face and body of the reef,
As if slashed by a knife:
But it stands there still
With a faint smile, gazing out at the sea.

July 25, 1954

(Translated by Eugene Chen Eoyang)

On This Side of the World

On this side of the world,
People embrace us so tightly
That we cannot breathe,
And kiss our faces fervently —

It is not because we are still young,
Nor because we are attractive,
But because we come from the same country,
A country born in blood;

Nor is it meeting old friends in a new place,
For many have never met before,
But in a kind of high devotion,
We are to each other as lovers long-separated.

The Chinese are welcome anywhere!
Our perseverance and courage are known to the world;
Six hundred million people march forward under one banner,
And on that banner one word is inscribed: Peace!

Santiago
July 1954

(Translated by Eugene Chen Eoyang)

Venus, the Morning Star

Yours is the moment
When light replaces darkness
When black night flees
And bright day follows in her wake

The stars have already retired
But you stand there still
Waiting for the sun to rise

Lit up by morning's first rays
Plunging into the ranks of light
Till no one can see you any more

August 1956

(Translated by Peng Wenlan)

Spring

1

The mountain song you sing
Far, near, its name well-known
Listen! Your song
Is clearer than the spring

2

Here, mountains are high
Waters come deep
Drink the water here
And soothe your singing throat

The common people
Don't come this way
No one has the patience
To climb such high peaks

And perched here
Are only two kinds of birds
Days, the Mongolian lark
Evenings, the nightingale

August 1956

(Translated by Marilyn Chin)

On a Morning When It Snows

The snow is falling, falling, without a sound
The snow is falling, falling, not stopping for a second
Clean white snow, totally covering the courtyard
Clean white snow, totally covering the rooftops
How peaceful the whole world is, how peaceful!

As I watch the snowflakes fluttering down
My thoughts drift off, far far away
I think of the forests of summer
Of dawn in those thick forests,
And of dew daubed on everything.
The sun has just risen:
A boy, his feet bare,
Walks out from the morning glow
His face is as fresh as a flower
A soft and gentle song on his lips
In his tiny hand, a bamboo staff.
He raises his small head,
His eyes all aglimmer,
And peers into the dense foliage,
To search out the cicada's sounds. . . .

In his other tiny hand,
He carries a string of something green
— Stalks of very long foxtails,
Strung with grasshoppers, beetles, and dragonflies.
All this
I remember oh so clearly.

We haven't been back to the forest for a long time,
There where it must be full of leaves already,
Where there's not a trace of a single soul,
But I shall always think of that boy
And the lilting sound of his song.
Just now, he is in some small room or other
Watching the snowflakes fluttering endlessly down.
Perhaps he has a mind to throw snowballs in the forest,
Or to skate on the iced-over lake:
But he certainly will not know
That someone thinks of seeing him
On such a morning when it snows.

November 27, 1956

(Translated by Eugene Chen Eoyang)

Plateau

The daytime here
Why so hot

Too high here
Close to the sun

The evening here
Why so cold

Too high here
Close to the moon

Why is it hot near the sun
Why is it cold near the moon

The sun is fire
The moon is ice

1956

(Translated by Marilyn Chin)

Presented to Ulanova

— composed after watching the ballet, *Serenade*

As soft and gentle as a cloud,
As light as the wind,
More brilliant than the moon,
More tranquil than the night —
A figure floats through the air;

She's not a fairy from heaven,
But a goddess from earth,
More beautiful than a dream,
More breathtaking than a vision,
The crystal of creative movement.

(Translated by Eugene Chen Eoyang)

Hope

Dream's friend
Illusion's sister

Originally your shadow
Yet always in front of you

As formless as light
As restless as wind

Between you and her
She keeps her distance always

Like flying birds outside the window
Like floating clouds in the sky

Like butterflies by the river
She is sly and lovely

When you rise, she flies away
You ignore her, and she nudges you

She is always with you
To your dying breath

(Translated by Eugene Chen Eoyang)

The Umbrella

In the morning I ask the umbrella,
"Do you prefer being baked in the sun
Or being drenched by the rain?"

The umbrella smiles. It says,
"This is not what I worry about."

I persist in my question:
"Then what are you worrying about?"

The umbrella says,
"What worries me is this:
In the rain I mustn't let people's clothes get wet;
In the sun I must serve as a cloud overhead."

1978

(From *Chinese Literature*)

Fish Fossil

With such agility in your movements,
Such buoyancy in your strength,
You leaped in the foam
And swam in the sea.

Unfortunately a volcano's eruption
Or perhaps an earthquake
Cost you your freedom
And buried you in the silt.

After millions of years
Members of a geological team
Found you in a layer of rock
And you still look alive.

But you are now silent,
Without even a sigh.
Your scales and fins are whole
But you cannot move.

So absolutely motionless,
You have no reaction to the world.
You cannot see the water or the sky,
You cannot hear the sound of the waves.

Gazing at this fossil,
Even a fool can learn a lot:
Without movement
There is no life.

To live is to struggle
And advance in the struggle;
Even if death is not at our doorstep,
We should use our energy to the fullest.

(From *Chinese Literature*)

The Mirror

Though just a plain surface,
Yet it seems unfathomable.

It loves truth deeply,
Never hiding defects.

It is honest with those who seek it,
Anyone can discover himself in it,

Whether one is flushed with wine
Or wears hair white as snow.

Some like it
Because they are good-looking.

Some avoid it
Because it is too frank.

There are even some
Who hate it and wish to smash it.

1978

(From *Chinese Literature*)

To the Soul of Danuska, My Friend

I place this poem on funerary urn No. 38 at the Ninth Sector
of Olśany Cemetery in Prague, the urn of my friend Danuska
Heroldova Stovickova.

In these confused, unsettled times,
Friendship is like a reed on a darkling day,
Trembling in the wind,
Sighing imperceptible sighs. . . .

How vast is space,
How infinite is time,
When I flip open memory's album,
The words seem almost rubbed off:

The first time you got off the plane,
You looked in the crowd
For a man known to write poems,
But he wasn't there to receive you.

You stayed in China three years,
Through spring bloom, autumn moon, warm winds, radiant
      sun,
You came to love this country,
And her ancient, simple people.

In the autumn of 1957,
Your contract fulfilled, you left Beijing;
Again, among those who saw you off,
Missing was the man who wrote poems.

In the vast, forsaken steppes,
I received a postcard from Prague;
For some time I hesitated, and then did not write,
Doubting that the frail dandelion would ever reach you.

Ten full years went by,
Then the banks of the Vltava were struck by an earthquake,
It was you I thought of first —
And the fate of someone, like you, with integrity;

You saw me in your library —
So much like the library a Chinese would have,
What has become of your projects, your translations?
And what about the *Complete Works of Lu Xun*?

Time passed, with unimaginable ordeals,
The air became polluted by the stench of blood. . . .

Twenty-one years have passed with no news,
Today, it's three full weeks into winter,
All of a sudden, the bitter cold seems to tell:
"Danuska is, alas, with us no more!"

You were killed in a car accident,
On October 30, 1976.
When I heard this news,
It was a full two years later.

I thought I saw a small pine sapling, green,
Uprooted violently by the wind;
I thought I saw a bridge, reaching for the other bank
Suddenly overwhelmed by a mountain torrent. . . .

How much you loved China,
You came to see her as your own country;
You defended her in her darkest hours,
You resisted pressures to vilify her.

Death has snatched from you any hope of seeing China again,
Snatched the hope of seeing once again your Chinese friends.

After an interminable twenty-one years,
I am, at last, restored to dignity.
How you would have been happy at this news,
You who never stopped being indignant at my plight!

Alas, you have already gone to your everlasting rest,
You will never again hear my songs,
You, who were so familiar with their sound —
Songs that, even in moments of joy, were soured by sorrow.

Now, on my desk,
I still have the ashtray you gave me;
It seems not to know anything,
And sparkles and shines just as before. . . .

A friendship like ours, in these times,
Is so precious, so hard to come by!

Like a photograph spared from the flames,
Like a shard of porcelain picked up after an earthquake,
Like the mast of a ship that has foundered,
With a wan and bitter smile, after all that's happened,
I see there's no way I can complete this poem, so full of
        remorse. . . .

Rest
Dear Danuska!

January 11, 1979

(Translated by Eugene Chen Eoyang)

To Welcome So Bewitching a Spring

1

I wonder if you have heard:
The last few nights, from the riverside
    Comes — bit by bit — a kind of cracking sound.
Ah! The river ice is thawing,
The waters can flow swiftly without restraint,
Huge blocks of ice bump together, jostle each other
Like streams of people in front of the theater
    Cheerfully surging into the distance.

The spring we've waited for so long is at last coming,
The season that gives birth to a million things is coming,
The season for sowing and sprouting is coming,
Who could possibly not love spring!
Even if, after the snow and ice have melted,
    The roads are muddy,
Even if we have to trudge through great marshlands,
We should go to greet her,
For she brings to us, one and all,
Warmth and hope.

2

We've had springs when we've been deceived,
We've had springs when we've been banished,
We've had springs when we've been imprisoned,
We've had springs when we've been choked with silent tears.

We used to be like snails,
Climbing slowly at the base of the wall;
We used to be like lamaist devotees,
Striking the wooden fish, reciting sutras to pass the time.

While the entire world outside,
Troops, in convoys, by the thousands and millions,
Flew along the highways at high speed,
While MIG-25 fighter planes
Could streak over at any time
      Across our sacred blue sky:
What we were faced with was an impossibly difficult test.

Having experienced such turmoil and strife,
We have at last awakened
At last broken through each layer of ice;
We now welcome an era of resounding progress.

3

We can live out our lives at last in justice,
We can spend our days in pride and satisfaction,
We have supremely resolute faith,
And like Kazakhs starting up their dance "Courting the
      Maidens", we welcome this spring.

She is here, really here.
You can smell her fragrance,
You can feel her warmth,
In the trees just now the birds are singing,
In the woods just now fawns are gamboling. . . .

We want to sound every siren,
      To welcome the dawn of this new era;
We want to fire a 21-gun salute,

To welcome the start of these years;
All you musicians, pluck your instruments,
All you poets, compose your verses,
All these instruments, melodies, and poems
 Now constitute one gigantic symphonic movement
To welcome so bewitching a spring!

(Translated by Peng Wenlan
and Eugene Chen Eoyang)

On the Crest of a Wave

— Written for Han Zhixiong and young friends
of his generation

1. "I Am Only Han Zhixiong"

Let me introduce you to the others:
"This is a hero."
You laugh and protest:
"No hero. I'm only Han Zhixiong."[1]

A self-seeking hero might prove embarrassing,
The people paid you their most glorious compliment —
Still, you could, quite without embarrassment,
Consider yourself the hero of "The Tiananmen Incident".

When the wolves bared their teeth, flashed their claws,
Right away, you dared to go up and pluck their whiskers,
You were brave in the fight,
Enough to bolster the pride of a generation!

And you were clear-headed,
Like an island steadfast against wind and wave,
Under the blue dome of the sky,
Silently watching ten thousand waves. . . .

---

[1] There is a pun in Chinese impossible to preserve in English. The
Chinese for "hero" is *yingxiong*; Han's name is *Zhixiong*, which means
"will-to-be-a-hero" — *Ed.*

151

2.   What Kind of Fight Is This?

It's almost no fight at all,
Yet everyone brandishes knives and guns,
Claiming they are "Probing to the Very Soul",[1]
Inflicting deaths by the millions;

"Understand, and then execute;
You don't understand; you must still execute."
One hundred percent lies,
Out-and-out deceits;

The most ruthless oppressions,
The most outrageous monopolies;
More absurd than religion,
More treacherous than assassination;

Some say: "Attack with culture, defend with arms!"[2]
Some say: "Light the fires, burn down the wilderness!"[3]
One side yells: "Down with law and order!"
One side urges: "Attack! Plunder! Loot!"

They announce: "Limit the Rights of the Bourgeoisie!"
They confiscate property by "Ransacking People's Homes";
Behind the smokescreen of "Down with Restoration"
They carry out their deranged pillaging.

Reason is strangled by instinct,
Presumptions hoodwink the people;

[1] A slogan coined by Lin Biao, which provided the pretext for repeated acts of extortion and forced confession — *Ed.*

[2] A slogan coined by the Gang of Four, which in time became the rationale for all sorts of verbal as well as physical abuses — *Ed.*

[3] This slogan was directed particularly at the People's Army, which Jiang Qing wanted to destroy because it would not follow her mandate — *Ed.*

Cunning shows off by flexing its muscles,
Against uprightness, false witness is sworn;

Savage hearts puff up in the dark of night,
Lusts of the flesh grow along with power,
Self-interest and conceit compete,
Conscience is put up for auction;

The bright become the cunning,
The honest turn into dullards;
Unchecked, rumor runs rampant,
While truth gets the third degree.

Is destruction the means
Or is destruction the end? —
As if someone were playing tricks,
Someone were putting on a carnival;

"Anti-Lin Biao, Anti-Confucius, Anti-Premier Zhou!"
"Down with Rightist-Deviationists Overturning of Correct
     Decisions!"
Whoever has authority must be toppled,
And contemptible clowns show supernatural powers;

Justice, trussed up, is put on public display,
Truth is exhibited, with blindfolds on,
Even the Commander-in-Chief is not spared trumped-up
     charges,
And the Premier, already dead, is falsely accused.

From the age of ten to the age of twenty —
The ten years of the Cultural Revolution —
Han Zhixiong was swept up by great wind and wave
Into the year 1976.

3. A Day of Tragedy

Beloved Premier Zhou
You have bid your farewells —
But the enemies hadn't expected
You would stir a grief so widespread.

The world has never seen one man
The recipient of so many poems;
There has never been a man in history
Who has received so many flower-wreaths!

A mountain of flowers, an ocean of flowers,
An ocean of poems, an ocean of tears,
A limitless, vast and awesome tide,
A tumultuous outpouring of the people's grief. . . .

How many treacherous schemes,
How many rumors, how many slanders,
How many frame-ups, how many false witnesses?
None of them could soil his image;

He is an immense, massive mountain —
The enemies find him hard to overcome;
His loftiness brings out their lowliness;
His radiance pierces right through their hearts;

The enemies won't let the people wear black veils,
The enemies forbid the people from sending wreaths,
The enemies crumple the lotus flowers,
The enemies trample down the noble orchids;

Still, the mountains far away,
The trees in front of the window,
The clear spring by the roadside,
All remind people of Premier Zhou;

Premier Zhou is like the air,
Like sunlight, like water,
It's as if he were everywhere,
No one gets very far from him;

The Premier belongs to everyone,
The air belongs to everyone,
The sunlight belongs to everyone,
The earth belongs to everyone.

4.   The Qingming Festival,[1] 1976

There has never been a Qingming Festival
Like the Qingming Festival of 1976, with so many tears,
When he was alive, no one was more selfless,
The devotion of the people never more steadfast;

Han Zhixiong, in front of Tiananmen
Listened to the poems being recited day after day —
Felt a sorrow so deep tears never ceased to flow,
Felt a fury that scorched dry his tears;

A million verses,
A million torches,
One torch lighting up yet another torch,
Shining into the early spring night;

In order to protect the truth,
One must join the battle —
Where thoughts are banners,
And words are bullets;

[1] One of the 24 solar periods of the year, which fell on April 5th in 1976, a festival on which people traditionally sweep the graves of their ancestors — *Ed.*

The poems that Han Zhixiong wrote
Were pasted on the east face of the Heroes' Monument,
Like the flames of a torch,
Like the shimmer of a swift sword;

"History has its memorial tablets,
History has its scaffold for villains,
History is a judge,
History takes the people's loyal ministers
    And pays its respects on a memorial plaque —
        to remain forever in memory,
History takes the people's evil ministers
    And shoves them up the scaffold — and executes them
    in wrath!

. . . .
. . . .

How does history tolerate these poisonous traitors?
The people pluck out the peacock feathers on these black
    crows,
And tear off their outer vestments of Marxism and Leninism.
In front of the Heroes' Monument,
In the midst of the people shouting,
The sentence on them was passed without pity —
    On a handful, on the dregs of the Chinese people!
History's Heroes' Monument is bequeathed forever,
Reaching out to the heavens from this earth;
It blares out in brave, stentorian tones:
    'If the devils spew forth noxious fumes,
    Then the people will seize the wicked, and lay the
    devils low.'

. . . .
. . . .

On the tablet, the Premier shows his spirit,
Called forth numberless masses to expel the villains."

Listen, Han Zhixiong's poem,
Splits the heavens like the sound of thunder. . . .

5. "I'd Rather Rot in Jail a Thousand Years!"

This young worker was arrested,
Right in front of the portrait of Lenin,
Two days before the Qingming Festival —
At twelve, midnight.

He was shoved into prison
And immediately stripped naked of his clothes,
Repeatedly pummeled and kicked,
He was then whipped all about his face and chest!

Those who interrogated him, were they countrymen?
They bound him up in "Maximum Security" to make him
        confess:
"Why was he mourning for Premier Zhou?
Why was he supporting Deng Xiaoping?"

There was in this another kind of "law",
Revolution was turned into "Counter-revolution",
Patriots were converted into "criminals",
All to carry out the orders of the "Empress";

Listen! What kind of language do they speak?
        "This bureau is the guardian of law and order,
Where counter-revolutionaries are crushed,
How does one get out? Wishful thinking! Don't talk
        nonsense!"

Han Zhixiong responded, steadfast and firm:
"I'd rather rot in prison a thousand years!"
It was as if he had fallen into the Middle Ages,
And was awaiting trial by the Inquisition!

6. "The Tiananmen Incident"

The people's Premier is dead,
Why aren't they allowed to mourn him?
Why are the memorial poems ripped away?
Why are the flower wreaths all removed?

Why are plainclothesmen sent out
To stir things up among the masses?
Who sent out lackeys to bark out anti-revolutionary slogans,
So that the anger of the masses could be diverted?

And who was it, cowering in some dark corner,
Spent their energies plotting "The Tiananmen Incident" —
Flogging a fourteen-year-old boy all the while,
Trying to force a confession of "arson" out of him?

And who decided to replay "The Reichstag Fire"[1]
In front of Tiananmen Square?
And who downgraded the revolution of the masses
As just another "Hungarian Incident"?

"The Tiananmen Incident"
Saw a conflict pitting brightness against darkness,
Democracy against autocracy,
Where bayonets were crossed between Revolution and
    Counter-revolution;

"The Tiananmen Incident"
Was a bolt of lightning flashing in the darkest cloud,
Lighting up the true face of evil,
Outlining the figures of hatchetmen;

---

[1] "The Reichstag Fire" of 1933 was the fire set to burn down the seat of government in Germany, which Hitler staged and attributed to his enemies so that he could seize the opportunity presented by the crisis and assume control over the government — *Ed.*

"The Tiananmen Incident"
Tolled the deathknell of the Gang of Four,
It hastened the downfall of the Gang of Four —
It brightened the eyes of the people;

"The Tiananmen Incident"
Is the most brilliant sheaf of poems,
It's the river-fork, where revolution and counter-revolution
        divide;
It's the turning point in Chinese history!

7. Revolutionary Fervor Burns Brighter the More It's Tempered

Having undergone eleven months in pitch darkness,
Han Zhixiong once again saw the sun,
Even if his body was riddled with injuries,
His revolutionary fervor burned the brighter.

Why, oh great motherland,
After the "Three Big Mountains"[1] were destroyed,
Should the likes of Lin Biao and the Gang of Four appear?
Leaving wounds that are deep even now?

Where do these vipers come from?
What kind of soil nurtures these vermin?
For those who still survive today,
Is it enough to make them wonder?

The struggle is far from over,
Our eyes have to be burnished bright —

[1] The "Three Big Mountains" are associated with the Nationalist
government of Chiang Kai-shek and refer to Imperialism, Feudalism and
exploitation by the "compradors" — Ed.

We must replace superstition with science,
And break out of our mental prisons!

We must never let ourselves be swindled again,
Never let ourselves be cheated again,
What we want must be the truth,
What we want must be the light of the sun!

We must not rely on the pity of the gods,
Nor wait upon the mercy of the heavens,
The people must protect their own rights,
For the people's rights are the weapons of revolution.

All Government policies must be carried out to the letter,
All injustices must be redressed,
Even if they have lain dormant for so long,
Reputations besmirched must be restored!

8.   Fly Bravely Over....

Now, you young drivers,
Drive your bulldozers,
Get on with the job,
Dispose of all the garbage that has piled up —

Dispose of all the obstacles —
Of everything that is feudal or fascist,
Superstitious or corrupt,
And clear the ground for the Four Modernizations!

Han Zhixiong underwent trial by fire,
Tested by the worst kind of typhoon,
He was a youth of the era of Mao Zedong,
A sea swallow on the raging crest of a political wave!

"Struggle for the benefit of the people"
That was his magnificent oath —
Han Zhixiong, soaring up there bravely,
Look, the Party is beckoning to you.

If someone were to ask:
"What, in the end, did the Cultural Revolution mean?"
The answer would be unmistakably clear:
China saw a new generation of youth emerge.

November 16, 1978

(Translated by Eugene Chen Eoyang)

Song in Praise of Light

Each man in his life,
Whether clever or slow-witted,
Whether lucky or unlucky,
When he leaves his mother's womb,
Follows the light with his eyes.

A world without light
Would be like a man without eyes,
A ship without a compass,
A gun without any sights;
How else to know of the snake by the roadside
Or the trap laid on the road ahead?

If there were no light in the world,
No spring with willow catkins drifting about,
No summer with flowers vying in beauty,
No autumn with golden fruit filling the orchards,
No winter with big snowfalls and flying snowflakes.

If there were no light in the world,
We could not see the turbulent rivers,
We could not see unbroken stretches of forest,
We could not see suddenly violent seas,
We could not see snowy peaks that look like old men.

If we could see none of these,
What attachments would we form in the world?

2

It is only because there is light
That our multifarious world
Manifests its beauty and color
And our lives appear more attractive.

Light gives us insight,
Light gives us imagination,
Light gives us passion,
Light helps create forms that are immortal.

How magnificent are the monuments of architecture!
Inside, they are even more glorious!
Those poems that move us deeply,
Who can read them and not shed tears?

Those wonderful sculptors
Giving warmth to cold marble!
Those brilliant painters
Drawing alluring eyes with the spirit of life!

Dances lighter than the wind,
Songs brighter than the pearl,
Fiery enthusiasm, loyalty hard as diamond —
All art, without light, has no life.

How beautiful the camp fires on the plain,
How beautiful the lighthouse near the harbor,
How beautiful the stars of a summer night,
How beautiful the fireworks in a celebration!
All these beautiful things are at one with light.

3

What a wondrous thing light is!
It is weightless but bright as gold,

Can be seen but cannot be grasped,
Goes everywhere in the world but has no form;
Wise and modest,
It abides with beauty.

It is born of clashes and frictions,
It comes from the process of burning and extinguishing;
It comes from fire, from electricity,
It comes from the eternally blazing sun.

Ah sun, the greatest source of our light!
From outer space millions of miles away.
It sends warmth to where we live,
So that all things grow in this world.
All creation pays it homage.
Because it is the light that never fades.

It is something unfathomable,
It is not solid, not liquid, not gas,
It comes without a trace, goes without a shadow, with in-
        finite range.
It makes no noise, settles anywhere
It's strong, with no show of strength,
It is silent dignity.

It is a great being,
Rich and benevolent,
Broad-minded and open-hearted,
Gives without hope of reward,
Selfless, it sends its radiance out everywhere.

4

But there are creatures that fear the light,
Creatures that harbor a hatred for the light,

Because the rays of the light
Prick their selfish eyes.
All the tyrants in history,
All the evil ministers of past dynasties,
All the avaricious people —
To steal wealth, to seize wealth —
Have tried their best to sequester light,
Because light can rouse the people awake.

All those who oppress others
Want the people to remain incapable,
Incapable to the point of not daring to utter a sound,
So that they can rule as gods.

All those who exploit men
Want everyone stupid.
So stupid that they cannot figure things out,
Not even what makes one plus one.

What they want are slaves,
Working tools that can talk.
They only want obedient livestock:
They are afraid of people with a will.

They think to damp out the fires,
So that in the unmitigated darkness,
In their mountaintop castles,
They can wield their bloodthirsty power.

They occupy powerful thrones,
Medals in one hand, a whip in the other,
Gold coins on one side, iron chains on the other,
Conducting their depraved "government business".
Then they prepare for a dance with demons
And a bloody banquet offering human flesh.

Looking back on human history,
How many generations past
Have been plunged into this abyss of misery
Where darkness hardens into granite.
Yet, how many heroes have there been among men,
Who charged headlong through the iron gates of hell?

Glory is for those who fight without regard for themselves,
Glory is for those who step into the breach when others fall.
The sound of thunder is especially loud in a stormy rain,
The flash of lightning is especially bright in the darkest cloud.
Only through the vigil of the long dark night
Can the bright fires of the sun blaze forth.

5

Ignorance is benightedness,
Wisdom is brightness,
Man has emerged out of ignorance,
The man who first went out to steal fire from the gods,
Was the first hero to appear.
He was not afraid of the eagles who guarded fire
Pecking away at both his eyes
Nor was he afraid of Zeus' anger
Or his devastating thunderbolt,
When he stole fire from the precincts of heaven.

After that, light was no longer monopolized,
And has since been conveyed to the world of men.

We have said goodbye to clearing the land with blade and
    fire;
The steam engine brought along the Industrial Revolution;
Nuclear physics gave birth to the atom bomb;

And today, we send out satellites the way one sent out
    pigeons. . . .

Light has brought us into a strange new world:
X-rays, that can shine into living flesh,
Laser beams, that can penetrate layers of steel,
Diffraction telescopes, that can track objects in the firma-
    ment,
The electronic computer
    which thrusts us into the twenty-first century.

Still, what is even more precious to us,
Is our own penetrating vision,
The vision of our early wise men.
This vision sees through everything, foretells everything,
It can penetrate the outer layers of flesh and blood
To see into our souls,
To see into the essence of things:
All the inner laws controlling things,
All the mutations in movement,
All the movements in mutation.
All growth and decline:
Even the serene Himalayas,
Continue to rise up inexorably.

There are no horizons to knowledge
Horizons exist where progress has stopped,
But knowledge knows no limits;
Man in tracking the external world,
Leaves his own footprints.

Application is the ladder of knowledge,
Science marches forward along the trail of practice.
On the road of progress,
One must break open lock after lock,

One must unshackle chain after chain.
Truth lives on forever only on the road of practice.

6

Light from immeasurable heights
Looks down on the long currents of man's history.
From Zhoukoudian[1] to Tiananmen Square,
A course like the rolling waves in a torrent,
We have passed how many dangerous rapids, how many
    hidden reefs,
We are riding in a boat that will never sink,
For we will always be led by the light shining down from
    heaven. . . .

We have been aroused from a thousand delusions,
We have learned wisdom after being fooled a thousand times,
Unity has its contradictions, progress its setbacks,
Movement its obstructions, revolutions its betrayers.

Even light has its darkness,
Even darkness its light.
Many things ugly and shameful
Are hidden from the light:
Poisonous snakes, rats, bedbugs, scorpions, spiders,
And innumerable species of the white moth.
They are all mothers who spawn venomous creatures.
We must be on guard all the time in our lives;
Enemies we can't see lie in wait for us.

Still, our dedication
Must be as strong as light —

---

[1] Site where the skull of Peking Man was found — *Ed.*

No matter how many disasters are sustained,
When we have passed through the long, dark night,
Man's future will be bright without end, bright forever.

7

Each person has one life,
That is but a tiny grain of dust in the galaxy of humanity.
Each grain of dust has its own power;
Innumerable grains of dust collect into a ray of light.
Each person, though he stands alone,
Reflects radiance off on each other,
Spinning without stop in the communal radiance,
Along with the spinning earth in space.

We burn up in this spinning,
Our lives are nothing but this burning.
We, in our own time,
Should be like the fireworks at holidays,
That shoot up into the sky to shouts of delight,
Then blossom out in glittering bursts of light.

Even if we are a candlestick,
We must "Burn to ashes before tears are dry".[1]
Even if we are only a matchstick,
We must catch flame to blaze in one crucial moment.
Even if we all rot away after we die,
We will turn into the phosphorus spark that sets off a brush
    fire

[1] Quote from a poem by Li Shangyin, a ninth-century Tang poet,
that reads in part: "Spring silkworms spin out their lives in silk, Wax
candles burn to ashes before tears are dry." — *Ed.*

8

To be an insignificant person,
A grain of dust among astronomical figures,
Even if one's life were as short-lived as a drop of dew,
Even if it were like the minute sands on the banks of the
     Ganges
It could reflect more light than it alone can produce
With a voice that was hoarse, I sang,
During all those months and years without freedom, I sang of
     freedom.
I am the oppressed people, and I sing the song of liberation.

In this immense world,
I have sung for those who have been humiliated,
I have sung for those who have been exploited,
I sing of rebellion, I sing of revolution,
In the darkest night, I offer hope along with the dawn,
In the savor of victory, I sing of the sun.

I am but one spark in a great fire,
Before the fire of my life is extinguished,
I plunge into the ranks of fires, the ranks of light;
The "one" and the "innumerable" I meld together,
And promote the struggle for truth,
And in this struggle march in step with the people.

I will sing the praises of light forever.
Light is something that belongs to the people,
The future belongs to the people,
Whatever wealth there is belongs to the people.

With light, we advance together,
With light, we triumph together.

Triumph belongs to the people,
Together with the people, we are invincible.

9

Our ancestors won glory,
They forged the road for us.
Along the way, they left indelible footprints
And on each footprint the traces of blood.

Now we are just starting a new Long March.
This Long March is not just 25,000 *li* long.
What we want to cross are not merely thousands of mountains,
What we want to climb is not only the thousand-*li* Minshan
    range,
What we want to capture is not only the Jinsha and Dadu
    Rivers,[1]
What we want to seize are crossings more important and
    more dangerous.
When we scale the heights, we will encounter bigger
    snowstorms, even more glaciers. . . .

But light summons us to march ahead,
Light encourages us, prods us;
Light provides us with the dawn of a new age,
Our people charge ahead on all sides, their voices raised in
    song.

Let faith and courage be our companions,
We are armed with the loftiest ideals,
We are together with the class most in the vanguard,
Our hearts are burning with hope,
The road of our progress basks in sunlight.

[1] These refer to two of the fiercest battles in the Long March — *Ed.*

Let every day of our lives
      Spin off like a pinwheel;
Let our lives emit the greatest energy,
Let us, like the force released from the earth's core,
      Spread out wings of light to the utmost limits,
      To soar in the vast, limitless universe.

Let us soar at the greatest speed,
Let us soar with a spirit that knows no fear,
Let us, taking off from today, soar off towards tomorrow,
Let us make of every day a new starting point.

Perhaps one day, there will come a time,
That our very ancient people,
Our most courageous social class
Will receive the invitation of light
To go knock open the doors shut tight
And visit all our neighbors in the universe.

Let us, starting from this planet,
Soar towards the sun. . . .

August to December 1978

(Translated in *Chinese Literature* and
      by Eugene Chen Eoyang)

Wall

A wall is like a knife
It slices a city in half
One half is on the east
The other half is on the west

How tall is this wall?
How thick is it?
How long is it?
Even if it were taller, thicker and longer
It couldn't be as tall, as thick and as long
As China's Great Wall
It is only a vestige of history
A nation's wound
Nobody likes this wall

Three meters tall is nothing
Fifty centimeters thick is nothing
Forty-five kilometers long is nothing
Even a thousand times taller
Even a thousand times thicker
Even a thousand times longer
How could it block out
The clouds, wind, rain, and sunshine of the heavens?

And how could it block out
The currents of water and air?

And how could it block out
A billion people

Whose thoughts are freer than the wind?
Whose will is more entrenched than the earth?
Whose wishes are more infinite than time?

Bonn
May 22, 1979

(Translated by Marilyn Chin)

The Tour Guide

Trèves is a very lovely old town
Trèves had a very lovely tour guide

I don't know her name
But she had beautiful eyes
From her delicate lips
Came the most ravishing sounds

She was like a shepherd girl
Affectionately herding her flock
She was also like a history instructor
With wide learning and great patience

From the palaces of enfeoffed lords
To the cathedrals of the Protestants
From the capital of the Eastern Roman Empire
To Emperor Constantine the Great

From the invasion of Napoleon
To the birth of Karl Marx
From the occupation of the Prussians
To the Trèves of today

With persistent wittiness and good humor
She draws laughter out of her tourists
And in the course of two short hours
She covers two thousand years of history

Then through the Porta Nigra, by the fountain
With a fleeting smile, she says goodbye
And no one ever sees her again
But in our hearts, we still hear her crystal clear voice.

Trèves (Trier)
May 23, 1979

(Translated by Eugene Chen Eoyang)

A Toast

One glass and another glass,
Are clinking together,
Making a "clink-clink" sound,
"Chin-chin", "Chin-chin", "Chin-chin".[1]

Your heart, my heart
Clinking together
Also make a "clink-clink" sound:
"Chin-chin", "Chin-chin", "Chin-chin".

For friendship, for peace
Let all our hearts together make
This "clink-clink" sound:
"Chin-chin", "Chin-chin", "Chin-chin".

Milan
June 25, 1979

(Translated by Eugene Chen Eoyang)

[1] In Italy, "Chin-chin" is a toast which means "Bottoms up!"
(This poem puns in Chinese on the words "Chin chin", which means
"love love" or "kiss kiss", and the words "ching-ching", which means
"lightly", translated here as "clink-clink" and "clinking" — *Translator*.)

The Great Cockpit of Ancient Rome

Maybe you've seen it?
This kind of spectacle.
In a small round earthenware jar
There are two crickets battling each other
Each beating its wings
Making a whirring metallic sound,
Opening their jaws, slashing out with their claws,
Twisting and wrestling, bumping and butting,
Strength pitted against strength in a long struggle.
In the end, there's always one who is stronger,
Who tears off the legs of the other,
Bites into the body — and kills it.

The Roman Colosseum
Is just such an arena.
Everyone can imagine
That heroic spectacle.

Ancient Rome is the famous "City of the Seven Hills"
East of the Palatine Hill
North of the Caelian Hill
South of the Esquiline Hill.
In the middle of that basin
There is — possibly
The world's largest cockpit:
It's like an old round city fortress;
From a distance, four storeys can be seen,
Each storey with high archways by the score,

And, inside, in a circle, stone steps
That can seat a hundred thousand or more.

If we think of the games taking place then,
Perhaps even on a day of celebration,
More boisterous than at a local fair:
The ancient Romans wear their opulent robes,
A horde of people — the whole city delirious,
As if celebrating victories in Asia and Africa.
Actually, they are watching a heartless tragedy,
Deriving from the agonies of others their own delight.

There's the sound of the trumpet
The God of the Dead appears

The gladiators are all captive-slaves,
Picked for their strength and sturdiness,
All prisoners of war from countries defeated,
Whose wives are long lost, sons dispersed, homes wrecked,
And who are now forced into the cockpit.
It seems there is no need to pass the death sentence:
They face the outcome of their own slaughter
Like livestock in a pen;
In the fight, there is neither hate nor hostility
Yet both combatants share a similar fate:
They must raise a blameless hand
To slaughter a blameless victim;
They know that they are bound to die
But they pin their hopes on the tips of their blades;

There are times they must battle with wild beasts,
Wild beasts — fearsome whether hungry
Or just eaten their fill —
What they thirst for is fresh warm blood;
The slaves, even if they come with courage,

It's courage that comes from desperation,
Because what is needed now is not wisdom,
But the strength that must knock the opponent down;

Look at those "henchmen" — how proud they are!
They are the hired hands in the arena.
One after another, with their ox-head helmets or horses masks
Holding an iron staff and a leather whip
(At first they wear masks
But they dispense with them after a while).
They shove the gladiators together so they can fight,
To struggle even in their death throes;
The most pitiable are the gladiators whose faces are covered
(Who knows what idle reveller
Came up with such a heartless idea?);
The combatants in the arena cannot see each other
And both thrust their short swords out blindly at the adversary
Attacking or defending alike, it's blind man's bluff —
A blind man's death, a blind man's victory.

With one round of combat over
Those "henchmen" enter the arena,
And with long hooks drag the corpses out,
The chunks of flesh soaking in blood.
Those who have been stabbed to death are pulled to one
    side,
Their weapons and whatever implement they used are re-
    moved;
Those who still gasp their dying breaths are dispatched;
Afterwards, water is used to rinse away the blood
So that, after a while, not a trace is left —
This is the way the "henchmen" carry out their orders:
They don't go and kill people directly,
But they are more heinous than executioners.

Let's look again at those who are watching in the stands.
Tens of thousands, crazed, relish the spectacle.
There are august figures, sitting apart,
People placed according to their power,
The emperor's family, the nobles, casual and complacent,
By their sides, toadies paying court,
The noble ladies made up to attract attention.
Some say their coming to watch the gladiators
Is nothing compared to the display they make of themselves,
Like the glistening of stars in the firmament shining down;
The nobles have their "glorious conquests", and live
In palaces built by the labor of slaves,
They rape the women of defeated countries;
Their eating implements are stained with blood,
They relish the smell of blood;
Those who can watch man and beast fight to the death
All show their own bestiality —
From the blood-letting combats, they derive their entertain-
      ment,
From the death-dealing struggles, they draw their laughter,
The more people suffer, the happier they are
(Have you not heard their laughter?);
The most hateful are those
Who use the agonies of others to speculate with,
People who take profits out of the river of blood,
Their wealth and their vileness together grow apace;

The combat of the slaves in the arena becomes more intense,
The people in the stands are getting worked up;
As the clamor for killing becomes louder
The more it can explode into raucous laughter;
In the stands, glint gold jewelry and silver,
In the arena, glint sword and dagger;
The two groups are not very far apart —

But there's a barrier, a wall that can't be scaled, between
    them.

This is the cockpit of ancient Rome.
It continued for so many centuries.
Who knows how many slaves and captives
Perished in this round pool?
Oh, gods! Oh, Zeus! Oh, Jupiter! Oh, Jesus!
All you "omnipotent gods", where are you?
Why do you not lift a hand to alleviate these miseries?
Oh, wind! Oh, rain, lightning, and thunder!
How can you allow this kind of atrocity?

Slaves are slaves as always.
Who is running things among us?
Who is the mastermind behind these "blood baths"?
The more distant in time, the clearer it seems:
Those who managed these combats were all slave-masters
Whether it was old Tarquinius
Or Sulla, Caesar, or Augustus . . .
All of these are slavemasters among slavemasters —
Bloodthirsty beasts, ruthless monarchs!

"We won't be slaves!
We want to be free!"
One man yells;
And thousands respond.
In order to change one's own destiny
One must destroy these vicious cockpits;
One must take those who gamble with people's lives
        And nail them up on a cross of shame.

A leader of slaves
Can only emerge from slaves;
He must share with them the same destiny,

Produce the same kind of thinking;
Share the same set of ideals
And convert them into enormous power.
Again and again, they raise the flag of just revolt,
They temper their strength in defeat;
The furious troops are like the huge waves of the Mediter-
       ranean,
Overwhelming palaces, toppling Arch of Triumph,
Knocking down Colosseums, vast and extensive.
The people, aroused, pour out their blood to irrigate the
       earth
To erect a haven of free and easy work.

As now, the ancient Roman Colosseum
Has become a relic of history, like the ruins of war,
Submerged in the twilight of a setting sun, like a fort.
I cannot help wondering and thinking:
Was it a glorious monument
Or a manifestation of shame?

Was it a tribute to the magnificence of Rome
Or the evidence of a barbaric civilization?
Was it something to elicit a cheap kind of "sympathy"
Or an attempt to draw sighs of pity from posterity?
It has been too long . . .
Even the marble sheds tears;

It has been too long . . .
Even the Arch of Triumph will bow;
The most pitiful scene of a slave society has been played out
The unjust slaughter has disappeared into the mists of history
But it has left a shameful memory on the conscience of
       humanity
And it has proclaimed a particular truth:
Blood-guilt sooner or later must be repaid with blood;

Those who gamble blood-money on other people's lives
Cannot achieve a brilliant end.

Actually, aren't there such absurdities —
In the world today
There are people, as before, who have the slavemaster com-
    plex
They see all of humanity as objects of enslavement
The entire globe as one big cockpit.

Beijing
July 1979

(Translated by Eugene Chen Eoyang)

Hush, a Voice Is Speaking ...

In the dead of night, when everyone is still
In the skies above China
There is the spirit of a woman —
Hush, a voice is speaking:

A

You are terrified of me
Because I am at one with the truth
You hate me
Because I am at one with the people

You won't let me speak
The dead are already dead,
The living do not speak out
There's not so much as a sound.

I need only open my mouth
And you begin to tremble
What my mouth spews forth is fire
Truth is inextinguishable fire

You flogged me with a leather whip
As if I were a beast of burden
You kicked me with your feet
As if you were kicking a football

You used my chest

To toughen up your fists
My body and its various nerves
You treated as if it were a rock

I didn't so much as move a hand
So why put handcuffs on me
I didn't so much as wiggle my feet
So why did you lock on leg-irons

I love brightness most of all
So you kept me from the sun
I love freedom most of all
So you took me and put me in jail

You won't let me sing
But I want to sing, and loud
My kind of song you wouldn't want to hear
My kind of song I sing for the people

You are using criminals to guard "criminals"
Fostering a breed of informers
Not satisfied with mortifying the flesh
You also want to corrupt the soul

Guarding me now is a woman
Who was a secret agent for the Kuomintang —
Before, she killed Communists stealthily
Now, she kills Communists in public

Incredibly, the blood of our Communist comrades
Is converted into your faith in her
The more ruthless she is to us
The happier you are with her

You trump up "crimes"
Then interrogate me

I am innocent
You are the ones who are guilty

You have made "Comrades" out of enemies
You have made enemies out of Comrades
You have let the enemy crush our Comrades
You have become yourselves the enemy

A Communist faithful
Has been exchanged for a KMT agent
I am sentenced to prison
While she is still at large

Actually you are all of the same ilk
A bunch of absurd freaks
Except that you are good at camouflage
And foment counter-revolution in the revolutionary camp

My heart is a ruby
My soul more transparent than crystal
You use force to make me submit
I use reason to overthrow you

You use death to intimidate me
I made up my mind long ago
If I don't die in prison
It will be on the field of battle

You have turned into raving lunatics
And think of putting an end to my life —
No matter whether I live or die
I will be witness to your crimes

In order to stop up my mouth
So that I won't cry out to the world

You raise your vicious hand
As if slitting a chicken you slit my throat

You are pretty good at slaughter now
I am number 46
You will slaughter some more
Try to silence all of us

My windpipe is not mine alone
My windpipe belongs to the people
My windpipe belongs to the Communist Party
My windpipe is a seamless iron pipe that broadcasts the truth

Hands manacled — not allowed to write
Feet in shackles — not allowed to walk
Windpipe cut — not allowed to cry out
But, I still have my thoughts —
     Furious shafts that shoot out with my withering gaze

If I look at you once
And you shake and tremble all over
If I look at you twice
It pierces you to your very heart

Under guard, you take me to the execution grounds
And thought that I would at last lower my head
But I raised my head even higher
Proudly welcoming my own death

Why are you afraid to look at me
Why is your hand trembling
You are lily-livered after all
You are ashamed of yourselves after all

You raise your guns
Aimed at my breast

But the one you kill is not me
The one you kill is the truth

Those who love me should not cry
Those who hate me need not laugh
It is not that I died a cruel death.
It is that I died too young.

Those I love will suffer as before
Those I hate will still be at large
Those who survive must be more vigilant
The enemy has not yet finished with their butchery.

B

I really didn't die
The enemies are mistaken
I will never die
I am eternal spring

As soon as a rifle fires
The shot reverberates again and again
Comes back the outraged roars of the people,
A thunderous sound in the sky

I am not just one
I am the sum total
All the victims of your false witness
Are my bulwark

I am we, and we are numberless
I am the incarnation of them all
I am one of millions and millions of individuals
I am Zhang Zhixin

When I was arrested
It was 1969
When I was shot to death
It was 1975

Don't worry that I was only 45
Death has its time like a flower
A six-year lifetime in prison
Even an iron tree will bring forth flowers

I fell, I rose
I stopped breathing, I spoke
I did not die, I have everlasting life
I am at one with the people, and have everlasting life —

One day the people will speak out for me
One day the people will make images of me
One day the people will write music for me
One day the people will sing songs for me

All the world is looking at me
I am but one star in a galaxy
All the world is listening to my voice
I am like the whistle that heralds the dawn

The people is a mirror of a billion faces
In the mirror there are traces of every face
Reflecting your every movement
Reflecting your repulsive soul

See how you brush off the dirt
And wipe off the blood on your hands —
How you construct your lies
To gain "good works" by fraud

The people are millions and millions of cameras
Every lens is focused directly on you —
The face of a Judas
The heart of a wolf

Harbin
August 1979

(Translated by Eugene Chen Eoyang)

Iowa

North of Missouri is Iowa. Here, the lush grasses sway back and forth, like great waves; the trees are full of dogwood blossoms and roses. The farmers and their families are, for the most part, from New England, New York, and Ohio, who came and settled in this scenic area. They all like living here because the climate and the vegetation reminded them of home.

Those who love freedom also appreciate the fact that there are no slaves here.

Everywhere there are farms.

— History of America[1]

Away from the clamor of the Eastern Seaboard
Away from the hubbub of the Pacific Coast
Away from the noise of Chicago
Stands Iowa City, a tiny town out there on the Midwest
    Prairie

Iowa
Beautiful name
I think the Indians called it that
The Indians who have long since been driven away
Those who came after to Iowa
Were settlers who moved here from the East
Who could possibly not like this place?
Where the plains are so vast, the soil so fertile

And trees and grasses stretch on and on
The pioneers who went westward

[1] A Chinese work. *— Tr.*

Came this far and went no further

Iowa's a place where the corn flourishes
One stretch after another, fields of corn
When a breeze blows over
The fields undulate like waves on the sea

In the state of Iowa
There is Iowa City
With maples and willows
And oaks and elms
A place where rabbits and squirrels scurry about
And once in a while a dappled deer
      gambols in a grove of trees

Iowa City
Is a corn-popping town

Iowa City
Is like a village maiden
Soft-spoken and hardworking
Who rarely gets to go to Chicago
Even though it's not very far

In the autumn
In the "Mayflower" apartment building
A number of foreigners are living
They have come, like migrating birds
Authors and poets who have been invited
      To the "International Writers Workshop"

Iowa
Is an ideal place for reflection
Not as crowded or as pressed as New York
Nor as spread out and as sprawling as Los Angeles

In Iowa City

The residents are mostly students
On the street
With their long hair
Book bags on their backs
Young people wearing cowboy jeans
When they see each other
Their greeting is a shy smile

There are no skyscrapers in Iowa City
It's like a large public park
With mountains and plains for scenery
And everywhere scattered about, houses in the shade:
Little wooden houses out of a Hans Christian Andersen fable

And the Iowa River
Winds its twisty course through Iowa City
And then flows east to the Mississippi

Iowa City
A tiny little city, like an unspoiled
Lyric, and as lovely
Who could possibly not like this place?

October 1980

(Translated by Eugene Chen Eoyang)

Chicago

On the dark fertile grasslands
By the shores of Lake Michigan
A town first settled by the Indians
In time, the white people from the East
Drove away all the redmen from this place

They used rifles
To occupy this land
Cut down logs to build their houses
Constructed roads, built tracks for trains
That reached out, like a spider web, every which way

There are fiery steelmills here, slaughterhouses
A black community blacker than coal
That's been called by poets "the pit of hell"

Here, for the length and breadth of America,
This was the crossroads, the center of shipping and trade
Like a huge octopus stretching out its tentacles
Drawing in wealth and riches.

Haplessly, like ancient Rome
A great fire, fanned by the wind
Burned the entire city to the ground
— Save for one water tower

The phoenix that rose again
Had sinews of steel
Wings of glass

The architects used marble and granite
Like so many toy blocks, piled up one on another
On the shores of Lake Michigan
They built scores and scores of skyscrapers

The black "Sears Tower"
The so-called "Summit of the World"
Stands one hundred and eleven storeys high
Even if one uses a telescope to scan the horizon
One still cannot see any signs of Indians
— Who knows where they've all gone?
Only at the Natural History Museum
Are relics of their culture to be found

And the black-skinned slaves
Who came from Africa and were freed
Multiplied very quickly
Their descendants
Now go in boisterous groups
To the exhibits at the Science Museum

There is also the Art Institute
Where the names "Picasso" and "Chicago"
Are linked together
Here, you'll find the university
Where the first atom bomb was built
That leveled the Japanese city of Hiroshima

Above the gorges lined with high buildings
There is a sliver of sky
The wind whistles overhead
And red and green lights regulate the flow below

Trains fly by
Trolleys fly by

Cars fly by
Squad cars fly by

Gazing out in the dark of night:
Chicago is an ocean of lights
An ocean of glittering lights
An ocean of a million glittering lights
An ocean of lights, like one bright column, standing straight
   up

Lake Michigan
Gives off the reflection of the lights —
With a rock-and-rolling accompaniment —
Burning up into the dawn

November 3, 1980

(Translated by Eugene Chen Eoyang)

New York

Standing at the mouth of the Hudson River
An entire metropolis
A huge, incomparable framework
Human lives in a maelstrom of steel

Steel vibrating
Steel rubbing together
Steel vaulting up
Steel flying through

Above the streets
Bridge buttresses intersect one another
Long bridge spans of steel
Stretch skyward
Like strong forearms
Joining together several little islands
Into one greater New York

Manhattan
Centerpiece of all the islands
With too many skyscrapers
Sheer cliffs and precipices of iron, steel, and glass
In their numberless gorges and valleys
The traffic of a million cars flows

In the canyons below
The sun can't be seen
Nor groves of trees

You'll not find wisteria
You'll not find ferns

Larks and nightingales
Are found here only in ornithology books

If steel be the sinews of a great city
Then electricity is its bloodline
Electricity courses through
Even the tiniest capillary
Electricity is the god of our age
It controls everything

Everyone is pressing, everything's a rush
And in this rush, people try to survive
Time is what enslaves the people
And it is money urging time on

All the different peoples of the world
May be found packed into this city
Along with hordes of black people
Times Square, Harlem
Night and day
All panting out their lusts of the flesh

The age of rock-and-roll
Mixed in with the cacophony
And competing, besides
To see who can make the loudest noise

Tonight, after nightfall
The residents of New York turn on lights by the millions
More dazzling than any vision
But
Who can live their lives on visions?

In the Museum of Modern Art
Steel sculptures
Electric canvasses
Create an uncanny mirage
All kinds of weird and eerie notions
Are embodied here
The epitome of materialism
Some will enter the halls of heaven
Some will drop into the pits of hell

And the goddess of Liberty
Is no more than a likeness
Standing alone
On an island out in the harbor
Gazing on vacantly, watching this great city

November 17, 1980

(Translated by Eugene Chen Eoyang)

Los Angeles

Enchanting Los Angeles
Has the look of a southern climate

But
The fog rises from out in the harbor
The fog creeps stealthily in
The fog is silent
Crawling onto the subtropical plants
Crawling by the masts on the sailboats
Crawling up the bell-towers on the churches

The fog weighs heavily
Lumbering and leaden mass
It seeps into the little stores selling fish
To come out
Doused in a powerful stench

The fog mixes with the smoke from the factories
The fog mixes with the exhausts from cars on the freeway
The fog occupies every corner of the city

The streetlamps are clouded over
The cars on highspeed highways crawl bumper-to-bumper

Los Angeles is vast:
Joining together seven satellite cities

Los Angeles is sprawling:
Joining together city and town

Yet the fog is vaster even than Los Angeles
The fog is even more sprawling
The fog is silent. . . .

December 1980

(Translated by Eugene Chen Eoyang)

Hong Kong

Like a mound of ants pried open
A landscape of hustle and bustle

Towering buildings in droves
Rise straight up row upon row
It's like an oven baking
So hot it's hard to catch your breath
It's like a concrete mixer churning
So loud as to be unsettling

How extraordinarily crowded!
But
In the gaps between buildings
One can see the mountain ranges
And the sunshine lights up the houses on the mountain
There are bridges that leap over space
There are electric cables that pierce the clouds
Taking tourists up Tai-ping Mountain
There are crowds of pleasure-seekers
Buzzing around in Ocean Park

This area was once seashore
Peaceful in the moonlight
With boats of fishermen
Moored among the reeds and rushes
When, suddenly, it was chosen
As the center of activity

Then, miraculously,
It emerged as this strange, uncanny city

With "freedom" as the siren song —
They all came, stowing away, swimming the sea,
Wearing themselves out for the sake of wealth

City of commerce
Stockmarket
Like a pool of polluted blood
They have congealed on this tiny island

The times you are in
And your geographical location
Along with your avarice and rapacity
Give you the glamor to dazzle people

Double-decker trolleys
Buses, trucks, taxis
Motorcycles forging ahead in the vanguard
Police cars rushing past, sirens screaming
Making thousands, ten thousands nervous
Gasping in the crannies between cars

At night, neon advertising signs
Burning on competition and speculation
Night clubs and pleasure quarters
Steaming up with the desires of the flesh
There's music and dance
Full of luxury and lust
In the midst of impoverished people
The most lavish feasts are spread out

Yet there is still no end to you
Every available space is grabbed

Unlimited your thrust toward the sky
In order to vaunt your wealth
You extend your longings out to the sea

Still, this flower of a harbor
Radiant in every direction
Which I want to praise
Millions of compatriots have lived here
They have worked and struggled here
You are the conduit in and out of the motherland
You are the marketplace for the exchange of goods
You are the bridge that leads to the four seas, the five continents
For how many years have you — for the motherland —
Created incalculable wealth and riches

First draft, August 25, 1980
Revised, February 21, 1981

(Translated by Eugene Chen Eoyang)

The Hunter Who Drew Birds

There was a man who wanted to learn to hunt. So he went to a hunter and asked him to be his teacher. He said to the hunter, "A man must acquire a skill, and out of all the things one can do, I have chosen to be a hunter. I wish to take my gun into the woods and shoot the birds I choose to shoot."

The hunter looked at the pupil's gun. It was a good gun and his pupil also seemed very determined. So he told him about the characteristics of various birds and a little about how to take aim and fire a gun, and also advised him on the importance of practicing on different kinds of birds.

When the man heard this, he now thought he knew how to hunt, and so off he went into the woods with his gun. But, as soon as he entered the woods, and before he could even raise his gun, all the birds flew away.

He returned to the hunter and said, "The birds are too clever. They saw me before I could even see where they were, and by the time I had lifted my gun, they had all flown off already."

The hunter asked, "Would you rather shoot a bird that cannot fly?"

The man answered, "Well, to tell the truth, it would be wonderful if birds would not fly away when I want to shoot them."

The hunter said, "Go home and get a piece of cardboard. Draw a bird on it and then hang the cardboard on a tree. Then, when you aim at the bird, you can't miss."

The man went home and did exactly as the hunter had

instructed him. He fired a few shots but not a single one hit the target. He went back to see the hunter again. He said to him, "I followed your instructions, but I still failed to hit the bird." When the hunter asked him why he had missed, the man said, "Perhaps it was because I drew the bird too small, or perhaps because I was standing too far from it."

The hunter thought seriously for a moment and said, "I am deeply moved by your perseverance. I'll tell you what, go back and get a larger piece of cardboard and hang it on the tree. Just fire at the cardboard; this time you can't fail."

The man asked anxiously, "From the same distance as before?"

The hunter said: "That's up to you."

The man then asked, "Should I draw another bird on the piece of cardboard?"

The hunter answered: "No."

The man smiled wryly and said, "In that case, I should be firing only at a piece of cardboard."

The hunter then said to him in a solemn tone, "What I have in mind is this: First, just concentrate on firing at the cardboard. When you have done that, you can draw a bird around each hole. Draw as many birds as the holes you make on the paper. This is your best bet!"

(Translated by Peng Wenlan
and Eugene Chen Eoyang)

The Gardener's Dream

There was a man who planted in his courtyard several hundred species of roses that bloomed at different times. He thought that only in this way would he be able to see flowers blooming all year round. There were diverse types of roses, and friends from all over found ways to send them to him, knowing how fond he was of roses. When the flowers bloomed, the different colors of flowers with the same form endowed the courtyard with a sort of boring boisterousness. The gardener took a lot of painstaking care to raise these flowers, and every day he would water them, loosen the soil, add fertilizer and prune the stems.

One night, he suddenly had a dream. He dreamt that just as he was trimming off the old stems of his rose bushes he saw a whole multitude of flowers entering his courtyard. It seemed as though flowers from all over the world had come: they looked at him with sad frowns on their faces, and tears in their eyes. The gardener stood up, astounded, and looked around at all the flowers.

The first to speak was Peony. She said, "Out of self-respect, I should certainly not be willing to come without an invitation to your courtyard. I came today because my sisters invited me."

Water Lily was the next to speak: "As I woke in my pond at the edge of the wood, I heard my sisters crossing over in a great clamor, so I followed along."

Morning Glory arched her delicate body and opened her mouth: "You can't say we aren't beautiful, too."

Pomegranate, somewhat agitated, said: "Indifference shows disdain."

White Orchid said: "You must appreciate beauty of character."

Cactus said: "Those who love only the meek are themselves feeble; but we have indomitable spirits."

Winter Jasmine said: "I bring forth faith."

Orchid said: "I value friendship."

Each flower spoke her piece. Finally, in unison, they said: "To be understood is to be blessed."

At that moment, the roses spoke: "To tell the truth, we feel very lonely here. If we could be together with all of you, we'd be much happier."

All the other flowers said: "Those who are doted upon are fortunate. We have been ignored for such a long time and we stand in the shadow of the lucky ones. We have complaints beyond counting." As soon as they finished speaking, they disappeared all at once.

When the gardener awoke, his heart was oppressed and he paced up and down his courtyard. He thought to himself: "Flowers have wills of their own, and they have the right to bloom. Because I have shown favoritism to one type of flower only, I have caused discontent among all the other types of flowers. I am becoming more and more convinced that my world is too narrow. With no point of comparison, many ideas will become confused. Only beside the short can we recognize the long; only beside the small can we recognize the big; only beside the ugly can we recognize the beautiful.... From this day on, my courtyard shall become a 'kingdom of many fragrances'. May we lead our lives even more intelligently and let all the flowers blossom in their own time."

July 6, 1956

(Translated by Peng Wenlan
and Eugene Chen Eoyang)

Notes on the Translation

page 26　　"Dayanhe — My Wet-nurse"
　　　　　　"Dayanhe" — The original reads 大堰河, and is
　　　　　　the name of a village in Zhejiang; the Chinese is,
　　　　　　in turn a corruption of 大葉荷 — "Big-leaved
　　　　　　Lotus" — which was, presumably, a feature of the
　　　　　　local flora that originally suggested the name for
　　　　　　the village.

page 26　　"Wet-nurse" — The original reads 褓母 which
　　　　　　actually refers to "a dry nurse". However, in the
　　　　　　poem, it is quite clear that Dayanhe was both a
　　　　　　奶母 — "a wet-nurse" — as well as a 褓母 — "a
　　　　　　dry nurse". The translation of 褓母 as "nurse"
　　　　　　would be most misleading; in English, "nurse"
　　　　　　has the primary meaning of a hospital attendant,
　　　　　　or someone who offers medical services generally.
　　　　　　Such a person would be called a 護士 in Chinese.

page 28　　"And the beautiful young bride called her
　　　　　　affectionately 'Mother'" — The original for
　　　　　　"'Mother'" is 岳母 which in English would be
　　　　　　"mother-in-law". However, "Mother-in-law" has
　　　　　　a somewhat unfortunate association, and is not
　　　　　　entirely affectionate, so the more intimate
　　　　　　"'Mother'" has been chosen. In English, no one
　　　　　　addresses their mother-in-law "Mother-in-law",
　　　　　　though the practice of calling one's mother-in-law
　　　　　　"Mother" is not uncommon.

page 56　　"Facing the Sun"; IV. "Sunrise"
　　　　　　"The sun has risen . . ./ When it appears. . . ./
　　　　　　'The cities beckon to it from the distance/With
　　　　　　electricity and steel'" — Although these lines are
　　　　　　identified as a quote from an earlier poem, "The
　　　　　　Sun", only the last two lines — not the entire

211

epigraph — are to be found in "The Sun". A slight adjustment has been made in the translation ("beckon" for "beckoning") to accommodate the quote for use in the epigraph.

page 74   "And the soldiers in their ash-gray uniforms"

page 76   "In the forward surge of soldiers"

page 77   ". . . of soldiers with guns firing . . ."

— In each case, for "soldiers" the original reads 人群 which means "people" or "a group of people"; in the Chinese, it is clear from their "ash-gray uniforms" that these "people" are soldiers. The phrase 人群 has been translated more explicitly as "soldiers" for two reasons: (1) it is not as clear in English as it is in Chinese that "people in ash-gray uniforms" are indeed soldiers; (2) metaphoric use of "soldiers" in English (as in "Onward Christian Soldiers") is now so commonplace, that the word admits a reading of non-military as well as military combatants.

page 105   "Highway"

— This poem was published in 1940, some forty years before Ai Qing actually visited the United States.

page 134   "Venus, the Morning Star"

". . . the Morning Star" — this phrase has been added to the title to distinguish the star from the goddess. In Chinese, entirely different words to designate the two.

page 146   "To the Soul of My Friend, Danuska"

". . . three full weeks into winter" — The original reads 三九 ("The third 'nine' "), which refers to a familiar farmers' way of reckoning the different phases of winter, each phase consisting of nine days. The following rough equivalent of a ditty recording this bit of folk wisdom may be helpful:

"First 'nine', second 'nine', don't show your hand,

Third 'nine', fourth 'nine', snow covers the land,

Fifth 'nine', sixth 'nine', Look! willows on the
   strand;
Seventh 'nine', a thaw follows,
Eighth 'nine', comes the swallows,
Ninth 'nine' plus 'nine', oxen can now plow the
   land."
The "third 'nine'" refers to the coldest weeks
   of the winter.

(Translated by Eugene Chen Eoyang)

Chronology

1910   Ai Qing is born on March 27th, in the county of Jinhua, Zhejiang Province. His original name was Jiang Haicheng. He has also used the pen-names "E Qie", "Ko Ah", "Na Yung", and "Lin Bi".

1915   At the age of five, Ai Qing returns to his family after being raised by the wet-nurse, "Dayanhe".

1928   He is admitted to the National "West Lake" Fine Arts Institute in Hangzhou.

1929   He leaves Shanghai in the spring and goes by steamer to France, where he takes up residence near Paris, moving into the Vaugirard area of Paris a little later. To earn money he works as an apprentice in a private atelier in Montparnasse.

1932   He leaves Marseilles on January 28th for home, arriving in Shanghai in April after a stopover in Hong Kong.

        On the evening of July 12th, at the Spring Soil Art Research Institute, he is arrested along with thirteen others. On August 16th, a high court of the Kuomintang government in Jiangsu convicts him of activity not in accord with the "Three Principles of the People" (*San-min zhu-yi*) and he is sentenced to six years imprisonment. In prison, he writes "Dayanhe — My Wet-nurse" on January 14, 1933.

1934   At the end of the year, after serving a third of his sentence, according to regulations, he is transferred to the Suzhou Detention Center (Suzhou "Confession" Court).

        "Dayanhe — My Wet-nurse" is published in *Spring Radiance* under the pen-name "Ai Qing", the first time he uses this pen-name.

1935   He is released in October 1935.

1936   In the first half of the year, he teaches Chinese and painting in a Teachers' College in Jiangsu, but he is released at the start of the second term. He returns to Shanghai. With the help of friends, he publishes a collection of poems under the title *Dayanhe.*

On March 27th, the Chinese Writers and Artists Anti-Aggression Association is formed. Ai Qing is one of the hundred founding members, which also include Mao Dun and Feng Naizhao.

1939   He edits the supplement "The South" in the *Guangxi Daily.*

He publishes, at his own expense, his second collection of poems, *The North.*

1941   In January, after the outbreak of "The Anhui Incident", the Kuomintang initiates its third anti-Communist campaign. All the writers in Chongqing are kept under surveillance by Kuomintang agents. Through the good offices of Zhou Enlai, and using the cover of a high staff officer of the Governor of the Suiyuan and Mongolia Autonomous Region, he is able to pass through 47 Kuomintang checkpoints, arriving at last in Yan'an in March.

In October, he becomes the editor of *Shikan* (Poetry).

1945   For the first part of the year, he teaches at the Lu Xun Institute of Literature and Art. He joins the Chinese Communist Party.

1949   He publishes a volume of prose, *On the Road to Victory.*

In October, he becomes associate editor of *Renmin Wenxue* (People's Literature).

1950   His third collection, *The Selected Poems of Ai Qing,* is published.

In July, he visits the Soviet Union with a delegation from the Central Chinese Communist Propaganda Section.

1954   In July, he is invited by the head of Chile's House of Representatives to visit Chile. En route, he visits Moscow, Prague, Vienna, Geneva, Lisbon,

　　　　Dacca, Rio de Janeiro, and Buenos Aires. He composes a sequence of poems entitled "South American Travels".

1956　From February 27th to March 6th, the Chinese Writers Association holds its second (expanded) administrative meeting. Ai Qing is censured.

The Renmin Wenxue Chubanshe (People's Literature Publishing House) issues *Spring*, his fourth collection of poems.

In June, he receives Pablo Neruda and Jorge Amado; he accompanies them to Chongqing, Wuhan, and Beijing.

Ai Qing is censured in the "Anti-Rightist Movement". In December, he is stripped of his membership in the Party.

1959　In November, he is sent to the Xinjiang Uygur Autonomous Region.

1960　In the spring, Ai Qing finishes "The Story of Su Changfu", which is published by the Xinjiang Qingnian Chubanshe (Xinjiang Young People's Publishing House).

1967　He is sent to a "farm" for "work rectification". He sleeps in a cellar; he is assigned to the latrine detail.

1973　In the spring, he goes to Beijing to seek medical attention for his eyes. After a brief visit home to Jinhua, he returns to Xinjiang.

1975　He returns to Beijing again as the trouble with his eyes flares up again. This time, he stays on in Beijing.

1978　On April 30th, he publishes a poem, "Red Flag" in Wenhui Daily in Shanghai. This is the first poem published after his restitution.

1979　*Renmin Wenxue* publishes Ai Qing's long poem, "In Praise of Light".

In March, the Organizing Ministry of the Central Committee of the Chinese Communist Party makes restitution (*ping-fan*) to Ai Qing, restores his Party membership, restores his reputation, and reinstates him at his former wage scale.

In May, Ai Qing visits West Germany, Austria, and Italy with the Chinese People's Association for Friendship with Foreign Countries.

In August, he is invited by the writers in Harbin for a month's visit. The Heilongjiang Provincial Association of Literature and Art organizes a public reading of Ai Qing's works, which is attended by thousands.

In September, the Renmin Wenxue Chubanshe issues a new edition of the *Selected Poems of Ai Qing*.

In November, he is chosen to participate in the Fourth Congress of the All-China Association of Literature and Art; he also becomes Vice-Chairman of the Chinese Writers Association.

1980   The Foreign Languages Press in Beijing publishes *Poèmes,* a selection of Ai Qing's verse translated into French.

In May, the Sichuan Publishing House issues *Songs of Return,* a collection of 66 poems written since his "return from silence".

In June, Ai Qing is invited by Paul Engle and Nieh Hualing of the International Writers Program to visit the University of Iowa.

On June 10th, at the invitation of the Singer-Bolibachek Foundation, he arrives in Paris to attend the International Symposium on Chinese Literature During the Sino-Japanese War, which is held from June 16th to June 19th. After the conference he visits Italy with a delegation from the Chinese Writers Association.

On August 24th, he visits the United States for four months and is invited to various American universities, including the University of Iowa, the University of California at Los Angeles, and Indiana University.

(Translated by Eugene Chen Eoyang)

In a suburb of Paris, 1929
在巴黎郊區玫瑰村（1929年）

With a labour model in
the Shaanxi-Gansu-Ningxia
Border Region, 1944
在定邊鹽池和邊區勞模在一
起（1944年）

In the rostrum of Tiananmen, Beijing, 1949 (*Ai Qing on the right*)
在北京天安門城樓上（1949年）

In Beijing, 1950
在北京（1950年）

In Prague, July 1954
在布拉格（1954年7月）

With his wife, Gao Ying, in Shanghai, April 1957
和他的妻子高瑛在上海（1957年4月）

With his wife, Gao Ying, in Shihezi, Xinjiang, 1960
和他的妻子高瑛在新疆石河子（1960年）

In Austria, June 1979

在奧地利（1979年6月）

At Dachau Concentration Camp,
Munich, June 1979

在慕尼黑達豪集中營（1979年6月）

In Austria, June 1979

在奧地利（1979年6月）

艾 青 詩 選

目　　録

寓言兩則：

作 者 自 序

一

　"我們找你找了二十年，我們等你等了二十年……"

　"在'四人幫'橫行的日子裏，不知你怎麼樣了，我總是想：大概死了……"

　　上面引的都是讀者來信中的話，這樣的話幾乎每封信裏都有。這是今年四月底，我發表了第一首詩之後，讀者對我的關切。

　"作家沒有作品，或者沒有發表作品，等於不存在……"

　　不存在等於死亡，而我並沒有死亡。

　　多少年來，林彪、"四人幫"總想禁錮歌聲，他們把不屬於自己幫派體係的作品都列爲禁書，束之高閣。

　　但是，只要歌聲是屬於人民的，人民就會保護歌聲。

　"爲了買你的詩集，我曾跑遍了很多地方也沒有買到……"

　"我們到處找你的詩集，找到了就互相傳抄，抄好了就東藏西藏……"

　　"爲了保存你的詩集，我用塑料布裹起來，藏在米缸裏……"

　　"唐山地震之後，我在櫃子底下找到了你的詩集……"

　　最近一個朋友給我看了四十二年前出版的《大堰河》，並且要我簽名作爲紀念。

　　我在那本書的扉頁上寫了一首"詩"：

　　　好像一個孤兒
　　　失落在人間
　　　經歷了多少烽火硝煙
　　　經歷了多少折磨和苦難
　　　相隔了四十多年
　　　終於重新相見——
　　　身上粘滿斑斑點點
　　　却保持了完好的容顏——
　　　可眞不簡單！

　　開灤煤礦的一個工人來信說：

　　"我不懂詩，我是一個生在農村的人，看到你的詩會勾起我回憶童年時代的農村和可憐我童年時代的農村……爲什麼詩的魅力這麼大呢？……我只知我這個普通工人經常懷念你，經常關心你！……只要你收到這封信，看到一個二十多年來經常把你懷念的人的感情，也就使我心安理得了……"

　　幾乎所有來信都對我寫詩表示高興："現在好了"，"你終於出來了"，"你還健在，你應該歌唱！"

我今年六十八歲。按年齡說並不算老，但是，有許多年輕的朋友都死在我前面，而我却像一個核桃似的遺失在某個角落——活着過來了。

二

我生於一九一零年陰曆二月十七日，是浙江金華人，老家在山區。

據說我是難產的，一個算卦的又說我的命是"克父母"的，我成了一個不受歡迎的人，甚至不許叫父母"爸爸媽媽"，只許叫"叔叔嬸嬸"。我等於沒有父母。這就使我討厭算卦，反對迷信，成了"無神論者"。

從少年時代起，我從美術中尋求安慰。

"五四運動"開始的時候，我已經九歲。小學課本裏已有啓蒙思想——要求民主和科學。

女學生們開始"放足"了。

中學老師第一次出的作文題是《自修室隨筆》，我寫了一篇《一個時代有一個時代的文學》，反對唸文言文。老師的批語是："一知半解，不能把胡適、魯迅的話當作金科玉律"。老師的批語並沒有錯，我却在他的批語上打了一個"大八叉"！

"山雨欲來風滿樓"。學生們經常上街遊行、搖旗吶喊，搗毀賣仇貨的商店，衝進賣鴉片的"禁煙處"……革命的風暴震撼着南方的古城。不知哪兒來的一本油印的《唯物史觀淺說》，使我第一次獲得了馬克思主義階級鬥爭的觀念——這個觀念終於和我的命運結合起來，構成了我一生的悲歡離合。

　　一九二八年暑假初中畢業後，我考入國立西湖藝術院（即現在的杭州美術學院）繪畫系。沒有唸完一個學期，院長發現了我。他說："你在這裏學不到什麼，你到外國去吧。"

　　第二年春天，我就懷着浪漫主義的思想到法國去了。

　　我在巴黎是一個窮學生。家裏不願意接濟我，我就在一家工藝美術的小廠工作，一邊進行自學，到蒙巴那斯一個"自由畫室"去畫人體速寫。我也讀了一些中文翻譯的哲學和文學的書；俄羅斯批判現實主義的小說、蘇維埃十月革命的小說和詩歌；有時也到工人區的"列寧廳"看禁演的電影。同時也讀了一些法文現代的詩。而我最喜歡、受影響較深的是比利時大詩人凡爾哈侖的詩，它深刻地揭示了資本主義世界的大都市的無限擴張和廣大農村瀕於破滅的景象。總之，我在巴黎度過了精神上自由、物質上貧困的三年。

三

　　一九三一年的"九一八事變"，使中國的民族危機深刻化了。

　　一九三二年的"一二八事變"那一天，正好是我從馬賽動身囘國的那一天。

　　但是，四月上旬輪船到香港停了四天——國民黨忙於和日本帝國主義談判"淞滬協定"。

　　到上海的時候戰爭已結束──祖國依然呻吟在屈辱中……我茫然回到老家，住了不到一個月就離開了。

　　五月我到上海，加入"中國左翼美術家聯盟"，和大家一同組織了一個"春地畫會"。

　　早在巴黎的時候，我就試着寫詩，在速寫本裏記下一些偶然從腦際閃過的句子。

　　在從巴黎回國的途中也寫了一些短詩。但從來沒有想要當一個"詩人"。

　　一天，同房住的一個詩人在桌子上看到我寫的一首詩《會合》，是記錄反帝大同盟東方支部在巴黎開會的場景的，他自作主張地寫了個條子："編輯先生，寄上詩一首，如不錄用，請退回原處"，寄到當時"左聯"的刊物《北斗》。想不到居然發表了。這件小事，却使我開始從美術向文學移動，最後獻身於文學。

　　六月，"春地畫會"在上海基督教青年會樓上舉行展覽會，得到了魯迅先生的支持，把他珍藏的德國女畫家珂勒惠支的版畫借來一同展出。魯迅自己也來參觀，簽了一個很小的名。看完之後捐了五元──會場要出租錢。我把"收條"給他，他悄悄一揉就扔掉了。

　　我和魯迅見面只這一次。

　　七月十二日晚上，"春地畫會"正在上世界語課，突然遭到法租界巡捕房密探的襲擊，進行了半個小時的搜查之後，我和其他十二個美術青年一同被捕。

　　國民黨以臭名昭著的"危害民國緊急治罪法"控告這一羣手無寸鐵的青年"顛覆政府"！

　　在看守所的時間特別長。我寫了不少詩。有些詩通過律師的談話、親友的探望，偷偷把稿子帶到外面發表。

　　爲了避免監獄方面的注意，從一九三三年開始，我改用“艾青”這個筆名，寫了《大堰河——我的褓姆》。這個筆名到今天，已整整用了四十五年。

　　一九三五年十月我出獄，三六年出版了第一本詩集《大堰河》。

四

　　一九三七年七月七日爆發了抗日戰爭。我在前一天在預感中，寫了《復活的土地》：

　　　　……

　　　　我們的曾經死了的大地，
　　　　在明朗的天空下
　　　　已復活了！
　　　　——苦難也已成爲記憶，
　　　　在它溫熱的胸膛裏
　　　　重新漩流着的
　　　　將是戰鬥者的血液。

　　中國人民，偉大的中華民族，以自己的鮮血來洗刷近百年來被奴役的耻辱。

　　我從上海到武漢，從武漢到山西臨汾，從臨汾到西安，又折囘到武漢，到桂林，在《廣西日報》編副刊《南方》。出版了詩集《北方》。

　　一九三九年下半年在湖南新寧敎了一個學期的書之後到重慶。

　　一九四零年春天，我帶了長詩《火把》到重慶——當時的所謂"大後方"的文化中心。

　　不久，我得到周恩來同志的接見。那是在重慶郊區北碚，在事先約定的時刻，他從濃蔭覆蓋的高高的石階上健步下來，穿一身淺灰色的洋布幹部服，顯得非常整潔。

　　他在育才學校的講話中，明確地提出希望我到延安去，"可以安心寫作"。那時，大家都親切地稱他"周副主席"（軍委副主席）。

　　一九四一年初發生了震驚中外的"皖南事變"，國民黨發動了第三次"反共高潮"。在重慶的進步作家受到了恐嚇與監視。我幸虧得到周恩來同志的幫助，和另外的四個作家一起，擺脫了國民黨特務的跟踪，沿途經過四十七次的檢查，安然到達延安。

　　初夏的一個夜晚，得到通知，我們在楊家嶺的窰洞裏，第一次見到了自己所生活的時代的傑出的人物——中國人民的偉大領袖毛澤東同志。在我的腦子裏留下了永遠不會消失的一個既魁梧又和藹的身影與笑容。

　　十一月，我被選為陝甘寧邊區參議會的參議員。我第一次寫了歌頌領袖的詩《毛澤東》。

　　一九四二年春天，毛主席多次接見我。最初他來約我"有事商量"，我去了。

　　他和我談了"有些文章大家看了有意見，你看怎麼辦？"老實說，我當時並沒有看出有什麼嚴重性。我很天眞地說："開個會，你出來講講話"。他說："我說話有人聽嗎？"我說："至少我是聽的。"

　　接着他來信說："前日所談文藝方針諸問題，請你代我收集反面的意見……"在"反面的"三個字下面加了三個圈。

我沒有收集什麼反面的意見，只是把自己的意見正面提出了。

他看了我的意見之後來信說："深願一談"。在談話中，他提出包括文藝與政治、暴露與歌頌等等問題。我根據他的指示進行了修改，以《我對目前文藝工作的意見》為題發表了。

五月，以毛主席的名義召開"延安文藝座談會"。會議進行了好多天，討論也很熱烈。

在會上，我記得的是朱總司令對我在文章中引用的李白的兩句話："生不用封萬戶侯，但願一識韓荆州"，作了最精闢的解釋："我們的韓荆州是工農兵。"實際上指出了文藝工作者的方向。

在會議結束的那一天黃昏，毛主席發表了著名的、經典性的《在延安文藝座談會上的講話》，把馬克思主義的文藝理論發展了，也明白無誤地重申了列寧對文學藝術的黨性原則。

在座談會之後，我寫信給毛主席提出想到前方去。他回信說："贊成你去晉西北，但不宜走得太遠，因同蒲路不好過"；"目前這個階段希望你蹲在延安學習一下馬列，主要是歷史唯物論，然後到前方，切實研究一下農村階級關係，不然對中國戰況總是不很明晰的……"

他指示我學習馬列——主要是歷史唯物論，實際上叫我投入接着不久就來到的"整風運動"，以馬克思主義為武器，去戰勝一切領域中的唯心主義。

五

一九四五年八月，日本投降。

十月，我隨華北文藝工作團到張家口，文工團併到華北聯合大學作爲文藝學院。不久就撤出張家口，轉移到冀中、冀南一帶。整個解放戰爭期間，我都在文藝學院搞行政工作。也曾參加過幾次土地改革工作。寫過組詩《布穀鳥》。

一九四九年初北京解放。我在進城後的第一件工作就是以"接管人員"的身份接管"中央美術學院"；參加全國文聯和作家協會的籌備工作；參加第一屆政治協商會議；最後當了《人民文學》的副主編。

一九五零年隨中共中央的一個代表團訪問蘇聯，所寫的詩均收入《寶石的紅星》裏。

一九五三年囘老家一次，收集了抗日戰爭期間在浙東一帶的歷史，但以民歌體寫的敍事長詩《藏槍記》却失敗了。

一九五四年七月，得到智利衆議院的邀請到智利訪問，寫了《南美洲的旅行》這組詩以及後來補寫的長詩《大西洋》。

一九五六年由人民文學出版社出版了我的第二個選集《春天》，我在"後記"中說：

> "……我的作品並不能反映這個偉大的時代。這個時代是要用許多的大合唱和交響樂來反映的。我只不過是無數的樂隊中的一個吹笛子的人，只是爲這個時代所興奮，對光明的遠景寄予無限的祝福而已。"

一九五七年，我先是計劃寫"匈牙利事件"，已完成

《弗洛拉》、《巴拉頓湖》兩個章段，因材料不足擱下了。接着到上海，收集了有關帝國主義在經濟上侵略中國的歷史資料，纔寫了《外灘》一節，又因事擱下了。

一九五八年四月，得到一個將軍的幫助，並經周恩來總理的同意，我到東北國營農場去"體驗生活"，當了一個林場的副場長，和伐木工人們一起生活了一年半；曾寫了長詩《踏破荒原千里雪》和《蛤螞通河上的朝霞》，可惜都已丟失了。

一九五九年冬我到新疆，在生產建設兵團的一個墾區度過了十六年。

我認識了不少新朋友。我也下決心要歌頌這些改造大自然的戰士們。我爲了要寫這個機械化的墾區積累了幾十萬字的材料。

一九七二年，經醫生檢查發現我的右眼因白內障而失明已經有四五年之久了。

一九七五年春天，我經上級批準到北京醫治眼疾。

難忘的一九七六年！我國人民先後失去了三個領導人，整個國家處在危急中——萬惡的"四人幫"從四面八方伸出了黑手……感謝黨中央一舉粉碎了"四人幫"，使偉大的祖國轉危爲安。我也得到了第二次解放。

六

詩人必須說眞話。

常常有這樣的議論：某人的詩受歡迎，因爲他說了人們心裏的話。我以爲這種議論不夠全面。全面的說，某人的詩受歡迎，因爲某人說了眞話——說了心裏的話。

人人喜歡聽眞話。詩人只能以他的由衷之言去搖撼人們的心。詩人也只有和人民在一起，喜怒哀樂都和人民相一致，智慧和勇氣都來自人民，纔能取得人民的信任。

人民不喜歡假話。哪怕多麼裝腔作勢、多麼冠冕堂皇的假話都不會打動人們的心。

人人心中都有一架衡量語言的天平。

也有人誇耀自己的"政治敏感性"，誰"得勢"了就捧誰，誰"倒霉"了就罵誰。

這種人好象是看天氣預報在寫"詩"的。

但是，我們的世界是風雲變幻的世界。這就使得"詩人"手忙脚亂，像一個投機商似的奔走在市場上，雖然具有市儈的鬼精，也常常下錯了賭注。

"政治敏感性"當然需要──越敏感越好。但是這種"敏感性"又必須和人民的願望相一致。以個人自私的動機是嗅不出正確的東西的。

這就要求詩人旣要有和人民--致的"政治敏感性"，更要求詩人要有和人民一致的"政治堅定性"。

"不倒翁"只能當玩具，却不宜作爲做人的樣板。

誰也不可能對什麼都興奮。連知了也知道什麼時候纔興奮。

有人反對寫詩要有"靈感"。這種人可能是"人工授精"的提倡者，但不一定是詩人。

把自己不理解的、或者是不能解釋的東西，一律當做不存在、或者是認爲非科學，這樣的人只能居住在螺絲殼裏。

外面的世界是瞬息萬變的：有時刮風、有時下雨，人的感情也有時高興、有時悲哀。

所謂"靈感"，無非是詩人對事物發生新的激動、突然感到的興奮、瞬卽消逝的心靈的閃耀。所謂"靈感"是詩人的主觀世界與客觀世界最愉快的邂逅。"靈感"應該是詩人的朋友，爲什麼要把它放逐到唯心主義的沙漠裏去呢？

無差別卽無矛盾。

對一切都興奮就是對一切都不興奮。

詩人要忠於自己的感受。所謂感受就是對客觀世界的反映。

並不是每首詩都在寫自己；但是，每首詩都由自己去寫——就是通過自己的心去寫。

沒有興奮而要裝出興奮，必然學會撒謊。自己沒有感動的事不可能去感動別人。

當然，說眞話可能惹出麻煩、甚至會遇到危險；但是，旣然要寫詩，就不應該昧着良心說假話。

七

不要爲玩弄技巧而寫詩，而寫詩又必須有技巧。連說話也有說得中聽的和不中聽的。

人的思維活動所產生的聯想、想象，無非是生活經驗的復合。在這種復合的過程中產生了比喻。比喻的目的是經驗與經驗的互相印證。

> "觸覺和視覺是如此地互相補充，以致我們往往可以根據某一物的外形來預言它在觸覺上的性質。"

好一個"互相補充"！恩格斯在這裏所說的"互相補充"雖然只是不同感官的事，但它也同樣存在於事物與事物之間、思維與思維之間。它使世界萬物取得了溝通與聯係。

形象思維的活動，在於使一切難以捕捉的東西、一切飄忽的東西固定起來，鮮明地呈現在讀者的面前，象印子打在紙上一樣地清楚。

形象思維的活動，在於把一切抽象的東西，轉化爲具體的東西——可感觸的東西。

形象思維的活動，在於使所有滯重的物質長上翅膀；反之，也可以使流動的物質凝固起來。

通過形象思維，可以使相距萬里的攜起手來；反之，也可以使原來在一起的揮手告別。

形象思維的方法，是抽象與具體之間的“互相補充”的方法。

形象思維的方法，是詩、也是一切文學創作的基本的方法。

甚至在理論文章（也就是依靠“邏輯思維”所進行的文章）裏，也可以遇見形象思維的表達方法。例如在《共產黨宣言》裏：

> “爲了拉攏人民，貴族們把無產階級的乞食袋當作旗幟來揮舞。但是，每當人民跟着他們走的時候，都發現他們的臀部帶有舊的封建紋章，於是就哈哈大笑，一哄而散。”

至於莎士比亞，那是一個離開形象思維就不能工作的人。在他的所有的作品中，無時不在閃耀着形象思維的光輝。

例如“金錢”兩個字只是一個概念，但在他的《雅典的泰門》裏，“金錢”轉化爲許多具體的“人”了：

> 啊，你可愛的兇手，帝王逃不過你的掌握，親生的父子會被你離間！你燦爛的奸夫，淫汚了純潔的婚牀！你勇敢的戰

神！你永遠年靑韶秀、永遠被人愛戀的嬌美的情郎，你的羞顏
可以融化了狄安娜女神膝上的冰雪！你有形的神明，你會使冰炭
化爲膠漆，仇敵互相親吻！……

　　這就是通過一連串的比喻，對爲資本所統治的世界所
發出的最深刻、也是最辛辣的咒駡！

　　詩只有通過形象思維的方法纔能產生持久的魅力。

　　寫詩的人常常爲表達一個觀念而尋找形象。例如拙作
《珠貝》：

　　　　在碧綠的海水裏
　　　　吸取太陽的精華
　　　　你是虹彩的化身
　　　　璀璨如一片朝霞

　　　　凝思花露的形狀
　　　　喜愛水晶的素質
　　　　觀念在心裏孕育
　　　　結成了粒粒眞珠

　　“觀念”是抽象的，結成“粒粒眞珠”，就成了明亮
的、可以把握得住的物質了。

　　“反抗”兩個字是屬於精神範疇的、抽象的名詞。
“哪裏有壓迫，哪裏就有反抗”。反抗天然地產生於受迫
害的人。

　　難道還有迫害人的人需要什麽反抗嗎？

　　作爲一個民族，作爲一個要求生存權利的個人，遇到
連續的迫害該怎麽辦呢？

一個浪，一個浪
無休止地撲過來
每一個浪都在它脚下
被打成碎沫，散開……

它的臉上和身上
像刀砍過的一樣
但它依然站在那裏
含着微笑，看着海洋……

　　這也只是從受到"無休止地撲過來"的"礁石"的角
度上所應採取的態度——它還有什麼別的辦法嗎？
　　然而有人說礁石是"與大大小小的航船爲敵的"——
"自傲的態度"！按照他的說法，礁石應該"自己消滅"
和對一切"大大小小的航船"——自覺地讓開。他完全忘
掉礁石是不可能移動的，應該由"大大小小的航船"不要
去碰那頑固不化的礁石。這就是從兩種不同的角度看問題
的不同的結果。
　　由形象思維的活動所產生的一切比喻，都不是原來的
事，所以列寧說：一切比喻都是跛脚的。正因爲這樣，比
喻也最容易被人歪曲甚至誣陷——歷史上不少"文字獄"
都由比喻構成。

八

　　我所經歷的時代，是一個波瀾壯闊、絢麗多彩的時
代。我和同我差不多年紀的人們一樣，度過了各種類型、
不同性質的戰爭；也遇見了各種類型、不同性質的敵人。
眞是變幻莫測！

　　我在一九四一年冬天寫的《時代》那首詩裏的許多話，裏面最重要的話，這些年都得到了應驗：

　　　　——縱然我知道由它所帶給我的
　　　　並不是節日的狂歡
　　　　和什麼雜耍場上的哄笑
　　　　却是比一千個屠場更殘酷的景象，
　　　　而我却依然奔向它
　　　　帶着一個生命所能發揮的熱情。

　　　　…………

　　　　我要迎接更高的贊揚，更大的毀謗
　　　　更不可解的怨仇，和更致命的打擊——
　　　　都爲了我想從時間的深溝裏升騰起來……

　　　　…………

　　　　我忠實於時代，獻身於時代，而我却沉默着
　　　　不甘心地，像一個被俘虜的囚徒
　　　　在押送到刑場之前沉默着
　　　　我沉默着，爲了沒有足夠響亮的語言
　　　　象初夏的雷霆滾過陰雲密布的天空
　　　　抒發我的激情於我的狂暴的呼喊
　　　　奉獻給那使我如此興奮、如此驚喜的東西
　　　　我愛它勝過我曾經愛過的一切
　　　　爲了它的到來，我願意交付出我的生命
　　　　交付給它從我的肉體直到我的靈魂
　　　　我在它的面前顯得如此卑微
　　　　甚至想仰臥在地面上
　　　　讓它的脚象馬蹄一樣踩過我的胸膛

　　這樣的一首詩，再明顯不過的是一首歌頌時代的詩，歌頌的是我們爲之戰鬥、爲之獻身的時代，“我在它的面前顯得如此卑微”，“甚至想仰臥在地面上讓它的脚象馬蹄一樣踩過我的胸膛”！

這樣的一首詩却被文痞姚文元之流恣意歪曲，汚蔑爲“個人主義者自我擴張的嘶喊”，而且明目張胆地說成是一首攻擊延安的詩。

也是這個文痞，竟說我從來沒有歌頌過無產階級！可是在我的四首詩裏曾提到第一個無產階級的政權“巴黎公社”：

一九三二年的《巴黎》裏，有“公社的誕生”；一九四零年的《哀巴黎》裏，有“將有第二公社的誕生”；一九四五年的《悼羅曼·羅蘭》裏，有“把公社的子孫出賣變成俘虜”；一九四二年的《土倫的反抗》裏，有“公社的子孫將重新得到解放”！

這個冒牌的“馬克思主義理論家”，早在二十年前，已暴露他是反對馬克思主義的。

就在這個文痞的文章發表之後，我收到一個將軍給我的信，鼓勵我：“你是歌頌過公社的子孫的，你應該繼續寫詩。”

這兩件事形成了多麼鮮明的對照！

我曾不知多少次地提到無產階級的領導人，提到無產階級的武裝部隊……怎能說我從不歌頌無產階級——難道只有貼上“無產階級”四個字的標簽纔算是無產階級嗎？

文痞同樣歪曲我的長詩《向太陽》中的“太陽之歌”裏的話：

太陽
它使我想起……
…………

　　想起　《馬賽曲》《國際歌》
　　想起　華盛頓　列寧　孫逸仙
　　　　和一切把人類從苦難裏拯救出來的人物的名字

　　文痞說："但國際歌和列寧是平列在馬賽曲、華盛頓和孫逸仙中間，並不突出"因而對我做了個政治性的"結論"："所神往的不過是資產階級的自由民主而已"！好一個"而已"！

　　我的長詩《向太陽》寫於一九三八年四月，地點是國民黨統治下的武昌。那時正是國民黨消極抗戰、積極反共的時期，我提出自由民主難道也不應該嗎？

　　這個文痞在整整過了二十年之後，在一九五八年的上海，住在特務父親姚蓬子經營的"作家書屋"裏，大腿叠二腿地坐在沙發上來嘲笑一首在白色恐怖中所寫的詩，顯得多麼得意啊！他而且說我把"列寧"和"國際歌"寫上去，只是為了"點綴"！

　　都因為他享有亂打棍子、亂扣帽子的自由！

　　今天有機會重溫這個文痞發迹的歷史，可以更清楚地看到這些年來"四人幫"所實行的法西斯文化專制主義，早在二十年前已經進行了一次大規模的演習了。

　　像這樣的一個流氓竟能如入無人之境地橫衝直撞，成了"龐然大物"，騙取了我國文學藝術領域裏生殺予奪之權達幾十年之久，這件事難道不值得我們深思嗎？

　　可慶幸的是，這一切終究過去了。

　　如今，時代的洪流把我捲帶到一個新的充滿陽光的港口，在汽笛的長鳴聲中，我的生命開始了新的航程。

　　　　　　　　　　　　　　　　一九七八年十二月中旬。

透 明 的 夜

一

透明的夜。

……闊笑從田堤上煽起……
一羣酒徒，望
沉睡的村，嘩然的走去……
村，
狗的吠聲，叫顫了
滿天的疏星。

村，
沉睡的街
沉睡的廣場，衝進了
醒的酒坊。

酒，燈光，醉了的臉
放蕩的笑在一團……

"走
到牛殺場，去
喝牛肉湯……"

243

二

酒徒們，走向村邊
進入了一道燈光敞開的門
血的氣息，肉的堆，牛皮的
熱的腥酸……
人的囂喧，人的囂喧。

油燈像野火一樣，映出
十幾個生活在草原上的
泥色的臉。

這裏是我們的娛樂場，
那些是多諳熟的面相，
我們拿起
熱氣蒸騰的牛骨
大開着嘴，咬着，咬着……

"酒，酒，酒
我們要喝 。"

油燈像野火一樣，映出
牛的血，血染的屠夫的手臂，
濺有血點的
    屠夫的頭額。

油燈像野火一樣，映出
我們火一般的肌肉，以及

——那裏面的——
痛苦，憤怒和仇恨的力。

油燈像野火一樣，映出
——從各個角落來的——
夜的醒者
醉漢
浪客
過路的盜
偷牛的賊……

"酒，酒，酒，
我們要喝。"

三

…………
"趁着星光，發抖
我們走……"
闊笑在田堤上煽起……
一羣酒徒，離了
沉睡的村，向
沉睡的原野
　嘩然的走去……

夜，透明的
夜！

一九三二年九月十日

大堰河——我的褓姆

大堰河，是我的褓姆，
她的名字就是生她的村莊的名字，
她是童養媳，
大堰河，是我的褓姆。

我是地主的兒子；
也是吃了大堰河的奶而長大了的
大堰河的兒子。
大堰河以養育我而養育她的家，
而我，是吃了你的奶而被養育了的，
大堰河啊，我的褓姆。

大堰河，今天我看到雪使我想起了你：
你的被雪壓着的草蓋的墳墓，
你的關閉了的故居簷頭的枯死的瓦菲，
你的被典押了的一丈平方的園地，
你的門前的長了青苔的石椅，
大堰河，今天我看到雪使我想起了你。

你用你厚大的手掌把我抱在懷裏，撫摸我，
在你搭好了竈火之後，
在你拍去了圍裙上的炭灰之後，

在你嘗到飯已羹熟了之後，
在你把烏黑的醬碗放到烏黑的桌子上之後，
在你補好了兒子們的爲山腰的荆棘扯破的衣服之後，
在你把小兒被柴刀砍傷了的手包好之後，
在你把夫兒們的襯衣上的虱子一顆顆的搯死之後，
在你拿起了今天的第一顆雞蛋之後，
你用你厚大的手掌把我抱在懷裏，撫摸我。

我是地主的兒子，
在我吃光了你大堰河的奶之後，
我被生我的父母領回到自己的家裏。
啊，大堰河，你爲什麼要哭？

我做了生我的父母家裏的新客了！
我摸着紅漆雕花的家具，
我摸着父母的睡牀上金色的花紋，
我呆呆的看着簷頭的我不認得的“天倫敍樂”的匾，
我摸着新換上的衣服的絲的和貝殼的鈕扣，
我看着母親懷裏的不熟識的妹妹，
我坐着油漆過的安了火缽的炕凳，
我吃着碾了三番的白米的飯，
但，我是這般忸怩不安！因爲我
我做了生我的父母家裏的新客了。

大堰河，爲了生活，
在她流盡了她的乳液之後，
她就開始用抱過我的兩臂勞動了；

她含着笑，洗着我們的衣服，

她含着笑，提着菜籃到村邊的結冰的池塘去，

她含着笑，切着冰屑悉索的蘿蔔，

她含着笑，用手掏着豬吃的麥糟，

她含着笑，扇着燉肉的爐子的火，

她含着笑，背了團箕到廣場上去

　　曬好那些大豆和小麥，

大堰河，爲了生活，

在她流盡了她的乳液之後，

她就用抱過我的兩臂，勞動了。

大堰河，深愛着她的乳兒；

在年節裏，爲了他，忙着切那冬米的糖，

爲了他，常悄悄的走到村邊的她的家裏去，

爲了他，走到她的身邊叫一聲“媽”，

大堰河，把他畫的大紅大綠的關雲長

　　貼在竈邊的牆上，

大堰河，會對她的鄰居誇口讚美她的乳兒；

大堰河曾做了一個不能對人說的夢：

在夢里，她吃着她的乳兒的婚酒，

坐在輝煌的結采的堂上，

而她的嬌美的媳婦親切的叫她“婆婆”

………………

大堰河，深愛她的乳兒！

大堰河，在她的夢沒有做醒的時候已死了。

她死時，乳兒不在她的旁側，

她死時，平時打罵她的丈夫也爲她流淚，
五個兒子，個個哭得很悲，
她死時，輕輕的呼着她的乳兒的名字，
大堰河，已死了，
她死時，乳兒不在她的旁側。

大堰河，含淚的去了！
同着四十幾年的人世生活的凌侮，
同着數不盡的奴隸的悽苦，
同着四塊錢的棺材和幾束稻草，
同着幾尺長方的埋棺材的土地，
同着一手把的紙錢的灰，
大堰河，她含淚的去了。

這是大堰河所不知道的：
她的醉酒的丈夫已死去，
大兒做了土匪，
第二個死在砲火的煙裏，
第三，第四，第五
在師傅和地主的叱罵聲裏過着日子。
而我，我是在寫着給予這不公道的世界的呪語。
當我經了長長的飄泊囘到故土時，
在山腰裏，田野上，
兄弟們碰見時，是比六七年前更要親密！
這，這是爲你，靜靜的睡着的大堰河
所不知道的啊！

大堰河，今天，你的乳兒是在獄裏，

寫着一首呈給你的讚美詩，
呈給你黃土下紫色的靈魂，
呈給你擁抱過我的直伸着的手，
呈給你吻過我的脣，
呈給你泥黑的溫柔的臉顏，
呈給你養育了我的乳房，
呈給你的兒子們，我的兄弟們，
呈給大地上一切的，
我的大堰河般的褓姆和她們的兒子，
呈給愛我如愛她自己的兒子般的大堰河。

大堰河，
我是吃了你的奶而長大了的
你的兒子，
我敬你
愛你！

　　　　　　　一九三三年一月十四日，雪朝。

巴　黎

巴黎
在你的面前
黎明的，黃昏的
中午的，深宵的
——我看見
你有你自己個性的
憤怒，歡樂
悲痛，嬉戲和激昂！
整天裏
你，無止息的
用手捶着自己的心肝
捶！捶！
或者伸着頸，直向高空
嘶喊！
或者垂頭喪氣，鎖上了眼簾
沉於陰邃的思索
也或者散亂着金絲的長髮
澈聲歌唱，
也或者
解散了緋紅的衣褲
赤裸着一片鮮美的肉
任性的淫蕩……你！

盡只是朝向我

和朝向幾十萬的移民

送出了

强靭的，誘惑的招徠……

巴黎，

你患了歇斯底里的美麗的妓女！

…………

看一排排的電車

往長道的頂間

逝去……

却又一排排地來了！

聽，電鈴

叮叮叮叮叮地飛過……

羣衆的洪流

從大街流來

分向各個小弄，

又從各個小弄，折回

成爲洪流，

聚集在

大街上

廣場上

一刻也不停的

沖蕩！

沖蕩！

一致的呼嚷

徘徊在：

成堆成壘的

建築物的四面，

和紀念碑的尖頂

和銅像的周圍

和大商鋪的門前……

手牽手的大商場啊，

在陽光裏

電光裏

永遠的映照出

翩翩的

節日的

Severini[1]的 “斑斑舞蹈” 般

輝煌的畫幅……

從 Radio[2]

和拍賣場上的奏樂，

和沖擊的

巨大的力的

勞動的

叫囂——

豪華的贊歌，

光榮之高誇的詞句，

鋼鐵的詩章——

同着一篇篇的由

公共汽車，電車，地道車充當

響亮的字母，

柏油街，軌道，行人路是明快的句子，

---

[1] Severini，意大利現代畫家。

[2] Radio，法文；無綫電廣播。

輪子＋輪子＋輪子是跳動的讀點

汽笛＋汽笛＋汽笛是驚嘆號！——

所湊合攏來的無限長的美文

張開了：一切派別的派別者的

多般的嘴，

一切奇瑰的裝束

和一切新鮮的叫喊的合唱啊！

你是——

所有的"個人"

和他們微妙的"個性"

朝向羣衆

像無數水滴、消失了

和着萬人

匯合而成爲——

最偉大的

最瘋狂的

最怪異的"個性"。

你是怪誕的，巴黎！

多少世紀了

各個年代和各個人事的變換，

用

它們自己所愛好的彩色

在你的臉上加彩塗抹，

每個生命，每次行動

每次殺戮，和那跨過你的背脊的戰爭，

甚至於小小的婚宴，

都同着

路易十六的走上斷頭台
革命
暴動
公社的誕生
攻打巴士底一樣的
具有不可磨滅的意義!
而且忠誠地記錄着：
你的成長
你的年齡,
你的性格和氣質
和你的歡喜以及悲哀。
巴黎
你是健强的!
你火熖冲天所發出的磁力
吸引了全世界上
各個國度的各個種族的人們
懷着冒險的心理
奔向你
去愛你吻你
或者恨你到透骨!
——你不知道
我是從怎樣的遙遠的草堆裏
跳出,
朝向你
伸出了我震顫的臂
而鞭策了自己
直到使我深深的受苦!

巴黎

你這珍奇的創造啊

直叫人勇於生活

像勇於死亡一樣的魯莽！

你用了

春藥，拿破崙的鑄像，酒精，凱旋門

鐵塔，女性

盧佛爾博物館；歌劇院

交易所，銀行

招致了：

整個地球上的——

白痴，賭徒，淫棍

酒徒，大腹賈

野心家，拳擊師

空想者，投機者們……

啊，巴黎！

爲了你的嫣然一笑

已使得多少人們

拋棄了

深深的愛着的他們的家園，

迷失在你的曖昧的青眛裏，

幾十萬人

都化盡了他們的精力

流乾了勞動的汗，

去祈求你

能給他們以些須的同情

和些須的愛憐！

但是

你——

龐大的都會啊

却是這樣的一個

鐵石心腸的生物！

我們終於

以痛苦，失敗的沮喪

而益增强了

你放射着的光彩

你的傲慢！而你

却抛棄衆人在悲慟裏，

像廢物一般的

毫無惋惜！

巴黎，

我恨你像愛你似的堅强；

莫笑我將空垂着兩臂

走上了懊喪的歸途，

我還年輕！

而且

從生活之沙場上所潰敗了的

決不只是我這孤單的一個

——他們實在比爲你所寵愛的

人數要多得可怕！

我們都要

在遠離着你的地方

——經歷些時日吧

以磨練我們的筋骨

等時間到了
就整飭着隊伍
興兵而來！
那時啊
我們將是攻打你的先鋒，
當克服了你時
我們將要
娛樂你
擁抱着你
要你在我們的臂上
顛笑歌唱！
巴黎，你——噫，
這淫蕩的
淫蕩的
妖艷的姑娘！

太　陽

從遠古的墓塋
從黑暗的年代
從人類死亡之流的那邊
震驚沉睡的山脈
若火輪飛旋於沙坵之上
太陽向我滾來……

它以難遮掩的光芒
使生命呼吸
使高樹繁枝向它舞蹈
使河流帶着狂歌奔向它去

當它來時，我聽見
冬蟄的蟲蛹轉動於地下
羣衆在曠場上高聲說話
城市從遠方
用電力與鋼鐵召喚它

於是我的心胸
被火焰之手撕開

陳窩的靈魂
擱棄在河畔
我乃有對於人類再生之確信

一九三七年春

煤的對話

─A─Y.R.

你住在哪裏？

我住在萬年的深山裏
我住在萬年的岩石裏

你的年紀──

我的年紀比山的更大
比岩石的更大

你從什麼時候沉默的？

從恐龍統治了森林的年代
從地殼第一次震動的年代

你已死在過深的怨憤裏了麼？

死？不，不，我還活着──
請給我以火，給我以火！

一九三七年春

261

笑

我不相信考古學家——

在幾千年之後，
在無人跡的海濱，
在曾是繁華過的廢墟上
拾得一根枯骨
——我的枯骨時，
他豈能知道這根枯骨
是曾經了二十世紀的烈焰燃燒過的？

又有誰能在地層裏
尋得
那些受盡了磨難的
犧牲者的淚珠呢？
那些淚珠
曾被封禁於千重的鐵柵，
卻只有一枚鑰匙
可以打開那些鐵柵的門，
而去奪取那鑰匙的無數大勇
卻都倒斃在
守衛者的刀槍下了

如能檢得那樣的一顆淚珠
藏之枕畔，
當比那撈自萬丈的海底之貝珠
更晶瑩，更晶瑩
而徹照萬古啊！

我們豈不是
都在自己的年代裏
被釘上了十字架麽？
而這十字架
決不比拿撒勒人所釘的
較少痛苦。

敵人的手
給我們戴上荆棘的冠冕
從刺破了的慘白的前額
淋下的深紅的血點，
也不曾寫盡
我們胸中所有的悲憤啊！

誠然
我們不應該有什麽奢望，
卻只願有一天
人們想起我們，
像想起遠古的那些
和巨獸搏鬥過來的祖先，
臉上會浮上一片

安謐而又舒展的笑——
雖然那是太輕鬆了，
但我卻甘願
爲那笑而捐軀！

一九三七年五月八日

復活的土地

腐朽的日子
早已沉到河底，
讓流水沖洗得
快要不留痕跡了；

河岸上
春天的腳步所經過的地方，
到處是繁花與茂草；
而從那邊的叢林裏
也傳出了
忠心於季節的百鳥之
高亢的歌唱。

播種者呵
是應該播種的時候了，
爲了我們肯辛勤地勞作
大地將孕育
金色的顆粒。

就在此刻，
你——悲哀的詩人呀，
也應該拂去往日的憂鬱，

讓希望甦醒在你自己的
久久負傷着的心裏：

因爲，我們的曾經死了的大地，
在明朗的天空下
已復活了！
——苦難也已成爲記憶，
在牠溫熱的胸膛裏
重新漩流着的
將是戰鬥者的血液。

　　　　　　　　　一九三七年七月六日，滬杭路上。

他起来了

他起來了——
從幾十年的屈辱裏
從敵人爲他掘好的深坑旁邊

他的額上淋着血
他的胸上也淋着血
但他却笑着
——他從來不曾如此地笑過

他笑着
兩眼前望且閃光
像在尋找
那給他倒地的一擊的敵人

他起來了
他起來
將比一切獸類更勇猛
又比一切人類更聰明

因爲他必須如此

　　因為他

　　必須從敵人的死亡

　　奪回來自己的生存

　　　　　　　　　一九三七年十月十二日　杭州

雪落在中國的土地上

雪落在中國的土地上，
寒冷在封鎖着中國呀……

風，
像一個太悲哀了的老婦，
緊緊地跟隨着
伸出寒冷的指爪
拉扯着行人的衣襟
用着像土地一樣古老的話
一刻也不停地絮聒着……

那從林間出現的，
趕着馬車的
你中國的農夫
戴着皮帽
冒着大雪
你要到哪兒去呢？

告訴你
我也是農人的後裔——
由於你們的
刻滿了痛苦的皺紋的臉

我能如此深深地
知道了
生活在草原上的人們的
歲月的艱辛。

而我
也並不比你們快樂啊
——躺在時間的河流上
苦難的浪濤
曾經幾次把我吞沒而又捲起——
流浪與監禁
已失去了我的青春的
最可貴的日子，
我的生命
也像你們的生命
一樣的憔悴呀

雪落在中國的土地上，
寒冷在封鎖着中國呀……
沿着雪夜的河流，
一盞小油燈在徐緩地移行，
那破爛的烏篷船裏
映着燈光，垂着頭
坐着的是誰呀？

——啊，你
蓬髮垢面的少婦，

是不是
你的家
——那幸福與溫暖的巢穴——
已被暴戾的敵人
燒燬了麼？
是不是
也像這樣的夜間，
失去了男人的保護，
在死亡的恐怖裏
你已經受盡敵人刺刀的戲弄？

咳，就在如此寒冷的今夜，
無數的
我們的年老的母親，
都蜷伏在不是自己的家裏，
就像異邦人
不知明天的車輪
要滾上怎樣的路程……
——而且
中國的路
是如此的崎嶇
是如此的泥濘呀。

雪落在中國的土地上，
寒冷在封鎖着中國呀……

透過雪夜的草原

那些被烽火所嚙啃着的地域，
無數的，土地的墾植者
失去了他們所飼養的家畜
失去了他們肥沃的田地
擁擠在
生活的絕望的汚巷裏；
饑饉的大地
朝向陰暗的天
伸出乞援的
顫抖着的兩臂。

中國的苦痛與災難
像這雪夜一樣廣闊而又漫長呀！

雪落在中國的土地上，
寒冷在封鎖着中國呀……

中國，
我的在沒有燈光的晚上
所寫的無力的詩句
能給你些許的溫暖麼？

　　　　　　　　一九三七年十二月二十八日夜間

手　推　車

在黃河流過的地域
在無數的枯乾了的河底
手推車
以唯一的輪子
發出使陰暗的天穹痙攣的尖音
穿過寒冷與靜寂
從這一個山脚
到那一個山脚
徹響着
北國人民的悲哀

在冰雪凝凍的日子
在貧窮的小村與小村之間
手推車
以單獨的輪子
刻畫在灰黃土層上的深深的轍跡
穿過廣闊與荒漠
從這一條路
到那一條路
交織着
北國人民的悲哀

一九三八年初。

北　方

一天
那個珂爾沁草原上的詩人
對我說：
"北方是悲哀的。"

不錯
北方是悲哀的。
從塞外吹來的
沙漠風，
已捲去北方的生命的綠色
與時日的光輝
——一片暗淡的灰黃
蒙上一層揭不開的沙霧；
那天邊疾奔而至的呼嘯
帶來了恐怖
瘋狂地
掃蕩過大地；
荒漠的原野
凍結在十二月的寒風裏，
村莊呀，山坡呀，河岸呀，
頹垣與荒塚呀
都披上了土色的憂鬱……
孤單的行人，

上身俯前
用手遮住了臉煩，
在風沙裹
困苦了呼吸
一步一步地
掙扎着前進……
幾隻驢子
——那有悲哀的眼
　　　和疲乏的耳朶的畜生，
載負了土地的
痛苦的重壓，
牠們厭倦的脚步
徐緩地踏過
北國的
修長而寂寞的道路……

那些小河早已枯乾了
河底也已畫滿了車轍，
北方的土地和人民
在渴求着
那滋潤生命的流泉啊！
枯死的林木
與低矮的住房
稀疏地，陰鬱地
散佈在灰暗的天幕下；
天上，
看不見太陽，

只有那結成大隊的的雁羣

惶亂的雁羣

擊着黑色的翅膀

叫出牠們的不安與悲苦，

從這荒涼的地域逃亡

逃亡到

綠蔭蔽天的南方去了……

北方是悲哀的

而萬里的黃河

汹湧着混濁的波濤

給廣大的北方

傾瀉着災難與不幸；

而年代的風霜

刻畫着

廣大的北方的

貧窮與飢餓啊。

而我

——這來自南方的旅客，

却愛這悲哀的北國啊。

撲面的風沙

與入骨的冷氣

决不曾使我咒詛；

我愛這悲哀的國土，

一片無垠的荒漠

也引起了我的崇敬
——我看見
我們的祖先
帶領了羊羣
吹着笳笛
沉浸在這大漠的黃昏裏；
我們踏着的
古老的鬆軟的黃土層裏
埋有我們祖先的骸骨啊，
——這土地是他們所開墾
幾千年了
他們曾在這裏
和帶給他們以打擊的自然相搏鬥，
他們爲保衞土地
從不曾屈辱過一次，
他們死了
把土地遺留給我們——
我愛這悲哀的國土，
它的廣大而瘦瘠的土地
帶給我們以淳樸的言語
與寬闊的姿態，
我相信這言語與姿態
堅強地生活在大地上
永遠不會滅亡；
我愛這悲哀的國土，
　　古老的國土

　　——這國土
　　養育了爲我所愛的
　　世界上最艱苦
　　與最古老的種族。

　　　　　　　　　　一九三八年二月四日　潼關

補 衣 婦

補衣婦坐在路旁
行人走過路
路揚起沙土
補衣婦頭巾上是沙土
衣服上是沙土

她的孩子哭了
眼淚又被太陽曬乾了
她不知道
只是無聲地想着她的家
她的被炮火毀掉的家
無聲地給人縫補
讓孩子的眼
可憐的眼
瞪着空了的籃子

補衣婦坐在路旁
路一直伸向無限
她給行路人補好襪子
行路人走上了路

一九三八年二月　平漢路某站

向 太 陽

從遠古的墓塋
從黑暗的年代
從人類死亡之流的那邊
震驚沉睡的山脈
若火輪飛旋於沙坵之上
太陽向我滾來⋯⋯

——引自舊作《太陽》

一　我　起　来

我起來——
像一隻困倦的野獸
受過傷的野獸
從狼籍着敗葉的林藪
從冰冷的岩石上
掙扎了好久
纔支撐着上身
睜開眼睛
向天邊尋覓⋯⋯

我——
是一個

從遙遠的山地
從未經開墾的山地
到這幾千萬人
　　用他們的手勞作着
　　用他們的嘴呼嚷着
　　用他們的脚走着的城市來的
　　　　旅客，
我的身上
痠痛的身上
深刻地留着
風雨的昨夜的
長途奔走的疲勞

但
我終於起來了

我打開窗
用囚犯第一次看見光明的眼
看見了黎明
——這眞實的黎明啊

（遠方
似乎傳來了羣衆的歌聲）
於是　我想到街上去

二　街　　上

早安呵
你站在十字街頭

　　車輛過去時
　　　舉着白袖子的手的警察
早安呵
你來自城外的
　　挑着滿籮綠色的菜販
早安呵
你打掃着馬路的
　　穿着紅色背心的清道夫
早安呵
你提了籃子，第一個到菜場去的
　　棕色皮膚的年輕的主婦
我相信
昨夜
你們決不像我一樣
　　被不停的風雨所追蹤
　　被無止的惡夢所糾纏
你們都比我睡得好啊！

三　昨　天

昨天
我在世界上
用可憐的期望
餵養我的日子
像那些未亡人
披着襤褸
用可憐的回憶

餵養她們的日子一樣

昨天
我把自己的國土
　當作病院
——而我是患了難於醫治的病的
沒有哪一天
我不是用遲滯的眼睛
看着這國土的
　沒有邊際的悽慘的生命……
沒有哪一天
我不是用呆鈍的耳朵
聽着這國土的
　沒有止息的痛苦的呻吟

昨天
我把自己關在
精神的牢房裏
四面是灰色的高牆
沒有聲音
我沿着高牆
走着又走着
我的靈魂
不論白日和黑夜

永遠的唱着
一曲人類命運的悲歌

昨天
我曾狂奔在
陰暗而低沉的天幕下的
沒有太陽的原野
到山巔上去
伏倒在紫色的岩石上
流着溫熱的眼淚
哭泣我們的世紀

現在好了
一切都過去了

四　日　出

太陽出來了……
當他來時……
城市從遠方
用電力與鋼鐵召喚他

——引自舊作《太陽》

太陽
從遠處的高層建築
　——那些水門汀與鋼鐵所砌成的山

和那成百的煙突
成千的電綫桿子
成萬的屋頂
所構成的
密叢的森林裏
出來了……

在太平洋
在印度洋
在紅海
在地中海
在我最初對世界懷着熱望
而航行於無邊藍色的海水上的少年時代
我都曾看着美麗的日出

但此刻
在我所呼吸的城市
噴發着煤油的氣息
柏油的氣息
混雜的氣息的城市
敞開着金屬的胴體
礦石的胴體
電火的胴體的城市
寬闊地
承受黎明的愛撫的城市
我看見日出
比所有的日出更美麗

五　太陽之歌

是的
太陽比一切都美麗
比處女
比含露的花朶
比白雪
比藍的海水

太陽是金紅色的圓體
是發光的圓體
是在擴大着的圓體

灰鐵曼
從太陽得到的啓示
用海洋一樣開闊的胸襟
寫出海洋一樣開闊的詩篇

凡谷
從太陽得到啓示
用燃燒的筆
蘸着燃燒的顏色
畫着農夫耕犂大地
畫着向日葵

鄧肯
從太陽得到啓示

用崇高的姿態
披示給我們以自然的旋律

太陽
它更高了
它更亮了
它紅得像血

太陽
它使我想起　法蘭西　美利堅的革命
想起　博愛　平等　自由
想起　德謨克拉西
想起　馬賽曲　國際歌
想起　華盛頓　列寧　孫逸仙
　　和一切把人類從苦難裏拯救出來的人物的名字

是的
太陽是美的
且是永生的

六　太陽照在

初昇的太陽
照在我們的頭上
照在我們的久久地低垂着
　不曾擡起過的頭上
太陽照着我們的城市和村莊

照着我們的久久地住着

　屈服在不正的權力下的城市和村莊

太陽照着我們的田野，河流和山巒

照着我們的從很久以來

　到處都蠕動着痛苦的靈魂的

　田野、河流和山巒……

今天

太陽的眩目的光芒

把我們從絕望的睡眠裏刺醒了

也從那遮掩着無限痛苦的迷霧裏

刺醒了我們的城市和村莊

也從那隱蔽着無邊憂鬱的煙霧裏

刺醒了我們的田野，河流和山巒

我們仰起了沉重的頭顱

從濡濕的地面

一致地

向高空呼嚷

　"看我們

　我們

　笑得像太陽！"

七　在太陽下

"看我們

我們

笑得像太陽！"

那邊
一個傷兵
支撐着木製的拐杖
沿着長長的牆壁
跨着寬闊的步伐
太陽照在他的臉上
照在他純樸地笑着的臉上
他一步一步地走着
他不知道我在遠處看着他
當他的披着繡有紅十字的灰色衣服的
　　高大的身體
走近我的時候
這太陽下的眞實的姿態
我覺得
比拿破崙的銅像更漂亮

太陽照在
城市的上空

街上的人
這末多，這末多
他們並不曾向我們打招呼
但我向他們走去
我看着每一個從我身邊走過的人
對他們
我不再感到陌生

太陽照着他們的臉

照着他們的

　　光潔的，年輕的臉

　　發皺的，年老的臉

　　紅潤的，少女的臉

　　善良的，老婦的臉

和那一切的

　昨天還在慘愁着但今天卻笑着的臉

他們都匆忙地

擺動着四肢

在太陽光下

來來去去地走着

　——好像他們被同一的意欲所驅使似的

他們含着微笑的臉

也好像在一致地說着

　"我們愛這日子

　不是因爲我們

　　看不見自己的苦難

　不是因爲我們

　　看不見飢餓與死亡

　我們愛這日子

　是因爲這日子給我們

　帶來了燦爛的明天的

　最可信的音訊。"

太陽光

閃爍在古舊的石橋上……

幾個少女——

　那些幸福的象徵啊

背着募捐袋
在石橋上
在太陽下
唱着清新的歌
　"我們是天使
　健康而純潔
　我們的愛人
　年輕而勇敢
　有的騎戰馬
　有的駕飛機
　馳騁在曠野
　飛翔在天空……。"

　　　（歌聲中斷了，她們在向行人募捐）

現在
她們又唱了
　"他們上戰場
　奮勇殺敵人
　我們在後方
　慰勞與宣傳
　一天勝利了
　歡聚在一堂……"
她們的歌聲
是如此悠揚
太陽照着她們的
　驕傲地突起的胸脯
和袒露着的兩臂
和發出尊嚴的光輝的前額

她們的歌
飄到橋的那邊去了……

太陽的光
泛濫在街上

浴在太陽光裏的
　街的那邊
一羣穿着被煤煙弄髒了的衣服的工人
扛擡着一架機器
　　——金屬的棱角閃着白光
太陽照在
　他們流汗的臉上
當他們每一步前進時
他們發出緩慢而沉洪的呼聲
　"杭——唷
　杭——唷
　我們是工人
　工人最可憐
　貧窮中誕生
　勞動裏成長
　一年忙到頭
　爲了吃與穿
　吃又吃不飽
　穿又穿不暖
　杭——唷
　杭——唷

　自從八一三
　敵人來進攻
　工廠被炸掉
　東西被搶光
　幾千萬工友
　飢餓與流亡
　我們在後方
　要加緊勞動
　爲國家生產
　爲抗戰流汗
　一天勝利了
　生活纔飽暖
　杭——唷
　杭——唷……"
他們帶着不止的杭唷聲
　轉彎了……
太陽光
泛濫在曠場上

曠場上
成千的穿草黃色制服的士兵
　在操演
我們頭上的鋼盔
　和槍上的刺刀
閃着白光
他們以嚴肅的靜默
等待着

　　那及時的號令
現在
他們開步了
從那整齊的步伐聲裏
我聽見

　　"一！二！三！四！
　一！二！三！四！
　我們是從田野來的
　我們是從山村來的
　我們生活在茅屋
　我們呼吸在畜棚
　我們耕犂着田地
　田地是我們的生命
　但今天
　敵人來到我們的家鄉
　我們的茅屋被燒掉
　我們的牲口被吃光
　我們的父母被殺死
　我們的妻女被强姦
　我們沒有了鐮刀與鋤頭
　只有背上了子彈與槍砲
　我們要用閃光的刺刀
　搶回我們的田地
　回到我們的家鄉
　消滅我們的敵人
　敵人的脚踏到哪裏

敵人的血流到哪裏⋯⋯
　⋯⋯⋯⋯⋯

一！二！三！四！
一！二！三！四！
　⋯⋯⋯⋯⋯⋯⋯”

這眞是何等的奇遇啊⋯⋯

八　今　天

今天
奔走在太陽的路上
我不再垂着頭
　把手插在褲袋裏了
嘴也不再吹那寂寞的口哨
不看天邊的流雲
不徬徨在人行道

今天
在太陽照着的人羣當中
我決不專心尋覓
那些像我自己一樣慘愁的臉孔了

今天
太陽吻着我昨夜流過淚的臉頰
吻着我被人間世的醜惡厭倦了的眼睛
吻着我爲正義喊啞了聲音的嘴唇

吻着我這未老先衰的
啊！快要佝僂了的背脊

今天
我聽見
太陽對我說
　“向我來
　　從今天
　　你應該快樂些啊……”

於是
被這新生的日子所蠱惑
我歡喜淸晨郊外的軍號的悠遠的聲音
我歡喜擁擠在忙亂的人叢裏
我歡喜從街頭敲打過去的鑼鼓的聲音
我歡喜馬戲班的演技
　　當我看見了那些原始的，粗暴的，健康的運動
　　我會深深地愛着它們
　　——像我深深地愛着太陽一樣

今天
我感謝太陽
太陽召回了我的童年了

九　我向太陽

我奔馳
依舊乘着熱情的輪子
太陽在我的頭上

用不能再比這更强烈的光芒
燃灼着我的肉體
由於它的熱力的鼓舞
我用嘶啞的聲音
歌唱了：
　　"於是，我的心胸
　　被火焰之手撕開
　　陳窩的靈魂
　　擱棄在河畔……"
這時候
我對我所看見　所聽見
感到了從未有過的寬懷與熱愛
我甚至想在這光明的際會中死去……

　　　　　　　　一九三八年四月在武昌。

我愛這土地

假如我是一隻鳥，
我也應該用嘶啞的喉嚨歌唱：
這被暴風雨所打擊着的土地，
這永遠洶湧着我們的悲憤的河流，
這無止息地吹颳着的激怒的風，
和那來自林間的無比溫柔的黎明……
——然後我死了，
連羽毛也腐爛在土地裏面。

為什麼我的眼裏常含淚水？
因為我對這土地愛得深沉……

一九三八年十一月十七日。

乞　丐

在北方
乞丐徘徊在黃河的兩岸
徘徊在鐵道的兩旁

在北方
乞丐用最使人厭煩的聲音
吶喊着痛苦
說他們來自災區
來自戰地

飢餓是可怕的
它使年老的失去仁慈
年幼的學會憎恨

在北方
乞丐用固執的眼
凝視着你
看你在吃任何食物
和你用指甲剔牙齒的樣子

在北方
乞丐伸着永不縮回的手

烏黑的手

要求施捨一個銅子

向任何人

甚至那掏不出一個銅子的兵士

一九三九年春，隴海道上。

街

我曾在這條街上住過——
同住的全是被烽火所驅趕的人們：
女的懷着孕，男的病了，老人嗆咳着
老婦在保育着嬰孩……

每個日子都在慌亂裏過去；
無數的人由·卡車裝送到這小城，
街上擁擠着難民，傷兵，失學的青年，
耳邊浮過各種不同的方言；

街變了，戰爭使它一天天繁榮：
兩旁擺滿了各式各樣的貨攤，
豆窩店改爲飯店，雜貨鋪變成旅館，
我家對面的房子充做醫院。

一天，成隊黑翼遮滿這小城的上空，
一陣轟響給這小城以痛苦的痙攣；
敵人撒下的毒火燬滅了街——
半個城市留下一片荒涼……

看：房子被揭去了屋蓋，
牆和牆失去了連絡，

井被塞滿了瓦礫，
屋柱被燒成了焦炭。

人們都在悲痛裏散光了，
（誰願意知道他們到哪兒去？）
但是我卻看見過一個，
那曾和我住在同院子的少女——

她在另一條街上走過，
那麼愉快地向我招呼……
——頭髮剪短了，綁了裹腿，
她已穿上草綠色的軍裝了！

　　　　　　　　　一九三九年春，桂林。

吹 號 者

　　好像曾經聽到人家說過,吹號者的命運是悲苦的,當他
用自己的呼吸磨擦了號角的銅皮使號角發出聲響的時候,
常常有細到看不見的血絲, 隨着號聲飛出來⋯⋯
　　吹號者的臉常常是蒼黃的⋯⋯

一

在那些蜷臥在鋪散着稻草的地面上的
　　困倦的人羣裏,
在那些穿着灰布衣服的污穢的人羣裏,
他最先醒來──
他醒來顯得如此突兀
每天都好像被驚醒似的,
是的, 他是被驚醒的,
驚醒他的
是黎明所乘的車輛的輪子
滾在天邊的聲音。

他睜開了眼睛,
在通宵不熄的微弱的燈光裏
他看見了那掛在身邊的號角,
他困惑地凝視着它

303

好像那些剛從睡眠中醒來
第一眼就看見自己心愛的戀人的人
一樣歡喜——
在生活注定給他的日子當中
他不能不愛他的號角；

號角是美的——
它的通身
發着健康的光彩，
它的頸上
結着緋紅的流蘇。

吹號者從鋪散着稻草的地面上起來了，
他不埋怨自己是睡在如此潮濕的泥地上，
他輕捷地綁好了裹腿，
他用冰冷的水洗過了臉，
他看着那些發出困乏的鼾聲的同伴，
於是他伸手攜去了他的號角；

門外依然是一片黝黑，
黎明沒有到來，
那驚醒他的
是他自己對於黎明的
過於殷切的想望。

他走上了山坡，
在那山坡上佇立了很久，

終於他看見這每天都顯現的奇蹟：
黑夜收斂起她那神秘的帷幔，
羣星倦了，一顆顆地散去……
黎明——這時間的新嫁娘啊
乘上有金色輪子的車輛
從天的那邊到來……
我們的世界爲了迎接她，
已在東方張掛了萬丈的曙光……
看，
天地間在舉行着最隆重的典禮……

二

現在他開始了，
站在藍得透明的天穹的下面，
他開始以原野給他的清新的呼吸
吹送到號角裏去，
——也夾帶着纖細的血絲麼？
使號角由於感激
以清新的聲響還給原野，
——他以對於豐美的黎明的傾慕
吹起了起身號，
那聲響流盪得多麼遼遠啊……

世界上的一切，
充溢着歡愉
承受了這號角的召喚……

林子醒了
傳出一陣陣鳥雀的喧吵，
河流醒了
召引着馬羣去飲水，
村野醒了
農婦匆忙地從堤岸上走過，
曠場醒了
穿着灰布衣服的人羣
從披着晨曦的破屋中出來，
擁擠着又排列着……

於是，他離開了山坡，
又把自己消失到那
無數的灰色的行列中去。

他吹過了吃飯號，
又吹過了集合號，
而當太陽以轟響的光彩
輝煌了整個天穹的時候，
他以催促的熱情
吹出了出發號。

三

那道路
是一直伸向永遠沒有止點的天邊去的，
那道路

是以成萬人的脚踩踏着
成千的車輪滾輾着的泥濘鋪成的，
那道路
連結着一個村莊又連結一個村莊，
那道路
爬過了一個土坡又爬過了一個土坡，
而現在
太陽給那道路鍍上了黃金了，
而我們的吹號者
在陽光照着的長長的隊伍的最前面，
以行進號
給前進着的步伐
做了優美的拍節……

四

灰色的人羣
散佈在廣闊的原野上，
今日的原野呵，
已用展向無限去的暗綠的苗草
給我們佈置成莊嚴的祭壇了：
聽，震耳的巨響
響在天邊，
我們呼吸着泥土與草混合着的香味，
郤也呼吸着來自遠方的煙火的氣息，
我們蟄伏在戰壕裏，
沉默而嚴肅地期待着一個命令，

像臨盆的產婦
痛楚地期待着一個嬰兒的誕生，
我們的心胸
從來未曾有像今天這樣的充溢着愛情，
在時代安排給我們的
——也是自己預定給自己的
生命之終極的日子裏，
我們沒有一個不是以聖潔的意志
準備着獲取在戰鬥中死去的光榮啊！

五

於是，慘酷的戰鬥開始了——
無數千萬的戰士
在閃光的驚覺中躍出了戰壕，
廣大的，激劇的奔跑
威脅着敵人地向前移動……
在震撼天地的衝殺聲裏，
在決不回頭的一致的步伐裏，
在狂流般奔湧着的人羣裏，
在緊密的連續的爆炸聲裏，
我們的吹號者
以生命所給與他的鼓舞，

一面奔跑，一面吹出了那
短促的，急迫的，激昂的，
在死亡之前決不中止的衝鋒號，
那聲音高過了一切，

又比一切都美麗，
正當他由於一種不能閃避的啓示
任情地吐出勝利的祝禱的時候，
他被一顆旋轉過他的心胸的子彈打中了！
他寂然地倒下去
沒有一個人曾看見他倒下去，
他倒在那直到最後一刻
　　都深深地愛着的土地上，
然而，他的手
却依然緊緊地握着那號角；

在那號角滑溜的銅皮上，
映出了死者的血
和他的慘白的面容；
也映出了永遠奔跑不完的
帶着射擊前進的人羣，
和嘶鳴的馬匹，
和隆隆的車輛……
而太陽，太陽
使那號角射出閃閃的光芒……

聽啊，
那號角好像依然在響……

　　　　　　　　　　一九三九年三月末。

他死在第二次

一　异　床

等他醒來時
他已睡在异床上
他知道自己還活着
兩個弟兄抬着他
他們都不說話

天氣凍結在寒風裏
雲低沉而移動
風靜默地擺動樹梢
他們急速地
抬着异床
穿過冬日的林子

經過了燒灼的激劇的痛楚
他的心現在已安靜了
像剛經過了可怕的惡鬥的戰場
現在也已安靜了一樣
然而他的血
從他的臂上滲透了綳紗布

依然一滴一滴地
淋滴在祖國的冬季的路上

就在當天晚上
朝向和他的舁床相反的方向
那比以前更大十倍的莊嚴的行列
以萬人的脚步
擦去了他的血滴所留下的紫紅的斑跡

二　醫　院

我們的槍哪兒去了呢
還有我們的塗滿血漬的衣服呢
另外的弟兄戴上我們的鋼盔
我們穿上了綉有紅十字的棉衣
我們躺着又躺着
看着無數的被金屬的溶液
和瓦斯的毒氣所嚙蝕過的肉體
每個都以疑懼的深黑的眼
和連續不止的呻吟
迎送着無數的日子
像迎送着黑色棺材的行列
在我們這裏
沒有誰的痛苦
會比誰少些的
大家都以僅有的生命
爲了抵擋敵人的進攻

迎接了酷烈的射擊——
我們都曾把自己的血
流灑在我們所守衛的地方啊……
但今天，我們是躺着又躺着
人們說這是我們的光榮
我們却不要這樣啊
我們躺着，心中懷念着戰場
比懷念自己生長的村莊更親切
我們依然歡喜在
烽火中奔馳前進呵
而我們，今天，我們
竟像一隻被捆綁了的野獸
呻吟在鐵床上
——我們痛苦着，期待着
要到何時呢？

三　手

每天在一定的時候到來
那女護士穿着白衣，戴着白帽
無言地走出去又走進來
解開負傷者的傷口的綳紗布
輕輕地扯去藥水棉花
從傷口洗去發臭的膿與血
纖細的手指是那麼輕巧
我們不會有這樣的妻子

我們的姊妹也不是這樣的

洗去了膿與血又把傷口包紮

那末輕巧，都用她的十個手指

都用她那纖細潔白的手指

在那十個手指的某一個上閃着金光

那金光撤動在我們的傷口

也撤動在我們的心的某個角落……

她走了仍是無言地

她無言地走了後我看着自己的一隻手

這是曾經拿過鋤頭又舉過槍的手

爲勞作磨成笨拙而又粗糙的手

現在却無力地擱在胸前

長在負了傷的臂上的手啊

看着自己的手也看着她的手

想着又苦惱着

苦惱着又想着，

究竟是甚麼緣分啊

這兩種手竟也被擱在一起？

四　愈　合

時間在空虛裏過去

他走出了醫院

像一個囚犯走出了牢監

身上也脫去笨重的棉衣

換上單薄的灰布制服

前襟依然綉着一個紅色的十字
自由，陽光，世界已走到了春天
無數的人們在街上
使他感到陌生而又親切啊
太陽强烈地照在街上
從長期沉睡中驚醒的
生命，在光輝裏躍動
人們匆忙地走過
只有他仍是如此困倦
誰都不曾看見他——
一個傷兵，今天他的創口
已愈合了，他歡喜
但他更嚴重地知道
這愈合所含有的更深的意義
只有此刻他纔覺得
自己是一個兵士
一個兵士必須在戰爭中受傷
傷好了必須再去參加戰爭
他想着又走着
步伐顯得多麽不自然啊
他的臉色很難看
人們走着，誰都不曾
看見他臉上的一片痛苦啊
只有太陽，從電桿頂上
伸下閃光的手指
撫慰着他的慘黃的臉
那在痛苦裏微笑着的臉……

五　姿　態

他披着有紅十字的灰布衣服
讓兩襟攤開着，讓兩袖懸挂着
他走在夜的城市的寬直的大街上
他走在使他感到陶醉的城市的大街上
四周喧騰的聲音，人羣的聲音
車輛的聲音，喇叭和警笛的聲音

在緊迫地擁擠着他，推動着他，刺激着他，
在那些平坦的人行道上
在那些眩目的電光下
在那些滑溜的柏油路上
在那些新式汽車的行列的旁邊
在那些穿着豔服的女人面前
他顯得多麼襤褸啊
而他却似乎突然想把腳步放寬些
（因爲他今天穿有光榮的袍子）
他覺得他是應該
以這樣的姿態走在世界上的
也只有和他一樣的人纔應該
以這樣的姿態走在世界上的

然而，當他覺得這樣地走着
——昂着頭，披着灰布的制服，跨着大步
感到人們的眼都在看着他的腳步時
他的浴在電光裏的臉
却又羞愧地紅起來了

為的是怕那些人們
已猜到了他心中的秘密——
其實人家並不曾注意到他啊

六　田　野

這是一個晴朗的日子
他向田野走去
像有什麼向他召呼似的

今天，他的脚踏在
田堤的溫軟的泥土上
使他感到莫名的歡喜
他脫下鞋子
把脚浸到淺水溝裏
又用手拍弄着流水
多久了——他生活在
由符號所支配的日子
而他的未來的日子
也將由符號去支配
但今天，他必須再在田野上
就算最後一次也罷
找尋那像在向他召呼的東西
那東西他自己也不曉得是什麼
他看見了水田
他看見一個農夫
他看見了耕牛

一切都一樣啊
到處都一樣啊
——人們說這是中國
樹是綠了，地上長滿了草
那些泥牆，更遠的地方
那些瓦屋，人們走着
——他想起人們說這是中國
他走着，他走着
這是什麼日子呀
他竟這樣愚蠢而快樂
年節裏也沒有這樣快樂呀
一切都在閃着光輝
到處都在閃着光輝
他向那正在忙碌的農夫笑
他自己也不曉得為什麼笑
農夫也沒有看見他的笑

七 一 瞥

沿着那伸展到城郊去的
林蔭路，他在濃藍的陰影裏走着
避開刺眼的陽光，在陰暗裏
他看見：那些馬車，輕快地
滾過，裏面坐着一些
穿得那麼整齊的男女青年
從他們的嘴裏飄出笑聲
和使他不安的響亮的談話

他走着，像一個衰憊的老人
慢慢地，他走近一個公園
在公園的進口的地方
在那大理石的拱門的脚旁
他看見：一個殘廢了的兵士
他的心突然被一種感覺所驚醒
於是他想着：或許這殘廢的弟兄
比大家都更英勇，或許
他也曾顧望自己葬身在戰場
但現在，他必須躺着呻吟着
呻吟着又躺着
過他生命的殘年
啊，誰能忍心看這樣子
誰看了心中也要燒起了仇恨
讓我們再去戰爭吧
讓我們在戰爭中愉快地死去
却不要讓我們只剩了一條腿回來
哭泣在衆人的面前
伸着污穢的饑餓的手
求乞同情的施舍啊！

八　遞　換

他脫去了那綉有紅十字的灰布制服
又穿上了幾個月之前的草綠色的軍裝
那軍裝的血漬到哪兒去了呢
而那被子彈穿破的地方也已經縫補過了

他穿着它，心中起了一陣激動
這激動比他初入伍時的更深沉
他好像覺得這軍裝和那有紅十字的制服
有着一種永遠拉不開的聯係似的
他們將永遠穿着它們，遞換着它們
是的，遞換着它們，這是應該的
一個兵士，在自己的
祖國解放的戰爭沒有結束之前
這兩種制服是他生命的旗幟
這樣的旗幟應該激劇地
飄動在被踐踏的祖國的土地上……

九　歡　送

以接連不斷的爆竹聲作爲引導
以使整個街衢都激動的號角聲作爲引導
以擠集在長街兩旁的羣衆的呼聲作爲引導
讓我們走在衆人的願望所鋪成的道上吧
讓我們走在從今日的世界到明日的世界的道上吧
讓我們走在那每個未來者都將以感激來追憶的道上吧
我們的胸膛高挺
我們的步伐齊整
我們在人羣所砌成的短牆中間走過
我們在自信與驕傲的中間走過
我們的心除了光榮不再想起什麼
我們除了追踪光榮不再想起什麼
我們除了爲追踪光榮而欣然赴死不再想起什麼……

十　一　念

你曾否知道

死是什麼東西？

——活着，死去，

蟲與花草

也在生命的蛻變中蛻化着……

這裏面，你所能想起的

是什麼呢？

當兵，不錯，

把生命交給了戰爭

死在河畔！

死在曠野！

冷露凝凍了我們的胸膛

屍體窩爛在野草叢裏

多少年代了

人類用自己的生命

肥沃了土地

又用土地養育了

自己的生命

誰能逃避這自然的規律

——那末，我們爲這而死

又有什麼不應該呢？

背上了槍

搖搖擺擺地走在長長的行列中

你們的心不是也常常被那

比愛情更強烈的什麼東西所苦惱嗎？

當你們一天出發了，走向戰場

你們不是也常常

覺得自己曾是生活着，

而現在却應該去死

——這死就爲了

那無數的未來者

能比自己生活得幸福麼?

一切的光榮

一切的贊歌

又有什麼用呢?

假如我們不曾想起

我們是死在自己聖潔的志願裏?

——而這，竟也是如此不可違反的

民族的偉大的意志呢?

十一　挺　進

挺進啊，勇敢啊

上起刺刀吧，兄弟們

把千萬顆心緊束在

同一的意志裏:

爲祖國的解放而鬥爭呀!

什麼東西值得我們害怕呢——

當我們已經知道爲戰鬥而死是光榮的?

挺進啊，勇敢啊

朝向炮火最濃密的地方

朝向噴射着子彈的塹壕

看，胆怯的敵人

已在我們馳奔直前的步伐聲裏顫抖了！

挺進啊，勇敢啊

屈辱與羞恥

是應該終結了——

我們要從敵人的手裏

奪回祖國的命運

只有這神聖的戰爭

能帶給我們自由與幸福……

挺進啊，勇敢啊

這光輝的日子

是我們所把握的！

我們的生命

必須在堅強不屈的鬥爭中

才能衝擊奮發！

兄弟們，上起刺刀

勇敢啊，挺進啊！

十二　　他倒下了

竟是那末迅速

不容許有片刻的考慮

和像電光般一閃的那驚問的時間

在燃燒着的子彈

第二次——也是最後一次啊——

穿過他的身體的時候

他的生命

曾經算是在世界上生活過來的

終於像一株
被大斧所砍伐的樹似的倒下了
在他把從那裏可以看着世界的窗子
那此刻是蒙上喜悅的淚水的眼睛
永遠關閉了之前的一瞬間
他不能想起什麼
——母親死了
又沒有他曾親昵過的女人
一切都這末簡單

一個兵士
不曉得更多的東西
他只曉得
他應該為這解放的戰爭而死
當他倒下了
他也只曉得
他所躺的是祖國的土地
——因為人們
那些比他懂得更多的人們
曾經如此告訴過他

不久，他的弟兄們
又去尋覓地
——這該是生命之最後一次的訪謁
但這一次
他們所帶的不再是舁床
而是一把短柄的鐵鏟

　　也不曾經過選擇
　　人們在他所守衛的
　　河岸不遠的地方
　　挖掘了一條淺坑……

　　在那夾着春草的泥土
　　覆蓋了他的屍體之後
　　他所遺留給世界的
　　是無數的星布在荒原上的
　　可憐的土堆中的一個
　　在那些土堆上
　　人們是從來不標出死者的名字的
　　──即使標出了
　　又有什麼用呢？

　　　　　　　　　　　一九三七年春末

曠　　野

薄霧在迷濛着曠野啊……

看不見遠方——
看不見往日在晴空下的
天邊的松林，
和在松林後面的
迎着陽光發閃的白堊岩了；
前面只隱現着
一條漸漸模糊的
灰黃而曲折的道路，
和道路兩旁的
烏暗而枯乾的田畝……

田畝已荒蕪了——
狼籍着犂翻了的土塊，
與枯死的野草，
與雜在野草裏的
腐爛了的禾根；
在廣大的灰白裏呈露出的
到處是一片土黃，暗赭，
與焦茶的顏色的混合啊……
——只有幾畦蘿蔔菜蔬

325

以披着白霜的
稀疏的綠色，
點綴着
這平凡，單調，簡陋
與卑微的田野。

那些池沼毗連着，
爲了久旱
積水快要枯涸了；
不透明的白光裏
彎曲着幾條淡褐色的
不整齊的堤岸；
往日翠茂的
水草和荷葉
早已沉澱在水底了；
留下的一些
枯萎而彎曲的枝桿，
呆然站立在
從池面徐緩地升起的水蒸氣裏……

山坡橫陳在前面，
路轉上了山坡，
並且隨着它的起伏
而向下面的疏林隱沒……
山坡上，
灰黃的道路的兩旁，
感到陰暗而憂慮的

只是一些散亂的墓堆，
和快要被湮埋了的
黑色的石碑啊。

一切都這樣地
靜止，寒冷，而顯得寂寞……

灰黃而曲折的道路啊！
人們走着，走着，
向着不同的方向，
却好像永遠被同一的影子引導着，
結束在同一的命運裏；
在無止的勞困與飢寒的前面
等待着的是災難，疾病與死亡——
傍徨在曠野上的人們
誰曾有過快活呢？

然而
冬天的曠野
是我所親切的——
在冷徹肌骨的寒霜上，
我走過那些不平的田塍，
荒蕪的池沼的邊岸，
和褐色陰暗的山坡，
步伐是如此沉重，直至感到困危
——像一頭耕完了土地
帶着倦怠歸去的老牛一樣……

而霧啊——
灰白而混濁，
茫然而莫測，
它在我的前面
以一根比一根更暗淡的
電桿與電綫，
向我展開了
無限的廣闊與深邃……

你悲哀而曠達，
辛苦而又貧困的曠野啊……

沒有什麼聲音，
一切都好像被霧窒息了；
只在那邊
看不淸的灌木叢裏，
傳出了一片.
畏懾於嚴寒的
抖索着毛羽的
鳥雀的聒噪……

在那蘆蒿和荊棘所編的籬圍裏
幾間小屋擠聚着——
它們都一樣地
以牆邊柴木的凌亂，
與竹桿上垂掛的襤褸，
歎息着

徒然而無終止的勤勞；
又以凝霜的樹皮蓋的屋背上
無力的混合在霧裏的炊煙
描畫了
不可逃避的貧窮……

人們在那些小屋裏
過的是怎樣慘淡的日子啊……
生活的陰影覆蓋着他們……
那裏好像永遠沒有白日似的，
他們和家畜呼吸在一起，
——他們的床榻也像畜棚啊，
而那些破爛的被絮，
就像一堆泥土一樣的
灰暗而又堅硬啊……

而寒冷與飢餓，
愚蠢與迷信啊，
就在那些小屋裏
强硬地盤據着……

農人從霧裏
挑起籤籮走來，
籤籮裏只有幾束葱和蒜，
他的氈帽已破爛不堪了，
他的臉像他的衣服一樣污穢，
他的凍裂了皮膚的手

插在腰束裏，
他的赤着的脚
踏着凝霜的道路，
他無聲地
帶着扁擔所發出的微響，
慢慢地
在蒙着霧的前面消失⋯⋯

曠野啊──
你將永遠憂慮而容忍
不平而又緘默麼？

薄霧在迷濛着曠野啊⋯⋯

　　　　　　　　　一九四零年元月三日晨。

冬天的池沼

—— 給 W. I.

冬天的池沼，
寂寞得像老人的心——
飽歷了人世的辛酸的心；
冬天的池沼，
枯乾得像老人的眼——
被勞苦磨失了光輝的眼；
冬天的池沼，
荒蕪得像老人的髮；
像霜草般稀疏而又灰白的髮；
冬天的池沼，
陰鬱得像一個悲哀的老人——
佝僂在陰鬱的天幕下的老人。

　　　　　　一九四零年元月十一日。

樹

一棵樹　一棵樹
彼此孤離地兀立着
風與空氣
告訴着它們的距離

但是在泥土的覆蓋下
它們的根伸長着
在看不見的深處
它們把根鬚糾纏在一起

一九四零年春。

擡

請你們讓開
請你們走在人行道上
讓我們把他們擡起來
請你們不要擁擠
請你們站在街旁
讓我們把他們擡起來
請你們不要叫嚷
請你們用靜默表示悲哀
讓我們擡起他們來

這是一個婦人
她的腦蓋已被彈片打開
讓她閉着眼好好地睡
願她過一陣能慢慢地醒來
讓我們擡起她送回她的家
讓她的家屬用哭泣與仇恨安排

這是一個服務隊的隊員
灰色的制服上還掛得有他的臂章
你們認識他麼——他的臉已蒙上了土灰
無情的彈片打斷了他勤勞的臂
請你們讓開，請向他表示悲哀

他已爲了減少你們的犧牲而被殘害

請你們不要擠，這裏還有更多的
他們都是傷兵住在傷兵醫院裏
他們在前方受了傷躺在床上
等着傷好了再上戰場
現在無恥的敵人已把醫院炸倒
現在他們已受到了更大的創傷

請大家讓開
讓我們撞起他們來
請大家站在旁邊
讓我們撞着舁床的走來
請大家記住
這些都是血債！

一九四零年六月十一日，重慶。

哀 巴 黎

柏林十四日下午六時海通社急電；據官方公告："德軍今
　　晨已正式入巴黎。"

紅白藍的三色旗
卸下來；
代替它而飄揚於
塞納河畔
襲果德廣場上的
是綴着黑色卐字的血色的旗。

於是塞納河的水
將無日夜的鳴咽着，
緩流着
一個都市的淪亡的眼淚……

於是莊嚴的大廈傾倒了；
隨着傾倒的
是刻有"自由，平等，博愛"的
寬大的門額……

於是 Pantheon
與 Invalides 的門前

　　將舉行
　　比第一執政官時代更隆重的“凱旋式”
　　在那長長的肅穆的行列之間，
　　走過了一個
　　比拿破崙更冒險的人物；
　　盧梭，服爾泰，丹頓的銅像；
　　將被無情的鐵錘擊落
　　在他們的位置上，
　　將站立起
　　希特勒，戈貝爾，戈林的
　　兩手插着腰身的姿態

　　人類的歷史
　　將加上一頁
　　充滿詼諧與幽默的記載；
　　而在那歷史的背面
　　暗暗地流着
　　純潔與嚴肅的眼淚

　　法蘭西——
　　這被讚頌民主的詩人
　　讚頌爲“世界上最美麗的名字”，
　　如今，日耳曼人的手
　　要來塗改，並且
　　將代之以含糊的齒音：
　　德意志
　　我昔日也曾徘徊過的街道上

不再看見尋覓歡樂的美利堅人，

慣於把謊話和接吻混合在一起的貴婦人

帶走了化裝跳舞的綢製的假面

和黑絲的網形的手套，

將遁跡於北非洲剛果河畔。

平坦而寬闊的

香榭莉樹

你瑪格麗特駕着

馬車散步的道上，

正馳過標幟着

卍字的鋼甲坦克，

和呼嘯着"希特勒萬歲"的輕騎兵隊……

國社黨的黨員來了！

他們的長統靴上的馬刺

從街頭響過刺耳的聲音

他們闖進了已關閉了一個禮拜的啡咖店

喝叱着那顫抖着的老婦

給他們以足够的混合酒。

文化與藝術的都市啊，

今天挺進隊的隊員

來扣開你博物院的門

他們用刺刀戳穿了

德拉克羅亞與大衛德的畫幅；

又把昂格爾的土耳其浴堂，

攜回到總司令部；
在所有圖書館與美術館裏
將散佈着我的奮鬥
與巴黎進軍圖。

巴黎，你懦庸的統治者
已放棄你——
達拉第與雷諾說：
"苟被迫自歐陸撤退
則當遷往北非，
一旦必要時
擬遷往美洲之屬地。"
——他們依然
沉醉在統治的夢想裏；

而你們——
善良而正直的
法蘭西的人民啊
終於流徙了
"扶老攜幼之難民
……猶如一極偉大之長蛇，
蜿蜒不絕……"
而我所哀傷的
也就是你們啊……

不！
法蘭西的人民是勇敢的。
普魯士軍隊進入巴黎

也不只這一次，
每次擊退侵略者的
是法蘭西的人民自己。
法蘭西的光榮的歷史
是它的勇敢的人民的血寫成的。

我們依然信任時間——
它將會給愛自由，愛民主的
法蘭西人民以勝利。

當此刻，
我沉湎在對於巴黎之囘想時，
我的耳際
還在響着
馬賽曲，國際歌的歌聲；
我的眼前
還映現從列寧廳出來的
勞動者的壯大的行列……
我相信：當達拉第，雷諾
捲帶了法蘭西的財富以及美女與香水
從波爾多遷往北非或美洲時，
法蘭西人民將更堅强起來，
他們將在街頭
重新佈置障礙物
爲了抵抗自己的敵人
將有第二公社的誕生！

　　　　　　一九四零年六月十五日，重慶。

公　路

像那些阿美利加人
行走在加里福尼亞的大道上
我行走在中國西部高原的
新闢的公路上

我從那隱蔽在羣山的夾谷裏的
一個卑微的小村莊裏出來
我從那陰暗的，迷蒙着柴煙的小瓦屋里出來
帶着農民的耿直與痛苦的激情
奔上山去——
讓空氣與陽光
和展開在山下的如海洋一樣的曠野
拂去我的日常的煩瑣
和生活的苦惱
也讓無邊的明朗的天的幅員
以它的毫無阻礙的空闊
松懈我的長久被窒息的心啊……

綿長的公路
沿着山的形體
彎曲地，伏貼地向上伸引

人在山上慢慢地升高
慢慢地和下界遠離

行走在大氣的環繞裏
似乎飄浮在半空
我們疲倦了
可以在一顆古樹的根上
坐下休息
聽山澗從巉巖間
奔騰而下
看鷹鷟與雕鴿
呼叫着又飛翔着
在我們的身邊……

而背上負着煤袋的騾馬隊
由衣着襤褸的人們帶引着
由倦怠的喝叱和無力的鞭打指揮着
凌亂地從這裏過去
又轉進了一個幽僻山峽裏去
我們可以隨着它們的步伐
揣摹着在那山峽裏和衰敗的古廟相毗連
有着一排製造着簡陋的工業品的房屋
那些載重的卡車啊
帶着愉快的隆隆之聲而來
車上的貨物顛簸着
那些年輕的人們
朝向我這步行者

揚臂歡呼
在這樣的日子
卽使他們的振奮
和我的振奮不是來自同一的原由
我的心也在不可抑制地激動啊

更有那些輕捷的汽車
掙着從金屬的反射
所投射出來的白光之翅
陶醉在疾行的速度裏
在山脈上
勇敢地飛馳
鼓舞了我的感情與想像
和它們比翼在空中

於是
我的靈魂得到了一次解放
我的肺腑呼吸着新鮮
我的眼瞳爲遠景而擴大
我的脚因歡忭而跛行在世界上

用堅强的手與沉重的鐵鎚所劈擊
又用爆烈的炸藥轟開了巖石
在萬丈高的崖壁的邊沿
以石塊與泥土與水門汀
和成千成萬的勞動者的汗
凝固成了萬里長的道路

上面是天穹

——一片令人看了要昏眩的藍色

下面是大江

不止地奔騰着江水

無數的烏暗的木船和破爛的布帆

幾乎是靜止地飄浮在水面上

從這裏看去

渺小得只成了一些灰黯的斑點

人行走在高山之上

遠離了煩瑣與陰暗的住房

可憐的心，誠樸的心啊

終於從單純與廣闊

重新喚醒了

一個生命的崇高與驕傲——

卽使我是一顆螞蟻

或是一隻有堅硬的翅膀的蚱蜢

在這樣的路上爬行或飛翔

也是最幸福的啊……

今天，我穿着草鞋

戴着麥稈編的涼帽

行走在新闢的公路上

我的心因爲追踪自由

而感到無限地愉悅啊

鋪呈在我的前面的道路

是多麼寬闊！多麼平坦！

多麼沒有羈絆地自如地

向遠方伸展——
我們可以清楚地看見
它向天的邊際蜿蜒地遠去
那麼豪壯地絡住了地面
當我在這裏向四周凝望
河流，山丘，道路，村舍
和隨處都成了美麗的叢簇的樹林
無比調諧地浮現在大氣裏
竟使我如此明顯地感到
我是站在地球的巔頂

一九四零年秋

刈草的孩子

夕陽把草原燃成通紅了。
刈草的孩子無聲地刈草，
低着頭，彎曲着身子，忙亂着手，
從這一邊慢慢地移到那一邊……

草已遮沒他小小的身子了——
在草叢裏我們只看見：
一隻盛草的竹簍，幾堆草，
和在夕陽裏閃着金光的鐮刀……

一九四零年

老　人

在長長的瓜棚的旁邊
伸引着一條長長的泥地
一個駝背的老人翻掘着泥土
想在那兒播散新的種子

他是這樣困苦地工作着
他的背聳得比他的頭還高了
他翻掘一陣又檢理一陣
把野草和石塊都擲棄在兩邊

他的衣服像黑泥一樣烏暗
他的皮膚像黃土一樣灰黃
陽光從高空照着他的臉
臉上是樹皮似的繁雜的皺紋

他舉着鋤用力地繼續着翻掘
汗已從他的前額流到他的顎邊
微風吹過時他輕輕地咳了幾聲
明朗的陽光映出他陰鬱的臉

一九四零年八月十七日。

346

我的父親

一

近來我常常夢見我的父親——
他的臉顯得從未有過的"仁慈"，
流露着對我的"寬恕"，
他的話語也那麼溫和，
好像他一切的苦心和用意，
都為了要袒護他的兒子。

去年春天他給我幾次信，
用哀懇的情感希望我回去，
他要囑咐我一些重要的話語，
一些關於土地和財產的話語：
但是我拂逆了他的願望，
並沒有動身回到家鄉，
我害怕一個家庭交給我的責任，
會毀壞我年輕的生命。

五月石榴花開的一天，
他含着失望離開人間。

二

我是他的第一個兒子，
他生我時已二十一歲，
正是滿清最後的一年，
在一個中學堂裏唸書。
他顯得溫和而又忠厚，
穿着長衫，留着辮子，
胖胖的身體，紅褐的膚色，
眼睛圓大而前突，
兩耳貼在臉頰的後面，
人們說這是"福相"，
所以他要"安份守己"。

滿足着自己的"八字"，
過着平凡而又庸碌的日子，
抽抽水煙，喝喝黃酒，
躺在竹床上看《聊齋誌異》
講女妖和狐狸的故事。

他十六歲時，我的祖父就去世；
我的祖母是一個童養媳，
常常被我祖父的小老婆欺侮，
我的伯父是一個鴉片煙鬼，
主持着"花會"，玩弄婦女；
但是他，我的父親，
却從"修身"與"格致"學習人生——

做了他母親的好兒子，
他妻子的好丈夫。

接受了梁啓超的思想，
知道"世界進步彌有止期"，
成了"維新派"的信徒，
在那窮僻的小村莊裏，
最初剪掉烏黑的辮子。

《東方雜誌》的讀者，
《申報》的定戶，
"萬國儲蓄會"的會員，
堂前擺着自鳴鐘，
房裏點着美孚燈。

鎮上有曾祖父遺下的店舖——
京貨，洋貨，糧食，酒，"一應俱全"，
它供給我們全家的衣料，
日常用品和飲茶的點心，
憑了摺子任意拿取一切雜物；
三十九個店員忙了三百六十天，
到過年主人拿去全部的利潤。

村上又有幾百畝田，
幾十個佃戶圍繞在他的身邊，
家裏每年有四個僱農，
一個婢女，一個老媽子，

這一切造成他的安閑。

沒有狂熱！不敢冒險！
依照自己的利益和趣味，
要建立一個"新的家庭"，
把女兒送進教會學校，
督促兒子要唸英文。

用批煩和鞭打管束子女，
他成了家庭裏的暴君；
節儉是他給我們的教條，
順從是他給我們的經典，
再呢，要我們用功唸書，
密切地注意我們的分數，
他知道知識是有用的東西——
一可以裝點門面，
二是可以保衛財產。
這些是他的貴賓；
退伍的陸軍少將，
省會中學的國文教員，
大學法律系和經濟系的學生，
和鎮上的警佐，
和縣裏的縣長。

經常翻閱世界輿地圖，
讀氣象學，觀測星辰，
從"天演論"知道猴子是人類的祖先；

但是在祭祀的時候，
却一樣的假裝虔誠，
他心裏很清楚：
對於向他繳納租稅的人們，
閻羅王的塑像，
比達爾文的學說更有用處。

無力地期待"進步"，
漠然地迎接"革命"，
他知道這是"潮流"
自己却囘避着衝激，
站在遙遠的地方觀望……
一九二六年
國民革命軍從南方出發
經過我的故鄉，
那時我想去投考"黃埔"，
但是他却沉默着，
兩眼混濁，沒有囘答。

革命像暴風雨，來了又去了。

無數年輕英勇的人們，
都做了時代的奠祭品，
在看盡了恐怖與悲哀之後，
我的心像失去布帆的船隻
在不安與迷茫的海洋裏飄浮……

地主們都希望兒子能發財，做官，
他們要兒子唸經濟與法律；
而我却用畫筆蘸了顏色，
去塗抹一張風景，
和一個勤勞的農人。

少年人的幻想和熱情，
常常鼓動我離開家庭；
爲了到一個遠方的都市去，
我曾用無數功利的話語，
騙取我父親的同情。

一天晚上他從地板下面，
取出了一千圓鷹洋，
兩手抖索，臉色陰沉，
一邊數錢，一邊叮囑：
"你過幾年就回來，
千萬不可樂而忘返！"

而當我臨走時，
他送我到村邊，
我不敢用腦子去想一想
他交給我的希望的重量，
我的心只是催促着自己：
"快些離開吧——
這可憐的田野，
這卑微的村莊，

去孤獨地漂泊，
去自由地流浪！”

三

幾年後，一個憂鬱的影子
囘到那個衰老的村莊，
兩手空空，什麼也沒有——
除了那些叛亂的書籍，
和那些狂熱的畫幅，
和一個殖民地人民的
深刻的恥辱與仇恨。

七月，我被關進了監獄
八月，我被判決了徒刑；
由於對他的兒子的絕望
我的父親曾一夜哭到天亮。

在那些黑暗的年月，
他不斷地用溫和的信，
要我做弟妹們的“模範”，
依從“家庭的願望”，
又用衰老的話語，纏綿的感情
和安排好了的幸福，
來俘虜我的心。

當我重新得到了自由，
他熱切地盼望我囘去，

他給我寄來了
僅僅足够回家的路費。

他向我重復人家的話語，
（天知道他從那裏得來！）
說中國沒有資產階級，
沒有美國式的大企業，
沒有殘酷的剝削和榨取；
他說：“我對夥計們，
從來也沒有壓迫，
就是他們眞的要革命，
又會把我怎樣？”
於是，他攤開了賬簿，
攤開了厚厚的租穀簿，
眼睛很慈和地看着我
長了鬍鬚的嘴含着微笑
一邊用手指撥着算盤
一邊用低微的聲音
督促我注意弟妹們的前途。

但是，他終於激怒了──
皺着眉頭，牙齒咬着下唇，
顯出很痛心的樣子，
手指節猛擊着桌子，
他憤恨他兒子的淡漠的態度，
──把自己的家庭，
當做旅行休息的客棧，

用看穢物的眼光，
看祖上的遺產。

為了從廢墟中救起自己，
為了追求一個至善的理想，
我又離開了我的村莊，
卽使我的脚踵淋着鮮血，
我也不會停止前進……

我的父親已死了，
他是犯了鼓脹病而死的；
從此他再也不會怨我，
我還能說什麼呢？

他是一個最平庸的人；
因為膽怯而能安份守己，
在最動蕩的時代裏，
渡過了最平靜的一生，
像無數的中國的地主一樣：
中庸，保守，吝嗇，自滿，
把那窮僻的小村莊，
當做永世不變的王國；
從他的祖先接受遺產，
又把這遺產留給他的子孫，
不曾減少，也不曾增加！
就是這樣——
這就是為什麼我要可憐他的地方。

如今我的父親，
已安靜地躺在泥土裏
在他出殯的時候，
我沒有爲他舉過魂幡
也沒有爲他穿過粗麻布的衣裳；
我正帶着嘶啞的歌聲，
奔走在解放戰爭的煙火裏⋯⋯

母親來信囑咐我回去，
要我爲家庭處理善後，
我不願意埋葬我自己，
殘忍地違背了她的願望，
感激戰爭給我的鼓舞，
我走上和家鄉相反的方向──
因爲我，自從我知道了
在這世界上有更好的理想，
我要效忠的不是我自己的家，
而是那屬於千萬人的
一個神聖的信仰。

一九四一年八月

獻給鄉村的詩

我的詩獻給中國的一個小小的鄉村——
它被一條山崗所伸出的手臂環護着。
山崗上是年老的常常呻吟的松樹；
還有紅葉子像鴨掌般撐開的楓樹；
高大的結着戴帽子的菓實的欅子樹
和老槐樹，主幹被雷霆劈斷的老槐樹；
這些年老的樹，在山崗上集成樹林，
蔭蔽着一個古老的鄉村和它的居民。

我想起鄉村邊上澄清的池沼——
它的周圍密密地環抱着濃綠的楊柳，
水面浮着菱葉、水葫蘆葉、睡蓮的白花。
它是天的忠心的伴侶，映着天的歡笑和愁苦；
它是雲的梳妝臺，太陽、月亮、飛鳥的鏡子；
它是羣星的沐浴處，水禽的游泳池；
而老實又龐大的水牛從水裏伸出了頭，
看着村婦蹲在石板上洗着蔬菜和衣服。

我想起鄉村裏那些幽靜的菓樹園——
園裏種滿桃子、杏子、李子、石榴和林檎，
外面圍着石砌的圍牆或竹編的籬笆，
牆上和籬笆上爬滿了蔦蘿和紡車花；

那裏是喜鵲的家，麻雀的游戲場；
蜜蜂的釀造室，螞蟻的堆貨棧；
蟋蟀的練音房，紡織娘的彈奏處，
而殘忍的蜘蛛偷偷地織着網捕捉蝴蝶。

我想起鄉村路邊的那些石井──
青石砌成的六角形的石井是鄉村的儲水庫，
汲水的年月久了，它的邊沿已刻着繩迹，
暗綠而濡濕的青苔也已長滿它的周圍，
我想起鄉村田野上的道路──
用卵石或石板鋪的曲折窄小的道路，
它們從鄉村通到溪流、山崗和樹林；
通到森林後面和山那面的另一個鄉村。

我想起鄉村附近的小溪──
它無日無夜地從遠方引來了流水
給鄉村灌溉田地、菓樹園、池沼和井，
供給鄉村上的居民們以足够的飲料；
我想起鄉村附近小溪上的木橋──
它因勞苦削瘦得只剩了一副骨骼，
長年地赤露着瘦長的腿站在水裏，
讓村民們從它駝着的背脊上走過。

我想起鄉村中間平坦的曠場──
它是村童們的競技場，角力和摔跤的地方，
大人們在那裏打麥，摜豆，颺穀，篩米……
長長的橫竹竿上飄着未乾的衣服和褲子；

寬大的地席上鋪晒着大麥、黃豆和蕎麥；
夏天晚上人們在那裏談天、乘凉，甚至爭吵，
冬天早晨在那裏解開衣服找虱子、曬太陽；
假如一頭牛從山崖跌下，它就成了屠場——

我想起鄉村裏那些簡陋的房屋——
它們緊緊地挨擠着，好像冬天寒冷的人們，
它們被柴煙薰成烏黑，到處掛滿了塵埃，
裏面充溢着女人的叱罵和小孩的啼哭；
屋檐下懸掛着向日葵和蘿蔔的種子，
和成串的焦紅的辣椒，枯黃的乾荣；
小小的窗子凝望着村外的道路，
看着山巒以及遠處山脚下的村落。

我想起鄉村裏最老的老人——
他的鬚髮灰白，他的牙齒掉了，耳朵聾了。
手像紫荆藤緊緊地握着拐杖，
從市集回來的村民高聲地和他談着行情；
我想起鄉村裏最老的女人——
自從一次出嫁到這鄉村，她就沒有離開過，
她沒有看見過帆船，更不必說火車、輪船，
她的子孫都死光了，她却很驕傲地活着。

我想起鄉村裏重壓下的農夫——
他們的臉像松樹一樣發皺而陰鬱，
他們的背被過重的挑担壓成弓形，
他們的眼睛被失望與怨憤磨成混沌；

我想起這些農夫的忠厚的妻子——
她們貧血的臉像土地一樣灰黃，
她們整天忙着磨穀，舂米，燒飯，喂猪，
一邊納鞋底一邊把奶頭塞進嬰孩啼哭的嘴。

我想起鄉村裏的牧童們，
想起用汚手擦着眼睛的童養媳們，
想起沒有土地沒有耕牛的佃戶們，
想起除了身體和衣服之外什麼也沒有的僱農們，
想起建造房屋的木匠們、石匠門、泥水匠們，
想起屠夫們、鐵匠們，裁縫們，
想起所有這些被窮困所折磨的人們——
他們終年勞苦，從未得到應有的報酬。

我的詩獻給鄉村裏一切不幸的人——
無論到什麼地方我都記起他們，
記起那些被山嶺把他們和世界隔開的人，
他們的性格像野猪一樣，沉默而兇猛，
他們長久地被蒙蔽，欺騙與愚弄；
每個臉上都隱蔽着不曾爆發的憤恨；
他們衣襟遮掩着的懷裏歪插着尖長快利的刀子，
那藏在套裏的刀鋒，期待着復仇的來臨。

我的詩獻給生長我的小小的鄉村——
卑微的，沒有人注意的小小的鄉村，
它像中國大地上的千百萬的鄉村。
它存在於我的心裏，像母親存在兒子心裏。

縱然明麗的風光和汚穢的生活形成了對照，
而自然的恩惠也不曾彌補了居民的貧窮，
這是不合理的：它應該有它和自然一致的和諧；
爲了反抗欺騙與壓榨，它將從沉睡中起來。

　　　　　　　　　一九四二年九月七日

毛 澤 東

毛澤東在哪兒出現，
哪兒就沸騰着鼓掌聲——

"人民的領袖"不是一句空虛的頌詞，
他以對人民的愛博得人民的信仰；

他生根於古老而龐大的中國，
把歷史的重載馱在自己的身上；

他的臉常覆蓋着憂愁，
眼瞳裏映着人民的苦難；

是政論家，詩人，軍事指揮者，
革命者——以行動實踐着思想；

他不斷地思考，不斷地概括，
一手推開仇敵，一手包進更多的朋友；

"集中"是他的天才的戰略——
把最大的力量壓向最大的敵人；

一個新的口號決定一個新的方向：
"一切都爲了法西斯主義之死亡。。"

一九四一年十一月六日於邊區參議會

太 陽 的 話

打開你們的窗子吧
打開你們的板門吧
讓我進去，讓我進去
進到你們的小屋裏

我帶着金黃的花束
我帶着林間的香氣
我帶着亮光和溫暖
我帶着滿身的露水

快起來，快起來
快從枕頭裏擡起頭來
睜開你的被睫毛蓋着的眼
讓你的眼看見我的到來

讓你們的心像小小的木板房
打開它們的關閉了很久的窗子
讓我把花束，把香氣，把亮光，
　溫暖和露水撒滿你們心的空間。

一九四二年一月十四日

野　火

在這些黑夜裏燃燒起來
在這些高高的山巔上
伸出你的光熖的手
去撫捫夜的寬闊的胸脯
去撫捫深藍的冰涼的胸脯
從你的最高處跳動着的尖頂
把你的火星飛飈起來
讓它們像羣仙似地飄落在
那些莫測的黑暗而又冰冷的深谷
去照見那些沉睡的靈魂
讓它們卽使在縹緲的夢中
也能得一次狂歡的舞蹈

在這些黑夜裏燃燒起來
更高些！更高些！
讓你的歡樂的形體
從地面升向高空
使我們這困倦的世界
因了你的火光的鼓舞
甦醒起來！喧騰起來！
讓這黑夜裏的一切的眼
都在看望着你

讓這黑夜裏的一切的心
都因了你的召喚而震蕩
歡笑的火熖呵
顫動的火熖呵

聽呀從什麼深邃的角落
傳來了那贊頌你的瀑布似的歌聲……

　　　　　　　　　一九四二年，陝北。

黎明的通知

爲了我的祈願
詩人啊，你起來吧

而且請你告訴他們
說他們所等待的已經要來

說我已踏着露水而來
已借着最後一顆星的照引而來

我從東方來
從洶湧着波濤的海上來

我將帶光明給世界
又將帶溫暖給人類

借你正直人的嘴
請帶去我的消息

通知眼睛被渴望所灼痛的人類
和遠方的沉浸在苦難裏的城市和村莊

請他們來歡迎我——
白日的先驅，光明的使者

打開所有的窗子來歡迎
打開所有的門來歡迎

請鳴響汽笛來歡迎
請吹起號角來歡迎

請清道夫來打掃街衢
請搬運車來搬去垃圾

讓勞動者以寬闊的步伐走在街上吧
讓車輛以輝煌的行列從廣場流過吧

請村莊也從潮濕的霧裏醒來
爲了歡迎我打開它們的籬笆

請村婦打開她們的雞塒
請農夫從畜棚牽出耕牛

借你的熱情的嘴通知他們
說我從山的那邊來，從森林的那邊來

請他們打掃乾淨那些曬場
和那些永遠污穢的天井

請打開那糊有花紙的窗子
請打開那貼着春聯的門

請叫醒殷勤的女人
和那打着鼾聲的男子

請年輕的情人也起來
和那些貪睡的少女

請叫醒困倦的母親
和她身邊的嬰孩

請叫醒每個人
連那些病者與產婦

連那些衰老的人們
呻吟在牀上的人們

連那些因正義而戰爭的負傷者
和那些因家鄉淪亡而流離的難民

請叫醒一切的不幸者
我會一併給他們以慰安

請叫醒一切愛生活的人
工人，技師以及畫家

請歌唱者唱着歌來歡迎
用草與露水所滲合的聲音

請舞蹈者跳着舞來歡迎
披上她們白霧的晨衣

請叫那些健康而美麗的醒來
說我馬上要來扣打她們的窗門

請你忠實於時間的詩人
帶給人類以慰安的消息

請他們準備歡迎，請所有的人準備歡迎
當雄雞最後一次鳴叫的時候我就到來

請他們用虔誠的眼睛凝視天邊
我將給所有期待我的以最慈惠的光輝

趁這夜已快完了，請告訴他們
說他們所等待的就要來了

礁　石

一個浪，一個浪
無休止地撲過來
每一個浪都在它脚下
被打成碎沫、散開……

它的臉上和身上
像刀砍過的一樣
但它依然站在那裏
含着微笑，看着海洋……

一九五四年七月二十五日

在世界的這一邊

在世界的這一邊，
人們把我們抱得這樣緊，
緊得使我們透不過氣，
在我們的臉上使勁地親——

不是因為我們還年輕，
也不是因為我們長得英俊，
只因為我們來自一個國家，
那個國家從血泊裏誕生；

也不是他鄉遇見了故知，
許多人都從來不曾見面，
但在一種崇高的感情下，
個個都像是久別的愛人。

"中國人"到處受到歡迎！
我們的艱苦和英勇舉世聞名！
六萬萬人高舉着大旗前進，
大旗上寫着兩個大字：和平！

一九五四年七月，聖地亞哥

啓 明 星

屬於你的是
光明與黑暗交替
黑夜逃遁
白日追踪而至的時刻

羣星已經退隱
你依然站在那兒
期待着太陽上升

被最初的晨光照射
投身在光明的行列
直到誰也不再看見你

一九五六年八月

泉

一

你唱的山歌
遠近都聞名
聽你的歌聲
比泉水還清

二

這兒的山高
水也來得深
喝這兒的水
使歌喉圓潤

平常的人們
不到這兒來
爬這樣的山
誰也沒耐性

只有兩種鳥
到這兒留停
白天的百靈
夜晚的夜鶯

一九五六年八月

下 雪 的 早 晨

雪下着，下着，沒有聲音，
雪下着，下着，一刻不停，
潔白的雪，蓋滿了院子，
潔白的雪，蓋滿了屋頂，
整個世界多麼靜，多麼靜。

看着雪花在飄飛，
我想得很遠，很遠，
想起夏天的樹林，
樹林裏的早晨，
到處都是露水，
太陽剛剛上升，
一個小孩，赤着腳，
從晨光裏走來，
他的臉像一朵鮮花，
他的嘴發出低低的歌聲，
他的小手拿着一根竹竿，
他仰起小小的頭，
那雙發亮的眼睛，
透過濃密的樹葉，
在尋找知了的聲音……

他的另一隻小手，
提了一串綠色的東西，
——一根根長的狗尾草，
結了螞蚱，金甲蟲和蜻蜓，
這一切啊，
我都記得很淸。

我們很久沒有到樹林裏去了，
那兒早已鋪滿了落葉，
也不會有什麼人影；
但我一直都記着那個小孩，
和他的很輕很輕的歌聲，
此刻，他不知在那間小屋裏，
看着不停地飄飛着的雪花，
或許想到樹林裏去抛雪球，
或許想到湖上去滑冰，
他決不會知道
有一個人想看他，
就在這個下雪的早晨。

　　　　　　　　一九五六年十一月十七日

高　原

這兒的白天
爲什麼熱

這兒太高
離太陽近

這兒的夜晚
爲什麼冷

這兒太高
離月亮近

爲什麼離太陽近了熱
爲什麼離月亮近了冷

太陽是火
月亮是冰

一九五六年

給烏蘭諾娃

——看芭蕾舞《小夜曲》後作

像雲一樣柔軟，
像風一樣輕，
比月光更明亮，
比夜更寧靜——
人體在太空裏遊行；

不是天上的仙女，
却是人間的女神，
比夢更美，
比幻想更動人——
是勞動創造的結晶。

希　望

夢的朋友
幻想的姊妹

原是自己的影子
却老走在你前面

像光一樣無形
像風一樣不安定

她和你之間
始終有距離

像窗外的飛鳥
像天上的流雲

像河邊的蝴蝶
旣狡猾而美麗

你上去，她就飛
你不理她，她撞你

她永遠陪伴你
一直到你終止呼吸

傘

早晨，我問傘：
"你喜歡太陽曬
還是喜歡雨淋？"

傘笑了，它說：
"我考慮的不是這些。"

我追問它：
"你考慮些什麼？"

傘說：
"我想的是——
雨天，不讓大家衣服淋濕；
晴天，我是大家頭上的雲。"

魚 化 石

動作多麼活潑，
精力多麼旺盛，
在浪花裏跳躍，
在大海裏浮沉；

不幸遇到火山爆發，
也可能是地震，
你失去了自由，
被埋進了灰塵；

過了多少億年，
地質勘探隊員，
在岩層裏發現你，
依然栩栩如生。

但你是沉默的，
連嘆息也沒有，
鱗和鰭都完整，
却不能動彈；

你絕對的靜止，
對外界毫無反應，

看不見天和水，
聽不見浪花的聲音。

　　　＊　　　＊

凝視着一片化石，
傻瓜也得到教訓：
離開了運動，
就沒有生命。

活着就要鬥爭，
在鬥爭中前進，
卽使死亡，
能量也要發揮乾淨。

鏡　　子

僅只是一個平面
却又是深不可測

它最愛眞實
決不隱瞞缺點

它忠於尋找它的人
誰都從它發現自己

或是醉後酡顏
或是鬢如霜雪

有人喜歡它
因爲自己美

有人躲避它
因爲它直率

甚至會有人
恨不得把它打碎

致亡友丹娜之靈

謹以哀詩一首呈獻於
布拉格奧爾桑一號公墓九區
三十八號丹娜的骨灰盒前

動亂不安的年代，
友誼像陰天的蘆葦，
在風中哆嗦着，
發出聽不見的哀嘆……

空間多麼遼闊，
時間多麼漫長，
翻開記憶的本子，
字跡已模糊不清：

你第一次下飛機，
就在人羣里，
尋找一個寫詩的人，
但他沒有去歡迎。

你在中國度過了三年，
春花秋月，風和日麗，

383

你愛上這個國家，
和她的古樸的人民；

一九五七年秋天，
你受聘期滿離開北京，
在爲你送行的人羣裏面，
却少了一個寫詩的人；

我在甩袖無邊的大荒原，
收到來自布拉格的明信片；
我躊躇很久沒有給你回信——
不相信蒲公英會飄到你身邊。

整整過了十年，
維爾塔發河邊發生了地震，
我最先想到的是你——
一個正直人的命運；

我曾到過你的書房——
那完全是中國人的書房，
不知你所編譯的書怎麼樣？
不知魯迅全集怎麼樣？

歲月在經受不可知的折磨，
空氣被血腥所汚染……

二十一年的杳無音訊，

如今是三九嚴寒的第二天，
突然像寒流侵襲，
"丹娜已不幸離開人間！"

你因車禍身亡，
時間是一九七六年十月三十日。
這消息傳到我耳邊，
已遲了整整兩年！

我好像看見一株葱翠的小松樹，
突然被狂風連根拔走了；
我好像看見一座正在延伸的橋樑，
突然被山洪衝斷了……

你多麼熱愛中國
把她看做自己的國家，
在最困難的時候保衛她，
在各種壓力下拒絕反對她。

死亡奪去了你想再到中國的希望，
奪去了你和中國朋友們團聚的希望，

經過了漫長的二十一年，
我總算恢復了應有的尊嚴，
你聽到這消息該多麼高興，
因為你一直為我的處境憤憤不平。

但是，你已長眠於九泉之下

再也聽不見我的歌聲，
這歌聲你是熟悉的——
即使最歡樂的時候也有悲酸……

而在我的桌子上，
留着你送給我的煙灰缸，
它好像什麼也不知道，
依然閃閃發光……

我們這個時代的友情，
多麼可貴又多麼艱辛——

像火災後留下的照片，
像地震後揀起的瓷碗，
像沉船露出海面的桅桿，
一場浩劫之後的一絲苦澀的微笑，
永遠無法完成的充滿遺憾的詩篇……

安息吧，
親愛的丹娜。

一九七九年一月十一日

迎接一個迷人的春天

一

不知道你們聽見了沒有——
這些夜晚，從河流那邊
　　傳來了一陣陣什麼破裂的聲音。
呵，原來是河流正在解凍，
河水可以無拘束地奔流了，
大片大片的冰塊互相撞擊着，
　　　　　　互相擁擠着，
好像戲院門前的人流，
　　帶着歡笑擁向天邊。

久久盼望的春天終於來了，
萬物滋生的季節要來了，
播種與孕育的季節要來了，
誰能不愛春天呢！
即使冰雪化了以後，
　　道路是泥濘的，
即使要穿過一大片沼澤地帶，
我們也要去歡迎她，

387

因爲她給我們大家
　　帶來了溫暖和希望。

二

我們有過被欺騙的春天，
我們有過被流放的春天，
我們有過被監禁的春天，
我們有過嗚咽啜泣的春天。

我們曾經像蝸牛似的，
在牆脚根上慢慢地爬行；
我們曾經像喇嘛教徒似的，
敲着木魚，唸着經消磨時間。
然而，整個外面的世界，
成千上萬的車隊，
在高速公路上飛奔，
而米格25戰鬥機，
隨時都有可能像閃電劃過
　　我們神聖的藍天，
我們所面臨的是一場無比
　　嚴峻的考驗。

經歷了多少的動盪與不安，
我們終於醒悟過來了，
終於突破了層層堅冰，
迎來了萬馬奔騰的時間。

三

我們終於能理直氣壯地生活了，
我們能揚眉吐氣地過日子了，
我們具有無比堅強的信心，
像哈薩克族舉行"姑娘追"似的
　　來迎接這個春天。

她來了，眞的來了，
你可以聞到她的芬芳
你可以感到她的體溫，
就連樹上的小鳥也在歌唱，
就連林間的小鹿也在跳躍……

我們要拉響所有的汽笛，
　　來迎接這個新時代的黎明；
我們要鳴放二十一門禮炮，
　　來迎接這個歲月的元首；
所有的琴師撥動琴弦，
所有的詩人譜寫詩篇，
所有的樂器，歌聲，詩篇
組成最大的交響樂章，
　　來迎接一個迷人的春天！

在 浪 尖 上

——給韓志雄和他同一代的青年朋友

一、 "是韓志雄"

我把你介紹給別人：
"這是一個英雄。"
你却笑着否認：
"不是英雄，是韓志雄。"

自封的"英雄"當然可恥，
人民給的稱號最光榮——
你可以當之無愧的
是"天安門事件"的英雄。

豺狼張牙舞爪的時候
居然敢上去拔毛，
你在鬥爭中的勇敢
可以引爲一代人的驕傲！

而你是清醒的
像大風大浪中的一個島，

你在萬里晴空下，
寧靜地注視着萬頃波濤……

二、這是什麽戰争

好像不是戰争，
却都動用了刀槍
說的是"觸及靈魂"，
却造成了千萬人的傷亡；

"理解的要執行，
不理解的也要執行。"
百分之百的虛僞，
徹頭徹尾的欺騙；

最殘酷的迫害，
最大膽的壟斷，
比宗教更荒唐，
比謀殺更陰險；

一邊說："文攻武衛"，
一邊說："放火燒荒"，
一邊喊："砸爛公檢法"，
一邊煽動："打砸搶"；

唸的是"限制資產階級法權"，
侵吞的是"抄家物資"；

在"反復闢"的煙幕裏
進行瘋狂的掠奪;

理性被本能扼殺,
用武斷蠱惑人心;
奸詐的耀武揚威,
忠誠的受到誣陷;

野心在黑夜發酵,
情慾隨權力增長;
自私與狂妄賽跑,
良心走進拍賣行;

聰明的變狡猾,
老實的變傻瓜;
謠言通行無阻,
眞話倒要追查;

不知以破壞爲手段,
還是以破壞爲目的——
好像是在玩魔術,
好像是在演雜技;

"批林批孔批周公",
"反對右傾翻案風",
誰有威信打倒誰,
跳樑小醜顯神通;

正義被綁着示衆，
眞理被蒙上眼睛，
連元帥也被陷害，
總理也死而含冤。

從十歲到二十歲，
文化大革命的十年，
韓志雄被大風大浪，
送到了一九七六年。

三、悲哀的日子

敬愛的周總理
和我們告別了——
敵人沒有想到
會激起這麼大的哀悼：

世界上沒有一個人
得到過這麼多詩篇；
歷史上沒有一個人
得到過這麼多花圈！

花的山、花的海、
詩的海、淚的海、
無邊浩淼的大海
汹涌着人民的悲哀……

多少的陰謀詭計，
多少的造謠誹謗，
多少的栽贓誣陷
都無損於他的形像；

他是一架大山──
敵人難於逾越的屏障；
他的崇高顯出了敵人的卑鄙；
他的光芒刺痛了敵人的心臟；

敵人不準人民戴黑紗，
敵人禁止人民送花圈，
敵人揉碎了馬蹄蓮，
敵人踩爛了君子蘭；

但是，遠處的山，
窗前的樹，
路邊的清泉，
都使人想起周總理；

周總理像空氣，
像陽光，像水，
好像很平凡，
却誰也不能離開；

總理是大家的，
空氣是大家的，

太陽是大家的，
土地是大家的。

四、丙辰清明

從來沒有一個清明節，
像丙辰的清明節流這麼多的淚，

活着的時候越無私，
人民的懷念也最永恆；

韓志雄在天安門前
一天一天的聽朗誦詩篇——
悲痛止不住淚水，
憤怒把淚水燒乾；

千萬首詩，
千萬個火炬，
火炬又點燃火炬，
照徹了初春的夜晚；

為了維護眞理，
必須投入戰鬥——
思想是旗幟，
語言是子彈；

韓志雄寫的詩

貼在紀念碑東面，
像燃燒的火炬，
像閃光的寶劍；

"歷史有紀念碑，
歷史有斬妖台，
歷史是裁判員，
歷史將把人民的忠臣
　　敬在紀念碑上——永遠懷念！
歷史也將把人民的奸臣
　　押上斬妖台——怒斬！
……
……

歷史哪容這團妖霧橫行。
人民將把這些烏鴉身上的
　　孔雀毛拔去，
撕開馬列外衣。
在紀念碑前，
在人民的怒吼中
無情地判決他們——
　　一小撮民族的敗類！
歷史永垂的紀念碑
在地球上向着太空
發出了雄壯渾厚的聲音：
　　'倘若魔怪噴毒火，
自有擒妖打鬼人。'
……

……
碑上總理顯神靈，
喚來無數驅妖人。"

聽，韓志雄的詩，
像響徹長空的雷聲……

五、"我願坐牢一千年！"

這個青年工人被捕了，
地點是列寧像的下面，
時間是清明節前兩天——
夜晚十二點。

他被推進了牢監，
馬上被剝光了衣服，
接着拳打脚踢之後，
是蒙頭蓋腦的皮鞭！

審問的不知是哪國人，
銬上"緊銬"要他供認：
"爲什麼悼念周總理？
爲什麼擁護鄧小平？"

這兒有另外的"法律"，
把革命的打成"反革命"，

把愛國者當作"罪人",
這兒執行的是"女皇"的命令;

聽,他們說的是什麼語言:
"這兒是專政機關
鎮壓反革命的地方,
從這兒出去?別痴心妄想!"

韓志雄回答得多麼堅硬:
"我願坐牢一千年!"
他好像進入中世紀,
等待的是"宗教裁判"!

六、 "天安門事件"

人民的總理死了,
為什麼不讓悼念?
為什麼撕掉詩文?
為什麼撤走花圈?

為什麼放出便衣,
在羣衆中來回打轉?
誰指使走狗喊反動口號,
想把羣衆的憤怒扭轉?

是誰躲在陰暗的角落

精心策劃"天安門事件"——
拷打一個十四歲的少年，
逼他供認自己是"縱火犯"？

是誰想在天安門前
把"國會縱火案"重演？
是誰把羣衆的革命行動
汚蔑爲"匈牙利事件"？

"天安門事件"
是光明與黑暗、
民主與專制、
革命與反動的白刃戰；

"天安門事件"
像烏雲深處的閃電，
照出了鬼魅的原形，
畫出了劊子手的嘴臉；

"天安門事件"
敲響了"四人幫"的喪鐘，
加速了"四人幫"的滅亡——
把人民的眼睛擦亮；

"天安門事件"
是最輝煌的詩篇；

是革命與反革命的分水嶺；
是中國歷史的轉折點！

七、革命意志越燒越旺

經過十一個月的黑夜，
韓志雄重新見到太陽，
卽使身上有了創傷，
革命的意志越燒越旺。

爲什麼，偉大的祖國
在推翻了三架大山之後
會出現林彪、"四人幫"，
至今還留下深刻的內傷？

這些妖孽從何而來？
滋長他們的是什麼土壤？
如今還活着的人
怎麼不應該想一想？

鬥爭遠沒有結束，
要把眼睛擦得更亮——
要用科學代替迷信，
衝出一切精神牢房！

不容許再受蒙蔽了，
不應該再被欺騙了，

我們要的是眞理，
我們要的是太陽！

不依靠神明的憐憫，
不等待上帝的恩賜，
人民要保衛民主權利，
因爲民主是革命的武器。

一切政策必須落實，
一切冤案必須昭雪，
卽使已經長眠地下的，
也要恢復他們的名譽！

八、你勇敢的飛翔吧

如今，年輕的司機
開着一輛推土機，
正在加大油門，
清除長期積累的垃圾——

清除一切障礙物——
封建的、法西斯的、
宗教迷信的、窩朽的，
爲四個現代化騰出基地！

韓志雄經受了烈火的鍛煉，
經受了十二級台風的考驗，

是屬於毛澤東時代的青年，
是政治風暴浪尖上的海燕！

"爲人類的幸福而鬥爭"
這是他的光輝的誓言——
韓志雄，勇敢的飛翔吧，
看，黨中央在向你召喚。

要是有人問：
"文化大革命有什麼成果？"
這就是最明顯的一件：
中國出現了新的一代青年。

　　　　　　　　　一九七八年十一月十六日

光 的 讚 歌

一

每個人的一生
不論聰明還是愚蠢
不論幸福還是不幸
只要他一離開母體
就睜着眼睛追求光明

世界要是沒有光
等於人沒有眼睛
航海的沒有羅盤
打槍的沒有準星
不知道路邊有毒蛇
不知道前面有陷阱

世界要是沒有光
也就沒有楊花飛絮的春天
也就沒有百花爭妍的夏天
也就沒有金菓滿園的秋天
也就沒有大雪紛飛的冬天

世界要是沒有光
看不見奔騰不息的江河
看不見連綿千里的森林
看不見容易激動的大海
看不見像老人似的雪山
要是我們什麼也看不見
我們對世界還有什麼留戀

二

只是因爲有了光
我們的大千世界
才顯得絢麗多彩
人間也顯得可愛

光給我們以智慧
光給我們以想像
光給我們以熱情
創造出不朽的形象

那些殿堂多麼雄偉
裏面更是金碧輝煌
那些感人肺腑的詩篇
誰讀了能不熱淚盈眶

那些最高明的雕刻家

使冰冷的大理石有了體溫
那些最出色的畫家
描出色授魂與的眼睛

比風更輕的舞蹈
珍珠般圓潤的歌聲
火的熱情、水晶的堅貞
藝術離開光就沒有生命

山野的篝火是美的
港灣的燈塔是美的
夏夜的繁星是美的
慶祝勝利的熖火是美的
一切的美都和光在一起

三

這是多麽奇妙的物質
沒有重量而色如黃金
它可望而不可及
漫遊世界而無體形
具有睿智而謙卑
它與美相依爲命

誕生於撞擊和磨擦
來源於燃燒和消亡的過程

來源於火、來源於電
來源於永遠燃燒的太陽

太陽啊，我們最大的光源
它從億萬萬裏以外的高空
向我們居住的地方輸送熱量
使我們這裏滋長了萬物
萬物都對它表示景仰
因為它是永不消失的光

真是不可捉摸的物質——
不是固體、不是液體、不是氣體
來無踪、去無影、浩渺無邊
從不喧囂，隨遇而安
有力量而不劍拔弩張
它是無聲的威嚴

它是偉大的存在
它因富足而能慷慨
胸懷坦蕩、性格開朗
只知放射、不求報償
大公無私、照耀四方

四

但是有人害怕光
有人對光滿懷仇恨

因爲光所發出的針芒
刺痛了他們自私的眼睛

歷史上的所有暴君
各個朝代的奸臣
一切貪婪無厭的人
爲了偷竊財富、壟斷財富
千方百計想把光監禁
因爲光能使人覺醒

凡是壓迫人的人
都希望別人無能
無能到了不敢吭聲
讓他們把自己當做神明

凡是剝削的人
都希望別人愚蠢
愚蠢到了不會計算
一加一等於幾也鬧不淸

他們要的是奴隸
是會說話的工具
他們只要馴服的牲口
他們害怕有意志的人

他們想把火撲滅
在無邊的黑暗裏

在岩石所砌的城堡裏
永遠維持血腥的統治

他們占有權力的寶座
一手是勛章、一手是皮鞭
一邊是金錢、一邊是鎖鏈
進行着可恥的政治交易
完了就舉行妖魔的舞會
和血淋淋的人肉的歡宴

回顧人類的歷史
曾經有多少年代
沉浸在苦難的深淵
黑暗凝固得像花崗岩
然而人間也有多少勇士
用頭顱去撞開地獄的鐵門

光榮屬於奮不顧身的人
光榮屬於前赴後繼的人

暴風雨中的雷聲特別響
烏雲深處的閃電特別亮
只有通過漫長的黑夜
才能噴湧出火紅的太陽

五

愚昧就是黑暗
智慧就是光明

人類是從愚昧中過來
那最先去盜取火的人
是最早出現的英雄
他不怕守火的鷲鷹
要啄掉他的眼睛
他也不怕天帝的憤怒
和轟擊他的雷霆
於是光不再被壟斷
從此光流傳到人間

我們告別了刀耕火種
蒸汽機帶來了工業革命
從核物理誕生了原子彈
如今像放鴿子似的
放出了地球衛星……
光把我們帶進了一個
　　　光怪陸離的世界：
Ｘ光，照見了動物的內臟
激光，刺穿優質鋼板
光學望遠鏡，追踪星際物質
電子計算機
　　　把我們推到了二十一世紀

然而，比一切都更寶貴的
是我們自己的銳利的目光
是我們先哲的智慧的光
這種光洞察一切、預見一切

可以透過肉體的軀殼
看見人的靈魂

看見一切事物的底蘊
一切事物內在的規律
一切運動中的變化
一切變化中的運動
一切的成長和消亡
就連靜靜的喜馬拉雅山
也在緩慢地繼續上升

認識沒有地平綫
地平綫只能存在於停止前進的地方
而認識却永無止境
人類在追踪客觀世界中
留下了自己的脚印

實踐是認識的階梯
科學沿着實踐前進
在前進的道路上
要砸開一層層的封鎖
要掙斷一條條的鐵鏈
眞理只能從實踐中得以永生

六

光從不可估量的高空
俯視着人類歷史的長河

我們從周口店到天安門
像滾滾的波濤在翻騰
不知穿過了多少的險灘和暗礁
我們乘坐的是永不沉沒的船
從天際投下的光始終照引着我們⋯⋯

我們從千萬次的蒙蔽中覺醒
我們從千萬種的愚弄中學得了聰明
統一中有矛盾、前進中有逆轉
運動中有阻力、革命中有背叛

甚至光中也有暗
甚至暗中也有光
不少醜惡與無恥
隱藏在光的下面
毒蛇、老鼠、臭蟲、蝎子
和許多種類的粉蝶——
她們都是孵化害蟲的母親
我們生活着隨時都要警惕
看不見的敵人在窺伺着我們
然而我們的信念
像光一樣堅強——
經過了多少浩劫之後
穿過了漫長的黑夜
人類的前途無限光明、永遠光明

七

每一個人都是一個生命
人世銀河星雲中的一粒微塵
每一粒微塵都有自己的能量
無數的微塵匯集成一片光明
每一個人旣是獨立的
而又互相照耀
在互相照耀中不停地運轉
和地球一同在太空中運轉
我們在運轉中燃燒
我們的生命就是燃燒
我們在自己的時代
應該像節日的熖火
帶着歡呼射向高空
然後迸發出璀燦的光

即使我們是一支蠟燭
也應該“蠟炬成灰淚始乾”
即使我們只是一根火柴
也要在關鍵時刻有一次閃耀
即使我們死後尸骨都窩爛了
也要變成磷火在荒野中燃燒

八

即使生命像露水一樣短暫
即使是恆河岸邊的一粒細沙

也能反映出比本身更大的光
作爲一個微不足道的人
天文學數字中的一粒微塵
我也曾經用嘶啞的喉嚨歌唱
在不自由的歲月裏我歌唱自由
我是被壓迫的民族，我歌唱解放
在這個茫茫的世界上
爲被凌辱的人們歌唱
爲受欺壓的人們歌唱
我歌唱抗爭，歌唱革命
在黑夜把希望寄托給黎明
在勝利的歡欣中歌唱太陽

我是大火中的一點火星
趁生命之火沒有熄滅
我投入火的隊伍、光的隊伍
把“一”和“無數”融合在一起
爲眞理而鬥爭
和在鬥爭中前進的人民一同前進
我永遠歌頌光明
光明是屬於人民的
未來是屬於人民的
任何財富都是人民的

和光在一起前進
和光在一起勝利

　　勝利是屬於人民的
　　和人民在一起所向無敵

九

　　我們的祖先是光榮的
　　他們爲我們開辟了道路
　　沿途留下了深深的足迹
　　每個足迹裏都有血迹

　　現在我們正開始新的長征
　　這個長征不只是二萬五千里的路程
　　我們要逾越的也不只是十萬大山
　　我們要攀登的也不只是千里岷山
　　我們要奪取的也不只是金沙江、大渡河
　　我們要搶渡的是更多更險的渡口
　　我們在攀登中將要遇到
　　　　更大的風雪、更多的冰川……

　　但是光在召喚我們前進
　　光在鼓舞我們、激勵我們
　　光給我們送來了新時代的黎明
　　我們的人民從四面八方高歌猛進

　　讓信心和勇敢伴隨着我們
　　武裝我們的是最美好的理想
　　我們是和最先進的階級在一起

我們的心胸燃燒着希望
我們前進的道路鋪滿陽光

讓我們的每個日子
　都像飛輪似地旋轉起來
讓我們的生命發出最大的能量
讓我們像從地核裏釋放出來似的
　　　極大地撐開光的翅膀
　　　在無限廣闊的宇宙中飛翔

讓我們以最高的速度飛翔吧
讓我們以大無畏的精神飛翔吧
讓我們從今天出發飛向明天
讓我們把每個日子都當做新的起點

或許有一天，總有一天
我們這個古老的民族
我們最勇敢的階級
將接受光的邀請
去叩開千萬重緊閉的大門
訪問我們所有的芳鄰

讓我們從地球出發
飛向太陽……

　　　　　　　　一九七八年八月——十二月

牆

一堵牆，像一把刀
把一個城市切成兩片
一半在東方
一半在西方

牆有多高？
有多厚？
有多長？
再高、再厚、再長
也不可能比中國的長城
更高、更厚，更長
它也只是歷史的陳迹
民族的創傷
誰也不喜歡這樣的牆

三米高算得了什麼
五十厘米厚算得了什麼
四十五公里長算得了什麼
再高一千倍
再厚一千倍
再長一千倍

又怎能阻擋
天上的雲彩、風、雨和陽光？

又怎能阻擋
飛鳥的翅膀和夜鶯的歌唱？

又怎能阻擋
流動的水和空氣？

又怎能阻擋
千百萬人的
比風更自由的思想？
比土地更深厚的意志？
比時間更漫長的願望？

　　　　　　一九七九年五月二十二日　波恩

導　遊　人

特里爾是一個可愛的古城
特里爾有一個可愛的導遊人

我不知道她的姓名
她有一雙嫵媚的眼睛
從她薄薄的嘴唇裏
流出最悅耳的聲音

她像一個牧羊姑娘
熱心地帶領着羊羣
也像一個歷史教員
學識淵博而有耐心

從選侯的宮殿
說到新教的教堂
從西羅馬的都城
說到大帝康士坦丁

以及拿破侖的入侵
到馬克思的誕生
從普魯士人的占領
到特里爾的今天

不斷地以機智和幽默
博得了旅遊者的笑聲
在短短的兩個小時裏
說完了兩千年的事情

穿過黑城來到噴水池邊
她微笑着和大家告別
從此誰也沒有再見她
但心裏却響着泉水的聲音

　　　　　　一九七九年五月二十三日　　特里爾

祝　酒

杯子和杯子，
輕輕地相碰，
發出輕輕的聲音，
"親親"、"親親"、"親親"[1]。

你的心，我的心，
也輕輕地相碰，
也發出輕輕的聲音：
"親親"、"親親"、"親親"。

爲了友誼，爲了和平，
讓我們每個人的心，
都發出輕輕的聲音：
"親親"、"親親"、"親親"。

一九七九年六月二十五日　米蘭

---

1 意大利人敬酒時說"親親"，意卽"乾杯"。

420

古羅馬的大鬥技場

也許你曾經看見過
這樣的場面——
在一個圓的小瓦罐裏
兩隻蟋蟀在相鬥，
雙方都鼓動着翅膀
發出一陣陣金屬的聲響，
張牙舞爪撲向對方
又是扭打、又是衝撞，
經過了持久的較量，
總是有一隻更强的
撕斷另一隻的腿
咬破肚子——直到死亡。

古羅馬的大鬥技場
也就是這個模樣，
大家都可以想像
那一幅壯烈的風光。

古羅馬是有名的"七山之城"
在帕拉丁山的東面
在錫利山的北面
在埃斯揆林山的南面

421

那一片盆地的中間
有一座——可能是
全世界最大的鬥技場，
它像圓形的古城堡
遠遠看去是四層的樓房，
每層都有幾十個高大的門窗
裏面的圓周是石砌的看台
可以容納十多萬人來觀賞。

想當年舉行鬥技的日子
也許是一個喜慶的日子
這兒比趕廟會還熱鬧
古羅馬的人穿上節日的盛裝
從四面八方都朝向這兒
眞是人山人海——全城歡騰
好像慶祝在亞洲和非洲打了勝仗
其實只是來看一場殘酷的悲劇
從別人的痛苦激起自己的歡暢。

號聲一響
死神上場

當角鬥士的都是奴隸
挑選的一個個身強力壯，
他們都是戰敗國的俘虜
早已妻離子散、家破人亡，
如今被押送到鬥技場上

等於執行用不着宣佈的死刑
面臨着任人宰割的結局
像畜棚裏的牲口一樣；

相搏鬥的彼此無冤無仇
却安排了同一的命運，
都要用無辜的手
去殺死無辜的人；
明知自己必然要死
却把希望寄托在刀尖上；

有時也要和猛獸搏鬥
猛獸——不論吃飽了的
還是飢餓的都是可怕的——
它所渴求的是溫熱的鮮血，
奴隸到這裏即使有勇氣
也只能是來源於絕望，
因爲這兒所需要的不是智慧
而是必須壓倒對方的力量；

看那些"打手"多麼神氣！
他們是角鬥場僱用的工役
一個個長的牛頭馬面
手拿鐵棍和皮鞭
（起先還帶着面具
後來連面具也不要了）
他們驅趕着角鬥士去廝殺

進行着死亡前的掙扎；
最可憐的是那些蒙面的角鬥士
（不知道是哪個遊手好閑的
想出如此殘忍的壞點子！）
參加角鬥的互相看不見
雙方都亂揮着短劍尋找敵人
無論進攻和防禦都是盲目的──
盲目的死亡、盲目的勝利。

一場角鬥結束了
那些"打手"進場
用長鈎子鈎曳出屍體
和那些血淋淋的肉塊
把被戮將死的曳到一旁
拿走武器和其它的什物，
奄奄一息的就把他殺死；
然後用水冲刷污血
使它不留一點痕跡──
這些"打手"受命於人
不直接去殺人
却比劊子手更陰沉。

再看那一層層的看台上
多少萬人都在歡欣若狂
那兒是等級森嚴、層次分明
按照權力大小坐在不同的位置上，
王家貴族一個個悠閑自得

旁邊都有陪臣在阿諛奉承；
那些宮妃打扮得花枝招展
與其說她們是來看角鬥
不如說到這兒展覽自己的青春
好像是天上的星斗光照人間，
有"赫赫戰功"的，生活在
奴隸用雙手建造的宮殿裏
姦淫戰敗國的婦女；
他們的餐具都沾着血
他們讚賞血腥的氣味；
能看人和獸搏鬥的
多少都具有獸性——
從流血的遊戲中得到快感
從死亡的掙扎中引起笑聲，
別人越痛苦，他們越高興；
（你沒有聽見那笑聲嗎？）
最可恨的是那些
用別人的災難進行投機
從血泊中撈取利潤的人，
他們的財富和罪惡一同增長；

鬥技場的奴隸越緊張
看台上的人羣越興奮，
廝殺的叫喊越響
越能爆發狂暴的笑聲，
看台上是金銀首飾在閃光
鬥場上是刀叉匕首在閃光；

兩者之間相距並不遠
却有一堵不能逾越的牆。
這就是古羅馬的鬥技場
它延續了多少個世紀
誰知道有多少奴隸
在這個圓池裏喪生。
神呀，宙斯呀，丘比特呀，耶和華呀
一切所謂"萬能的主"呀，都在哪裏？
爲什麼對人間的不幸無動於衷？
風呀，雨呀，雷霆呀，
爲什麼對罪惡能寬容？

奴隸依然是奴隸
誰在主宰着人間？
誰是這場遊戲的主謀？
時間越久，看得越淸：
經營鬥技場的都是奴隸主
不論是老泰爾克維尼烏斯
還是蘇拉、凱撒、奧大維……
都是奴隸主中的奴隸主——
嗜血的猛獸、殘暴的君王！
"不要做奴隸！
要做自由人！"
一人號召
萬人響應
爲了改變自己的命運
就要搗毀萬惡的鬥技場；

把那些拿別人生命作賭的人
　　釘死在恥辱柱上！

奴隸的領袖
只有從奴隸中產生；
共同的命運
產生共同的思想；
共同的意志
匯成偉大的力量。
一次又一次地舉起義旗
鬥爭的才能因失敗而增長
憤怒的隊伍像地中海的巨浪
淹沒了宮殿，掀翻了凱旋門
衝垮了鬥技場，浩浩蕩蕩
覺醒了的人們誓用鮮血灌漑大地
建造起一個自由勞動的天堂！

如今，古羅馬的大鬥技場
已成了歷史的遺物，像戰後的廢墟
沉浸在落日的餘暉裏，像碉堡
不得不引起我疑問和沉思：
它究竟是光榮的紀念，
還是恥辱的標志？
它是誇耀古羅馬的豪華，
還是記錄野蠻的統治？
它是爲了博得廉價的同情，
還是謀求遙遠的嘆息？

時間太久了
連大理石也要哭泣；
時間太久了
連凱旋門也要低頭；
奴隸社會最殘忍的一幕已經過去
不義的殺戮已消失在歷史的煙霧裏
但它却在人類的良心上留下可恥的記憶
而且向我們披示一條眞理：
血債遲早都要用血來償還；
以別人的生命作爲賭注的
就不可能得到光彩的下場。

說起來多少有些荒唐——
在當今的世界上
依然有人保留了奴隸主的思想，
他們把全人類都看作奴役的對像
整個地球是一個最大的鬥技場。

一九七九年七月　北京

聽，有一個声音……

夜深人靜的時分
在中國的上空
有一個女人的幽靈——
聽，有一個聲音：

上

你們害怕我
因爲我和眞理在一起
你們仇恨我
因爲我和人民在一起

你們不讓我說話
死了的已經死了
活着的再不說話
就什麼聲音也沒有了

只要我一開口
你們就要發抖
我的嘴噴出的是火
眞理是永不熄滅的火

你們拿皮鞭抽我
就像抽牲口
你們用脚踢我
就像踢足球

你們拿我的胸部
鍛煉你們的拳頭
我身上是有神經的
你們把我看做石頭

我又沒有動手
爲什麼給銬上手銬
我又沒有動脚
爲什麼給我釘上脚鐐

我最愛光明
你們奪走了陽光
我最愛自由
你們把我關進牢房

你們不讓我歌唱
我偏要大聲地唱
我的歌你們不願意聽
我的歌是唱給人民的

你們用犯人管"犯人"
培養他們互相告密

你們不但要摧殘肉體
還要腐蝕靈魂

管我的是一個女人
國民黨中統女特務——
過去暗中殺共產黨員
現在公開殺共產黨員

居然以共產黨員的血
換取你們對她的信任
她對我越殘忍
你們越高興

你們編造罪行
然後審判我
我是無罪的
有罪的是你們

你們把敵人當同志
你們把同志當敵人
你們讓敵人折磨同志
你們自己就成了敵人

拿一個共產黨員
和中統女特務交換
把我判了徒刑
她却得到釋放

原來你們都是一伙
一批眞正的牛鬼蛇神
只是你們更善於僞裝
在革命陣營裏幹反革命

我的心是紅寶石
靈魂比水晶更透明
你們用暴力逼我投降
我用理智戰勝了你們

你們用死嚇唬我
我早已下定決心
不是死於監獄
就是死於戰爭

你們變得瘋狂了
想結束我的生命——
我無論活着還是死
都是你們的罪證

爲了堵住我的嘴
不能向世界呼喊
你們下毒手了
殺鷄似的割斷我的喉管

你們割得很熟練
我是第四十六名

你們還要割下去
讓人間沒有聲音

我的喉管不是我個人的
我的喉管是屬於人民
我的喉管是屬於共產黨的
我的喉管是傳播真理的無縫鋼管

銬上手銬——不讓寫
釘上脚鐐——不讓走
割斷喉管——不讓喊
但是，我還有思想——
　　通過目光射出憤怒的箭

我向你們看一眼
你們就渾身打顫
我向你們看兩眼
就連心肺都扎穿

你們把我押送到刑場
想讓我最後低下頭來
我把頭仰得更高
驕傲地迎接死亡

爲什麼不敢看我
爲什麼手在發抖

你們終究是膽怯的
你們終究是羞愧的

你們舉起了槍
對準了我的胸膛
你們槍斃的不是我
你們槍斃的是眞理

愛我的不要爲我哭
恨我的不要爲我笑
不是我死得太悲慘
而是我死得太早——

我愛的依然在受苦
我恨的依然在逍遙
活着的要提高警惕
敵人並沒有放下屠刀

下

我並沒有死
敵人想錯了
我是不會死的
我是永恆的靑春

一聲槍響之後
發出萬聲回音

人間在怒吼
天上響着雷霆

我不是一個單數
我是一個總和
所有被你們誣陷的
都在擁護我

我是我們，我們是無數
我是無數的化身
我是千千萬萬的一員
我叫張志新

我被捕的時間
是一九六九年
我被槍斃的時間
是一九七五年

別看我只四十五歲
死於如花的年華
六年的監獄生活
連鐵樹也會開花

我倒下了，我起來了
我停止呼吸，我說話了
我沒有死，我得到永生
和人民在一起，就得到永生——

人民將爲我說話
人民將爲我造像
人民將爲我譜曲
人民將爲我歌唱

全世界都在看着我
我是繁星中的一顆星
全世界都聽見我的聲音
我像汽笛歡呼着黎明

人民是千千萬萬面鏡子
每面鏡子都追踪着你們
照見你們的每一行動
照見你們醜惡的靈魂

看着你們在撲打灰塵
把手上的鮮血洗净
如何編造謊言
去騙取"功勛"

人民是千千萬萬個攝影機
每個鏡頭都對準着你們——
猶大的嘴臉
豺狼的心

　　　　　　　一九七九年八月　哈爾濱

衣 阿 華*

密蘇里以北卽是衣阿華。在這裏，草原上茂草擺動，有如大海；樹林裏滿開着野茱萸和野玫瑰。農人和農人的家眷多半是由新英格蘭、紐約、俄亥俄來到這個美麗的地方。他們都喜歡在這裏住，因爲這裏的氣候與種植差不多和他們舊邦裏的老家一樣。

愛自由的人也喜歡這裏没有奴工。

到處都是農田。

——《美國史》

離開了喧鬧的東海岸
離開了煩囂的西海岸
離開了噪聲的芝加哥
衣阿華，是一個失落在
　　西部草原上的小小的
　　　　小小的城鎮

衣阿華
美麗的名字
想是印第安人的稱呼
印第安人早已被趕跑了

----

*衣阿華卽愛荷華

衣　阿　華

來到衣阿華的
是從東部來的移民

誰能不喜歡這地方呢
大地是這麼遼闊而又肥沃
樹林和草地相連
向西開發的人流
流到這裏就不走了

衣阿華是產玉米的地方
大片大片的玉米地
微風吹過時
起伏得像海洋裏的波浪

衣阿華州
有個衣阿華城
一片丘陵
有楓樹林、楊樹林
橡樹林、欅子樹林
是兔子和松鼠跳躍的地方
偶然也有梅花鹿
　到樹林裏閑逛

衣阿華城
是個爆玉米花的城

衣阿華城
像一個鄉村姑娘

既勤勞又寧靜
難得逛一次芝加哥
雖然離得並不遠

秋天了
"五月花"公寓裏
住了許多外國人
他們都像是候鳥
受"國際寫作計劃"
　　邀請來的作家和詩人

衣阿華
是富於思考的地方
它不像紐約那麼擁擠
也不像洛杉磯那麼散漫無邊

衣阿華城裏
住的多半是大學生
街上走的
留着長髮的
背着書包的
穿牛仔褲的年輕人
見面的時候
含着微笑打招呼

衣阿華城沒有高層建築
它像一個大公園

有山野的風光
到處散佈着濃蔭覆蓋的
　安徒生童話裏的木板房

而衣阿華河
彎彎曲曲流過衣阿華城
再向東流到密西西比河

衣阿華城
像一首沒有被污染的
抒情詩一樣美的小小的城市
誰能不喜歡衣阿華呢？

　　　　　　　　　一九八〇年十月

芝加哥

密執安湖畔的
肥沃的黑草原
是印第安人的村落
從東面來的白種人
把紅種人趕跑了

他們用槍炮
占領了這個地方
砍伐木材蓋起了房子
修築公路、修築鐵路
像蜘蛛網通向四面八方

這兒有煉鋼廠、屠宰場
有比煤炭更黑的黑社會
被詩人稱作邪惡的地方

這兒成了廣袤的美利堅的
  交通樞紐、運輸和貿易中心
像章魚伸出了吸盤
把財富集中起來

不幸的是，像古羅馬
一場大火隨風飄蕩

除了一座水塔
把整個城市都燒光

再生的鳳凰
是鋼的軀幹
是玻璃的翅膀
建築師採用大理石、花崗岩
像壘積木似的
在密執安湖畔
蓋起了許多摩天大樓

黑色的"西爾斯公司大廈"
成了"世界之巔"
站在一百一十層上面
用望遠鏡向遠方眺望
再也看不見印第安人
——誰知道他們到哪兒去了
只有在自然歷史博物館裏
還保留了他們的文化遺迹

而被釋放了的
從非洲來的黑色奴隸
却繁殖得很快
他們的後裔
成羣結隊地喧鬧着
參觀科學館

也有美術館
於是畢加索和芝加哥
兩個名字連在一起
在這兒的大學裏
製造的第一顆原子彈
使日本廣島夷爲平地

高層建築的峽谷
上面是一綫天
風，呼嘯而過
下面開放的是紅綠燈

火車在飛奔
電車在飛奔
汽車在飛奔
警車在飛奔

當夜晚來臨
芝加哥是燈火的海洋
是浮游的燈火的海洋
是成羣的浮游的燈火的海洋
是成片地矗立着的燈火的海洋

密執安湖
有了燈火的倒影
搖滾音樂伴奏着
一直燃燒到黎明

　　　　　　　　一九八零年十一月三日

紐　約

矗立在哈得孫河口
整個大都市
是巨大無比的鋼架
人生活在鋼的大風浪中

鋼在震動
鋼在磨擦
鋼在跳躍
鋼在飛跑

公路上
橋樑與橋樑交叉在一起
那些伸向天邊的
長長的鋼的橋樑
像有力的臂腕
把許多島嶼連接起來
構成了一個大紐約

曼哈頓
所有島嶼的中心
太多的摩天大樓
鋼鐵與玻璃的懸崖絕壁

它們中間的無數峽谷裏
流淌着車輛的洪流

在削壁之下
看不見太陽
看不見林木
找不到長春藤
找不到鳳尾草

百靈鳥和夜鶯
只存在教科書裏

要是說鋼是大都市的肢體
那末電就是大都市的血液
任何一個毛細管
都漩流着電
電是我們時代的神
它支配着一切

一切都在追趕速度
人在追趕中求生存
時間在奴役着人類
金錢在驅趕着時間

世界上所有種族的人
都擁擠在這個都市裏
還有爲數衆多的黑人

時代廣場、哈林區
日日夜夜
蒸發着肉慾的氣息

搖滾音樂的時代
和一切噪音一起
而且比賽着
看誰的聲音更響亮

當夜幕下垂
大紐約的萬家燈火
比任何幻覺更絢麗
但是
有誰能靠幻覺生活呢

現代美術館
鋼的雕塑
電光的繪畫
構成奇麗的幻景
千百種的奇思怪想
都在這裏出現了
物慾世界的峯頂
有人進入天堂
有人進入地獄

而自由神
只是一個影子
孤單地挺立在
河流對岸的一個小島上
茫然地看着這個大都市

　　　　　　一九八零年十一月十七日

洛 杉 磯

明媚的洛杉磯
有南國的風光

但是
霧從港灣升起了
霧悄悄地來了
霧是無聲的動物
爬上了亞熱帶的植物
爬上遊艇的桅杆
爬上教堂的鐘樓

霧是有重量的
它移動笨重的軀體
走進了賣海鮮的鋪子
當它出來時
帶着濃重的腥味

霧到工廠和工廠的煙在一起
霧在馬路上和汽車的煙在一起
霧占領了整個城市

街燈變暗了

汽車在高速公路上慢慢地爬行

洛杉磯是廣闊的
七個衛星城連在一起

洛杉磯是散漫的
城市和鄉村連在一起

而霧比洛杉磯更廣闊
霧比洛杉磯更散漫
霧是無聲的……

　　　　　　　　　　一九八〇年十二月

香　港

像捅開了一個螞蟻窩
一派繁忙緊張的景像

衆多的高層建築
重重叠叠地矗立着
好像有爐火在烤灼
炎熱得喘不過氣
好像攪拌機在操作
喧鬧得令人不安

擁擠得出奇!
但是
在房子與房子的空隙處
可以看見羣山
陽光照耀着山上的房子
上空飛架着橋樑
穿越雲間的電纜
把遊客送上太平山
而尋找歡樂的人們
熙熙攘攘在海洋公園

這兒原是一片海灘
有月光下的幽靜

漁民的小船
停泊在蘆葦叢裏
忽然被選中了
成了進攻的堡壘
於是，像奇迹似的
出現了這個奇異的城市

以"自由"爲號召
一切敢於冒險的
偸渡、泅泳而來
爲金錢而疲於奔命

商業城市
股票市場
像凝聚一灘汚血
凝聚在這個小島上

你所處的時代
你的地理位置
以及你的奢取豪奪
帶給你炫人耳目的繁榮

雙層的電車
巴士、大卡車、出租汽車
衝鋒陷陣的摩托車

拉長了汽笛飛馳而過的警車
使得千千萬萬人提心吊膽
呼吸在車輛的夾縫裏

夜晚，霓虹燈的廣告
燃燒着競爭與投機
夜總會和遊樂場
蒸發着肉的氣息
音樂和舞蹈
彌漫着情慾……
在這貧困的人間
擺開豐盛的宴席

而你並沒有終止——
爲了爭奪每一立方的空間
無限地向空中升高
爲了誇耀自己的財富
把慾望伸向海底

然而，我要贊美的
光芒四射的
花一般的港灣
幾百萬同胞生活在這裏
工作和奮鬥在這裏
你是祖國進出口的孔道
你是貨物交流的場所

你是友好往來的紐帶
你是走向五洲四海的橋樑
多少年來，你爲祖國
創造了難以估量的財富

　　　　　一九八零年八月二十五日初稿
　　　　　一九八一年二月二十一日修改

寓 言 兩 則

畫鳥的獵人

一個人想學打獵，找到一個打獵的人，拜他做老師。他向那打獵的人說：“人必須有一技之長，在許多職業裏面，我所選中的是打獵，我很想持槍到樹林裏去，打到那我想打的鳥。”

於是打獵的人檢查了那個徒弟的槍，槍是一支好槍，徒弟也是一個有決心的徒弟，就告訴他各種鳥的性格，和有關瞄準與射擊的一些知識，並且囑咐他必須尋找各種鳥去練習。

那個人聽了獵人的話，以為只要知道如何打獵就已經能打獵了，於是他持槍到樹林。但當他一進入樹林，走到那裏，還沒有舉起槍，鳥就飛走了。

於是他又來找獵人，他說：“鳥是機靈的，我沒有看見它們，它們先看見我，等我一舉起槍，鳥早已飛走了。”

獵人說：“你是想打那不會飛的鳥麼？”

他說：“說實在的，在我想打鳥的時候，要是鳥能不飛該多好呀！”

獵人說：“你回去，找一張硬紙，在上面畫一隻鳥，把硬紙掛在樹上，朝那鳥打——你一定會成功。”

那個人回家，照獵人所說的做了，試驗着打了幾槍，却沒有一槍能打中。他只好再去找獵人。他說："我照你說的做了，但我還是打不中畫中的鳥。"獵人問他是什麼原因，他說。"可能是鳥畫得太小，也可能是距離太遠。"

那獵人沉思了一陣向他說："對你的決心，我很感動，你囘去，把一張大一些的紙掛在樹上，朝那紙打——這一次你一定會成功。"

那人很擔憂地問："還是那個距離麽？"

獵人說"由你自己去決定。"

那人又問："那紙上還是畫着鳥麽？"

獵人說："不。"

那人苦笑了，說："那不是打紙麽？"

獵人很嚴肅地告訴他說："我的意思是，你先朝着紙只管打，打完了，就在有孔的地方畫上鳥，打了幾個孔，就畫幾隻鳥——這對你來說，是最有把握的了。"

養花人的夢

在一個院子裏，種了幾百棵月季花，養花的認爲只有這樣纔能每個月都看見花。月季的種類很多，是各地的朋友知道他有這種偏愛，設法托人帶來送給他的。開花的時候，那同一形狀的不同顏色的花，使他的院子呈現了一種單調的熱鬧。他爲了使這些花保養得好，費了很多心血，每天給這些花澆水，松土，上肥，修剪枝葉。

一天晚上，他忽然做了一個夢：當他正在修剪月季花的老枝的時候，看見許多花走進院子，好像全世界的花都來了，所有的花都愁眉淚睫地看着他。他驚訝地站起來，環視着所有的花。

最先說話的是牡丹，她說："以我的自尊，決不願成爲你的院子的不速之客，但是今天，衆姊妹們邀我同來，我就來了。"

接着說話的是睡蓮，她說："我在林邊的水池裏醒來的時候，聽見衆姊妹叫嚷着穿過林子，我也跟着來了。"

牽牛彎着纖弱的身子，張着嘴說："難道我們長得不美嗎？"

石榴激動得紅着臉說："冷淡裏面就含有輕蔑。"

白蘭說："要能體會性格的美。"

仙人掌說："只愛溫順的人，本身是軟弱的；而我們却具有倔强的靈魂。"

迎春說："我帶來了信念。"

456

蘭花說：“我看重友誼。”

所有的花都說了自己的話，最後一致地說：“能被理解就是幸福。”

這時候，月季說話了：“我們實在寂寞，要是能和衆姊妹們在一起，我們也會更快樂。”

衆姊妹們說：“得到專寵的有福了，我們被遺忘已經很久，在幸運者的背後，有着數不盡的怨言呢。”說完了話之後，所有的花忽然不見了。

他醒來的時候，心裏很悶，一個人在院子裏走來走去，他想：“花本身是有意志的，而開放正是她們的權利。我已由於偏愛而激起了所有的花的不滿。我自己也越來越覺得世界太狹窄了。沒有比較，就會使許多概念都模糊起來。有了短的，纔能看見長的；有了小的，纔能看見大的；有了不好看的，纔能看見好看的……從今天起，我的院子應該成爲衆芳之國。讓我們生活得更聰明，讓所有的花都在她們自己的季節裏開放吧。”

一九五六年七月六日